The Process View
of Simulation

THE COMPUTER SCIENCE LIBRARY

Operating and Programming Systems Series
Peter J. Denning, *Editor*

OPERATING AND PROGRAMMING SYSTEMS SERIES

The Process View
of Simulation

W. R. Franta
University of Minnesota

NORTH-HOLLAND·NEW YORK

NEW YORK • AMSTERDAM • OXFORD

Elsevier North-Holland, Inc.
52 Vanderbilt Avenue, New York, New York 10017

North-Holland Publishing Company
P.O. Box 211
Amsterdam, The Netherlands

Library of Congress Cataloging in Publication Data

Franta, W   R
  The process view of simulation.
  (The Computer science library) (Operating and
programming systems series)
  Bibliography: p. 236
  Includes index.
  1. Digital computer simulation. 2. SIMULA (Computer
program language) I. Title.
QA76.9.C65F7   001.4'24   77-5868
ISBN 0-444-00221-9
ISBN 0-444-00223-5 pbk.

Manufactured in the United States of America

To Kathy

A system is a big black box
Of which we can't unlock the locks,
And all we can find out about
Is what comes in and what goes out
Perceiving input-output pairs,
Connected by parameters,
Permits us, sometimes, to relate
An input, output and a state.
If this relation's good and stable
Then to predict we may be able,
But if this fails us—heaven forbid!
We'll be compelled to force the lid!
                              Kenneth Boulding

Contents

Preface

A number of books are available on the subject of discrete event digital simulation. None of them seriously considers or develops the process view of, or as we prefer, the scenario approach to, model program development. In this text we develop a simulation system based on that approach. We assume that the reader is unfamiliar with the approach, although perhaps not with simulation, and in Chapters 1 to 3 we establish first a foundation for discourse, and then informally introduce the scenario or process view of model development. We then turn to the formal development of the machinery that our informal investigations have suggested might be desirable. The actual form such machinery takes may be highly varied. From those possible forms we have chosen to concentrate upon that one realized by the extant system SIMULA. Our reasons are as follows.

To be acceptable, the extant system must be highly structured, based upon, and support a small number of highly useful and flexible concepts, and be relatively secure and widely available. The SIMULA system satisfies these requirements. In Chapter 4 we give a simple yet reasonably complete accounting of the concepts supported by SIMULA. Then, in Chapter 5, we develop a complete and flexible simulation system based upon these concepts, building from them in a hierarchical fashion. In Chapter 5 we assume the reading and study of the included code segments an integral rather than ancillary part of the presentation. By so structuring the treatment, we foster familiarity with the constructs given in Chapter 4, and also provide a compact, complete, and highly structured development, these latter attributes promoting later use of the material in a reference rather than learning mode. In these chapters the subject of synchronization is all important and considerable attention is given it.

In Chapter 6 the tools developed in Chapters 4 and 5 are used to realize a series of relatively simple model programs. They are simple to encourage study, a study which we hope develops further facility with the constructs and also promotes our underlying contention that the scenario approach to model program development is natural in a variety of situations. Preceding this series of examples we present a brief discussion of data collection and analysis methodologies and review first the methods of replication, next the method of subruns, and finally the reasonably new and flexible regenerative method.

The last example of the chapter is more elaborate than the others and is taken directly from a reported study. In all cases, to avoid errors in presentation, the listings from tested model programs are included.

In Chapter 7 we examine how the machinery developed can be used to realize other simulation systems and synchronization constructs. Examined is the relationship between SIMULA and GPSS, between SIMULA and SIMSCRIPT, and finally between SIMULA and ASPOL. The chapter is closed by examining a mechanism for realizing a generalized imperative scheduling construct, that is, a construct in which events occur as soon as a specified system state obtains. For this chapter, a basic familiarity with GPSS and SIMSCRIPT is desirable but not necessary.

In Chapter 8, we examine the cost of simulation and develop and discuss (nonstatistical) steps that can be taken to minimize that cost. In particular, attention is focused on the event set physical data structure, and alternative structures are examined.

Our presentation is basically self-contained and includes the complete realization, as we hopefully demonstrate, of a powerful and flexible simulation system. Throughout we attempt to develop vocabulary and emphasize terms and phrases, especially at first encounter.

Our primary objective is to display the appeal of the scenario approach to simulation and to present only that material which is not found in other books on simulation. For these reasons, we do not develop random variate generation algorithms or certain statistical techniques. We consider the book appropriate reading for junior, senior, and graduate level courses in computer science, operations research, and management science. Additionally, we hope it is appealing to systems analysts and simulation practitioners in industry and government. Finally, because we do not consider this report a textbook in the classic sense, we have omitted exercises and have proceeded more rapidly than perhaps we might otherwise have done.

I would like to acknowledge the advice and assistance given by P. J. Denning, P. A. Houle, and David Nassimi. I would also like to thank Anna Moody and Judi Matheson for assistance in preparation of the manuscript, and express special thanks to Barbara Heyer, without whose help the manuscript would never have been completed.

CHAPTER 1

Basic Notions

SYSTEMS AND MODELS

Terms such as *system* and *simulation*, which often mean different things to different people, require precise definition. For our purposes we may begin by defining [Mirham, 1972a] a *system* as

> a collection of interdependent elements which act together in a collective effort to achieve some goal.

The elements of the system are generally referred to as components or entities.

We are often interested in the behavior of the system under the influence of various internal and environmental conditions. One approach to obtaining information about system behavior is to bring about the desired internal and environmental conditions and then observe the behavior of the actual system. This approach is often not feasible. As an alternative, we can construct a model of the system, which captures its *essence,* and then conduct experiments on the model rather than on the system itself. The latter alternative is especially appealing when manipulation of the actual system is undesirable or impossible. The process of preparing a suitable model, known as *modeling,* can be defined as

> the process of developing an internal representation and set of trans- formation rules which can be used to predict the behavior and relationships between the set of entities composing the system.

The internal representation requires identification of a sufficient set of *variables* (state variables) to be used to describe *system state;* these variables are changed by the application of the transformational rules. We will further require that the model account for dynamic behavior, that is, the time-dependent application of transformational rules.

1

SOLUTION METHODS

In order to answer questions (i.e., predict behavior) about the system represented by the model, we must "solve" the model. There are *analytic* and *numeric* solutions. For analytic solutions the transformational rules are stated using only the laws of formal mathematics (i.e., the laws of logic, calculus, etc.) so that the "solution" is given in terms of formulas. Models of this kind are particularly helpful because *functional* relationships between variables are identified. Often analytic solutions can be given *in principle only* because the transformational rules can be formally stated, but the formal operations necessary to acquire a solution are too difficult or cumbersome to perform. A *numeric* solution is then appropriate and is obtained by substituting numbers for input variables and parameters, and manipulating them via the formally stated transformational rules to obtain a numeric solution. An alternate approach to obtaining a numeric solution is given by simulation.

SIMULATION

For both formal and simulation models we identify *components, component interactions,* and system and component *state variables* as discussed. The difference between formal and simulation models lies in the methodology employed to specify *transformational rules* and *variable* (attribute) *relationships.* First, recall that analytic models are *formal symbolic* models and therefore require that all variable relationships, component interactions, and evolutionary mechanisms be specified using the formalism of logic, algebra, the calculus, and so on. In contrast, in simulation models it is not necessary for all symbols to be manipulated by a *well-formed discipline.* In simulation models, this additional degree of freedom is realized by permitting the inclusion of *representational* or *procedural* descriptions of variable and component interactions. It is, in fact, this single capability which gives *simulation* its *appeal* and *versatility* (at a price, of course). These facts may be summarized as in Betz et al. [1974] that

> the methodology of simulation involves a representational approach
> to phenomena.

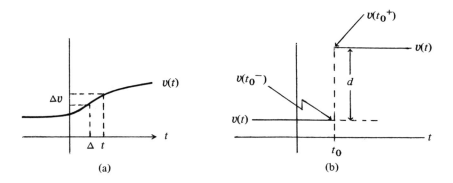

Figure 1.1   (a) Continuous and (b) Discrete simulations

Once stated, the above observations seem less than profound; however, if left unstated, they may go unnoticed.

Simulations can be further classified by the manner in which state
variables change values. *Continuous system simulations* are those in
which a variable $v(t)$, changes by an amount Δv in an increment Δt
of time (see Figure 1.1a). Discrete simulations are those in which
state variable values change by arbitrary amounts *only* at specified
time points (epochs). In Figure 1.1(b) the variable v changes by an
amount $d,$ at the epoch t_0. The epochs are determined by the proper
application of the transformational rules, and we define an *event* to
be *the instantaneous change in the value of one or more state variables.* Of the two kinds of simulations, the most flexible is discrete,
and it is the only type discussed in this book.

STOCHASTIC MODELS

A stochastic model is one in which one or more state variables are
stochastic, that is, take on values in accordance with a probability
distribution. The probability distribution may either vary or remain
constant with time.

The effects of stochastic state variables generally permeate the
entire model, so that the variables used to predict behavior (i.e., the
outputs) must also be considered stochastic in nature. We discuss the
ramifications of this situation in Chapter 6. Here we simply note that
stochastic variables are generally introduced as a method of dealing

with *uncertainty*; that is, when the values of a given state variable exhibit variation, but no discernible pattern in that variation can be found, then that variable may be best characterized by stochastic means.

EXAMPLE 1.1   Consider that we are developing a model of a service counter. As part of this endeavor we must characterize the manner in which customers arrive for service. Imagine further that we decide that the time between consecutive arrivals x is the appropriate characterization. We position ourselves by the counter and observe the time between customer arrivals so that we may parameterize our model. After a few observations we notice that consecutive values of x seem unrelated, and we suspect that the laws which govern x are quite complex. Try as we might, we may never discover a deterministic law governing the values of x. In the face of this uncertainty, we abandon the search for a deterministic characterization of x, and seek instead a probabilistic one. To that end we record the frequency with which x takes on a given value (if discrete variable) or the frequency with which the value is in a given subrange of observed values (if a continuous variable). On the basis of the data we then attempt to characterize x in terms of known probability distributions. To proceed we first identify candidate distributions, a task which is in part an art (see Martin [1962] for a discussion). Next, using statistical tests (e.g., the chi-square and Kolmogorov-Smirnov tests, see Fishman [1973]), we rank the appropriateness of our candidate distributions. These results are then used to select the appropriate distribution or to refine the procedure by suggesting additional candidate distributions. The procedure is continued until a selection is made.

QUEUEING THEORY

Many dynamic stochastic systems can be modeled by analytic machinery, especially those that may be viewed as "service systems."

The mathematical theory of stochastic service systems is known as queueing theory, and can be of considerable benefit to simulation. For this theory it is convenient to identify "customers," who arrive in a probabilistic manner at a service station. A backlog of customers is allowed to accumulate in a queue, and station servers attempt to

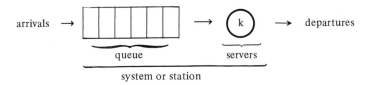

Figure 1.2 A service station

satisfy in some order, their probabilistic service requests. When we specify (1) the number of servers, (2) the nature of the arrival mechanism, and (3) the nature of the service times and queue selection mechanism we have, at least in principle, given sufficient information to answer all questions concerning the behavior of the service station.

For a single station system this information is given by specifying

1. The distribution $A(t)$ of interarrival times such that $A(t) = \Pr$ {time between consecutive arrivals $\leqslant t$}
2. The service time distribution $S(t) = \Pr$ {customer service time $\leqslant t$}
3. The number k of identical servers operating independently and in parallel
4. The queue selection discipline

Figure 1.2 depicts the situation.

Generally station behavior is characterized by

1. Distribution of queue length
2. Distribution of delay customers experience
3. Utilization of the servers

Queueing theory proceeds by declaring the *state* of the system to be given by the number $N(t)$ of customers who occupy it at time t. We say the system is in state E_n (at t) if it contains n customers. Because customer arrival and service requirements obey probabilistic laws, so will $N(t)$. It is thus natural to seek information on

$$P_n(t) = \Pr\{N(t) = n\}$$

from which information on items (1-3) above can be obtained.

A simple example will serve to introduce several notions.

EXAMPLE 1.2   Consider a system with $k = 1$, $A(t) = 1 - e^{-\lambda t}$, $S(t) = 1 - e^{-\mu t}$ (exponential distributions) and for which no queue is allowed to form. The latter condition is plausible if we agree that customers who arrive to find the server busy, immediately leave the system and thus have no effect upon it. The allowable states are E_0 and E_1. For this system it can easily be shown [Cooper 1972] that

$$P_0(t) = \frac{\mu}{\lambda + \mu} + \left(P_0(0) - \frac{\mu}{\lambda + \mu}\right)e^{-(\lambda + \mu)t} \qquad (1.1)$$

and

$$P_1(t) = \frac{\lambda}{\lambda + \mu} + \left(P_1(0) - \frac{\lambda}{\lambda + \mu}\right)e^{-(\lambda + \mu)t} \qquad (1.2)$$

where $P_0(0)$, $P_1(0)$ are the initial state probabilities.

The probabilities $P_0(t)$, $P_1(t)$ clearly vary with time, the variations being dependent in part upon the initial state probabilities.

As the system operates for a longer and longer period of time, however, the variations in the values of $P_0(t)$, $P_1(t)$ die out. Mathematically we can investigate the limiting situation, that is, as $t \to \infty$, and define

$$P_0 = \lim_{t \to \infty} P_0(t) = \frac{\mu}{\lambda + \mu} \qquad (1.3)$$

$$P_1 = \lim_{t \to \infty} P_1(t) = \frac{\lambda}{\lambda + \mu} \qquad (1.4)$$

We are assured that as t, the operation time of the system, increases, $P_0(t)$, $P_1(t)$ approach P_0 and P_1, respectively. Thus, after the system has been in operation for a sufficiently long time, the state probabilities become (nearly) independent of the initial conditions and for practical purposes assume the values given by Equations (1.3) and (1.4). For this reason we refer to the probabilities given by Equations (1.1) and (1.2) as transient, and those given by Equations (1.3) and (1.4) as equilibrium or stationary. The speed or rate with which $P_0(t) \to P_0$ and $P_1(t) \to P_1$ is, of course, dependent on the constant associated with exponential decay term in Equations (1.1) and (1.2).

Note also that the equilibrium distribution is stationary in the sense that if the system enters equilibrium at time t_0, it is in equilibrium for all $t > t_0$. That is, once the system enters equilibrium it stays in equilibrium, and its state probabilities remain constant in time.

If system operation is begun with say $P_0(0) = 1$, $P_0(0) = 0$ rather than with Equations (1.3) and (1.4), we can identify two distinct phases of system behavior. During the first or transient phase, the state probabilities vary with time, and during the second, statistical equilibrium nearly prevails. The boundary which separates the two phases is not sharp, but certainly for t greater than some (unknown) T_0, equilibrium essentially prevails. This observation is of direct importance to the conduct of simulation, and we shall return to it in Chapter 6.

For general service systems a mathematical determination of $P_n(t)$, $t > 0$, is all but impossible. Fortunately in a number of cases for which steady-state solutions *exist*, determination of P_n, $n \geqslant 0$, is possible, and queueing theory is concerned chiefly with equilibrium results.[1]

The values P_n, and so the other behavioral measures, are heavily dependent on the load placed on the system. If $T_a = 1/\lambda$ is the mean of the interarrival distribution $A(t)$, and $T_s = 1/\mu$ is the mean of the service time distribution $S(t)$, then ρ, the load per server (valid for systems in which all arrivals wait for service) is given by

$$\rho = \frac{\lambda}{\mu k} \tag{1.5}$$

and represents the utilization (fraction of time busy) of each server. As a utilization we must have $0 < \rho < 1$, and in fact it can be shown that the equilibrium distribution exists only if ρ is so bounded. For $k = 1$ we also have $P_0 = 1 - \rho$.

Additionally, most system behavioral measures are also dependent on the distributional forms of $A(t)$, $S(t)$, and the queue discipline. One very useful result, known as Little's result, is valid for arbitrary $A(t)$, $S(t)$, and almost all conceivable scheduling disciplines, because its validity essentially depends only on the existence of steady-state or equilibrium conditions. The result is usually presented in the form

$$L_s = \lambda W_s \tag{1.6}$$

---

[1] Some service systems never reach statistical equilibrium.

where L_s is the expected number of customers in the system, W_s is the expected time a customer spends in the system, and λ is $1/T_a$ as before. Further, since T_s is the average time a customer spends in service, the average time W_q a customer waits (in queue) for service is given by

$$W_q = L_s/\lambda - T_s \tag{1.7}$$

and the average number of customers in queue, L_q, is given by

$$L_q = L_s - k\rho. \tag{1.8}$$

EXAMPLE 1.3   Among the systems which succumb to analysis are those for which $A(t) = 1 - e^{-\lambda t}$, $S(t) = 1 - e^{-\mu t}$, that is, for which the interarrival and service times are exponentially distributed. From among those we present results for the system with a FCFS queue discipline and k servers. If all arrivals wait for service, then it can be shown (see Kleinrock [1975]) that

$$P_n = \begin{cases} \dfrac{1}{n!}\left(\dfrac{\lambda}{\mu}\right)^n P_0 & n = 0, 1, ..., k \\[3mm] \dfrac{1}{k^{n-k}\,k!}\left(\dfrac{\lambda}{\mu}\right)^n P_0 & n = k+1, k+2, ... \end{cases} \tag{1.9}$$

with

$$P_0 = \left[\sum_{n=0}^{k} \frac{1}{n!}\left(\frac{\lambda}{\mu}\right)^n + \frac{(\lambda/\mu)^{k+1}}{kk!\,(1 - \lambda/(k\mu))}\right]^{-1}$$

since we must have $\sum_{n=0}^{\infty} P_n = 1$. Notice that $P_n \to 0$ as $n \to \infty$. Then

$$L = \sum_{n=0}^{\infty} nP_n \tag{1.10}$$

and from Equations (1.6), (1.7), (1.8) W, W_q, and L_q are easily obtained. When $k = 1$, (1.9) reduces to

$$P_n = \rho^n(1 - \rho) \qquad n = 0, 1, ... \tag{1.11}$$

Similar results for variants of this example are summarized by Kleinrock [1975, Chapter 3]. As we deviate from exponential

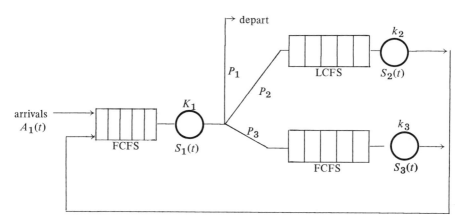

Figure 1.3 A network of service stations

distributions and an FCFS queue discipline, results are more difficult to obtain, and when obtained do not take as simple a form as Equations (1.9) or (1.11). Again Kleinrock [1975] should be consulted for a summary.

Whenever it is possible for customers departing one service station to immediately enter another, a queueing network results. If we call each network service station a node (each node having the form given in Figure 1.2), then characterization of an m node network requires specification of $A_i(t)$, $S_i(t)$, $i = 1, m$ and customer node to node traversal patterns.

EXAMPLE 1.4 Consider the network of service stations given in Figure 1.3. Customers enter the network at node 1, and following service there migrate to node 2, node 3, or exit the network with probabilities P_2, P_3, and P_1, respectively. Following service at nodes 2 and 3 they return to node 1. Since customers enter and depart the network it is called *open*. (When a fixed number of customers circulate endlessly within a network it is called *closed*.) The state of an m node network is given by the vector

$$n = (n_1, n_2, ..., n_m)$$

with the components n_i specifying the number of customers in node i.

Network operation can often be characterized by a transient and equilibrium phase, so it becomes meaningful to seek the equilibrium distribution *Pn*. As reported by Kleinrock [1975] the *Pn* are known for a variety of open and closed networks. Given *Pn*, Equation (1.6) can then be applied to the network as a whole (if open) or to each node.

Queueing theory benefits simulation in several ways. First, if the behavior of a system is known from queueing theory, its simulation is unnecessary. Second, simulation models are not easy to interpret with respect to cause and effect relationships between model parameters and behavioral measures. Therefore, even if a given situation is not represented exactly by queueing theoretic results, they may give insights into such relationships and aid in the construction and use of a simulation model. We discuss these issues in Chapter 6, and close this chapter with a recipe for the development of model programs.

STAGES OF SIMULATION MODEL DEVELOPMENT

The development of a simulation model of a real or proposed system is a *purposeful, orderly* activity. It is purposeful in that certain modeling goals are defined and understood. It is planned in that a well-defined, partially iterative procedure is available for model development and thus the realization of the stated goals. The initial stage of the modeling process (the zero-th) requires a clear statement of the objectives of the modeling effort. This includes enumeration of the questions for which the model must ultimately provide answers, together with performance measures appropriate for answering them. In short, the 0th stage defines the problem statement. The goals and measures identified in this stage must be realistic, taking into account the feasibility of obtaining model parameters and results. Following the initial stage, model development is governed by five additional stages which are given by Mirham [1972] as follows:

1. *System Analysis*. The initial stage of development, during which the salient components, interactions, relationships, and dynamic behavior mechanisms of a system are isolated;
2. *System Synthesis*. That stage of development during which the model of the system's behavior is organized in accordance with the findings of the preceding System Analysis stage, and

during which appropriate support data is delineated and collected;

3. *Verification*. The third stage of development, during which the model's responses are compared with those which would have been anticipated if *indeed* the model's structure was prepared as intended;

4. *Validation*. That stage of development during which the responses emanating from the verified model are compared with corresponding observations of, and measurements from, the actual system in order to establish the verisimilitude of the model and the modeled system;

5. *Inference*. The final stage of development, concerned with the definition of experiments with, and comparison of the responses from, the verified and validated model.

As elaboration and clarification of the above stages we observe the following:

1. Stage 1 identifies model entities. This is followed by a specification of entity attributes, or descriptors. Once the mechanisms by which they change values are identified, the state variables and transformational rules are enumerated.

2. This stage realizes the model. Since the computer language influences the realization, it must be selected at this stage.

3. This stage debugs. Debugging is complicated by the outputs of the model program being stochastic variables. Theoretical results often are useful for comparing with the simulation results to test for consistency with known cases. One sample statistical tests must be employed for stochastic models. Failure of model program outputs to compare favorably with predicted theoretical values implies a deficiency in the model structure and thus a necessary return to the task of stage 2. This feedback or iteration, as well as others, is depicted in Figure 1.4.

4. This stage compares with reality. Failure of the model to compare favorably with data collected from the subject system implies a return to stage 2. In the case of stochastic models, two sample statistical tests can be useful in determining the favorability of the comparison. An improper comparison

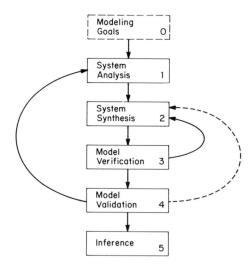

Figure 1.4   The modeling process

may force us to rethink the abstractions arrived at during stage 1.

The object of our discourse is an orderly procedure for the development and use of model programs. The procedure is none other than the classical scientific method. A more complete discussion of these matters can be found, for example, in Mihram [1972, 1974, all entries].

CHAPTER 2

A General View of Simulation and Simulation Systems

In Chapter 1 we touched upon simulation, and from among the activities that could be so labeled, focused our attention on the activity in which state variable values change (by arbitrary amounts) instantaneously at *specified* epochs. In Chapter 1 we called these changes *events* and now designate their occurrence epochs as *event times.* Operationally, then, discrete simulation consists of a sequence of events e_i occurring at event times t_i. This behavior can be realized by one of two general approaches, each requiring maintenance of a clock t. Either:

1. We can proceed by continually advancing the clock by one time unit ($t \leftarrow t + 1$), "checking" if any events are eligible to occur during the intervening interval, and if so, performing the required transformations. We call this the *unit advance* approach.

2. Alternately, we can maintain a collection of *records*

$$(e_1, t_1)(e_2, t_2) \dots (e_n, t_n)$$

in which e_i identifies an event and t_i its occurrence time, with $t_1 \leqslant t_2 \leqslant \dots \leqslant t_n$. Associate $t := t_1$ with the current time making e_1 the current event. Execution of the transformation rule identified by e_1 may cause the generation of additional (e_i, t_i) pairs (i.e., the *scheduling* of additional events) or cancellation of existing pairs (i.e., the cancellation of pending events). Upon completion we set $t := t_2$ and repeat.

The merits of these two approaches are discussed in Chapter 8. Here we simply note that the second is generally preferred, and simulations that employ it are characterized by the phrase *event list driven, event driven,* or *discrete event.*

13

We can, therefore, view simulation as an activity concerned with the generation and cancellation of event notices, transformational rule selection, and clock maintenance. It is a valid view, in fact, the correct view if we are concerned with *implementing* a simulation system. But from the viewpoint of model program development, it is too detailed and offers no *conceptual framework* to guide the effort. Thus, a second viewpoint more appropriate to the user or *analyst* is necessary. The two views are entangled, of course, since the analyst must develop simulations *using* the concepts and machinery developed by an implementer. For purposes of exposition we momentarily separate them.

ANALYST'S VIEW

The analyst's tasks were delineated in the last section of the preceding chapter. In summary he or she must (a) understand the nature of subject system elements and their interactions, and then (b) express these interactions (transformations) in a clear and simple way (as a computer program). Next, using (c) parameters and distributions determined from collected data and/or theoretical considerations he or she must, (d) perform simulations, collect data, and interpret results. The result of step (b) is the model program upon which the *act* of simulation depends.

As noted earlier, simulation models are based on representational descriptions of entity interactions and state variable transformations that must be specified in the computer (model) program which, when executed, *traces* or *mimics* the dynamic behavior of the modeled system. This program is, then, the realization of the model (as contrasted with the realization of the modeled system). Further, the specification of the computer program, that is, the model realization, must be made within the *confines* of the *abstractions* or *concepts* supported by the computer language selected to *implement* the model. Thus, the language choice greatly influences the way the modeled system is viewed.

Model programs have been realized using assembly language, FORTRAN, ALGOL, and many other general purpose languages. In fact evidence suggests that up to 70 percent of all simulations are realized using FORTRAN. The reasons are clear; namely, it is simple to learn, widely available, and its compilers generally produce very efficient object code.

As every reader knows there are also several languages expressly designed to support the simulation activity, and for that activity they are superior to general purpose languages. They achieve their status by supplying language concepts and support machinery directly applicable to the simulation activity. They occasionally fail to enjoy their sought status by requiring unduly long execution times. We shall turn to this latter point in Chapter 8, and return now to the first.

There are several ways in which simulation languages are designed to facilitate that activity; that is, they are designed (see Dahl [1968]):

1. To aid the model builder by presenting a *conceptual frame-work* for *precise thinking*. The elements of the language are *abstractions* which apply to a wide class of phenomena. Their application consists of identifying and describing the system being modeled in terms of the given language concepts.

2. To provide a notation for the description of dynamic behavior.

3. To serve as a programming aid; to facilitate the detection and correction of logical errors. (This feature has also been termed *security* (see Rogeberg [1973]).

4. To facilitate the generation of stochastic variates. This implies multiple random number streams and variate generators.

5. To aid in the dynamic collection, analysis, and display of statistical data.

6. To efficiently trace the dynamic behavior of model programs.

All six points are important and each is discussed in subsequent chapters. Here we elaborate on the first, for it bears heavily on the viability and general applicability of the language. If the conceptual framework supported by a language is at the heart of the description of a variety of situations, then the language exhibits a system to model closeness which makes use of the language both natural and easy. This in turn decreases development costs, increases the readability of the model program, and provides a self-documenting feature. The difficult part is to identify those concepts and abstractions (for inclusion in a simulation language) which are rich enough to be useful in a variety of situations, yet exhibit model closeness in all of them. In summary, a language that successfully meets the objectives in the preceding six points offers a major time advantage in the preparation and use of a model program. Reductions by a factor of ten have been reported [Emshoff, 1970]. Note also that, realistically, availability is as important a factor as 1 through 6 above. To be useful, a simulation language must be available on most if not all major computers, and a compatability between machine implementations is essential.

IMPLEMENTER'S VIEW

The implementer must provide machinery necessary to support the activities of the preceding six points; that is, he or she must

(a) Keep a record of pending events and their times of occurrence.
(b) Provide mechanisms for the generation and cancellation of event records.
(c) Provide routines to generate samples from common distributions.
(d) Provide routines for gathering data and for displaying output statistics.

The manner in which the implementer meets the demands of (a) through (d) determines the division of labor between the model program and the simulation system, and does much to determine the flexibility and applicability of the system. Here we concentrate on the requirements of (b), because their realization determines the conceptual framework of the simulation system. To that end we expand upon (b) and note that the simulation system (and/or language) must support

1. The concept and realization of a clock to record the passage of simulated time. As stated it is advanced in discrete jumps, and when updated is made to reflect the time of the next most imminent event.
2. Constructs that allow model program statements to specify the time at which an event is to occur, or alternately, to designate a Boolean function, such that the event is to occur at the first time point for which the function is logically true.

3. A support routine to insure that events occur in proper sequence at the proper epochs. This support routine is generally known as the *control program.*

The manner in which various simulation languages (systems) supply these functions is highly varied. Three approaches predominate, however, and they have come to be known as *activity scanning, event,* and *process interaction.* No matter which approach is used, execution of the model program is governed by the control program as depicted in Figure 2.1 until the execution *termination* criterion is reached.[2]

The code segments constitute the model program. Their number and structure are determined by the approach to sequencing the language supports, which also determines whether the segments are procedures or coroutines.

For the activity approach each segment has a preamble which contains a Boolean function, the segment being eligible for execution at each epoch for which the function value is logically true. Events are thus implicitly rather than explicitly scheduled. For the event approach, events are generally explicitly scheduled, (i.e., their occurrence times are specified). The code segments then correspond to the specifications of the transformational rule which accompany or define each identifiable event. These are known as *event routines.*

For the process interaction approach the segments are generally coroutines to be *reactivated* at specified epochs. This approach constitutes the main subject of this text, and its specific treatment is begun in the next chapter. Examples of extant simulation languages which employ each of the three approaches are given in Table 2.1.

Our reason for pursuing the process interaction approach is that

---

[2] Control program activation of a segment is based on the (e_i, t_i) records, which are commonly called event notices. Each notice identifies a code segment (via e_i) and the clock time t_i for its next activation or reactivation. The notice may also contain certain ancillary information. The notices are ordered in the *event list* by increasing clock time and are used to insure proper sequencing of events by ordering the activations of code segments. A notice is thus added to the event list to *schedule* an event (activation of a code segment) and is generally deleted when the specified event (activation) has occurred. This method is very effective when the event times can be predicted, but makes *direct* Boolean function specification of activation or reactivation impossible. We shall elaborate on this point in Chapter 7.

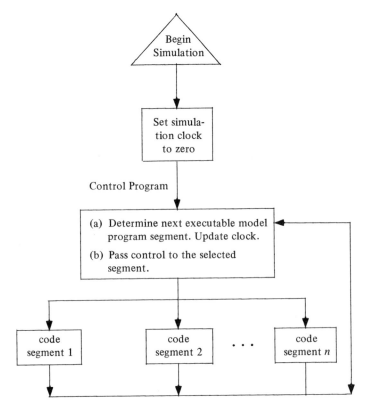

Figure 2.1 Basic sequencing procedure

Table 2.1
Sequencing Approaches Employed by Various Simulation Languages

Event-oriented Languages	Activity-oriented Languages	Process-oriented Languages
GASP [Pritscher, 1969]	AS [Parslow, 1967]	GPSS (all versions) [Gordon, 1975]
SEAL [IBM, 1968]	CSL [IBM, 1966]	NSS [Parente, 1966]
SIMCOM [GE, 1964]	ESP [Williams, 1964]	OPS [Greenberger, 1965]
SIMPAC [Bennett, 1962]		SIMPLE [Donovan, 1968]
SIMSCRIPT (all versions) [Kiviat, 1968]		SIMULA
	SILLY [U.S. Steel, 1968]	SOL [Knuth, 1964]
	SIMON [Jills, 1967]	SPL [Petrone, 1967]
		ASPOL [MacDougall, 1973]

we believe it to be most "natural" in a variety of modeling situations. We shall develop this approach from both the analyst and implementer views, even though they are entangled. Nevertheless we can characterize the subsequent chapters by the principal view from which they are developed. In summary we have: *Analyst's View,* Chapters 3, 5, 6, 7; *Implementer's View,* Chapters 4, 5, 8.

CHAPTER 3

The Scenario Approach to Simulation

THE NOTION OF A SCENARIO DESCRIPTION

In this chapter we begin our discussion of the process approach to simulation. For the moment we will not worry about language availability or detailed language implementation considerations. Instead we shall consider the following approach to the construction of model programs.

Let us assume that stage 1 development has been completed. For stage 2, we begin by examining system behavior from the view of a selected component, and thus develop a *scenario* of behavior by that component. The scenario includes, of course, the transformational rules which that component applies, together with an accounting of its possible need to request or react to application of transformational rules which are naturally part of the scenario descriptions of other components. The model program is then given by the scenario descriptions of possibly several components, and it is complete when an accounting has been made of all component interactions (synchronizations) and transformational rules which were identified during stage 1 development.

AN ATTEMPTED DEVELOPMENT

In further pursuit of these vague ideas we select a simple system and attempt to develop a scenario description model program. The system selected is a service station with a single server which serves arriving units on a first-come-first-served (FIFO) basis. Units arriving when the server is busy serving an earlier arrival join a queue to await their turn. We will assume that service times and unit interarrival times are specified by exponential variates.

A number of scenarios which describe the system can be written. A seemingly natural starting point is the scenario specification of the system from the server's view. Placing ourselves in the position of the server, logically we must

1. Establish the queueing mechanisms (assuming the queue is to be associated with the server) then repeat the following steps until the simulation termination criteria is met.
2. Examine the queue for empty. If queue is empty, skip to step 6.
3. Remove unit from queue.
4. Perform service (via *delay*) for selected unit.
5. Go to step 2.
6. *Wait* for next unit to arrive. When unit arrives return to step 2.

Notice that our scenario has the form of an algorithm. This is apt if the scenario is to be part of a model program executable by a computer. Hence, we might label our result a *scenario algorithm.* In such algorithms, the service is represented as a delay. For the scenario approach, the implication is that the code segment containing the delay can not be further executed until the clock has been advanced by an amount equal to the service time. That is, following the execution of the delay statement, execution of the code segment is temporarily abandoned and the control routine is again executed (see Figure 2.1). (Execution of the delay must result in the entry of an event notice into the event list specifying that execution of the abandoned segment is to be *continued,* from point of departure, at the completion of the service delay.) The statement following the statement specifying the delay is the first executed at continuation and is known as a *reactivation point.* Further, when segment execution is continued it is said to be *reactivated.*

The effect of step 6, that is, wait, is slightly different. It signals a delay with the same continuation rule as for the delay statement, except that its duration is not specified. [Because only events whose occurrence times are known can be represented in the events list, no notice can be generated in the "wait" case. The control program *reactivates* a segment only upon encountering an event notice in the list which dictates that it do so. (Note that the delay statement thus allows a segment to *schedule* its own reactivation time).] Thus, once the segment executes step 6, its reactivation can occur only by virtue of *another* segment having generated a notice on its behalf. (We say that the activity of the segment is *suspended.*) But what other segment? No account has been given of the arrival mechanism for the system being modeled. The other necessary segment will be given by specifying the scenario of the arrival mechanism. The fact that there is no physical "arrival" component does not keep us from the task. In fact, if we consider the arrival mechanism as a *logical* rather than physical system component, any possible objection is removed. Moreover, it was never stated or implied that scenarios had to be based on the behavior of *physical* system components. We proceed then by examining the behavior of the arrival mechanism which produces the scenario algorithm:

1. Generate and save interarrival time.
2. Generate a job (a data object).
3. Place the job in the server queue.
4. If the server scenario execution is discontinued in step 6, generate an event notice for its continuation (for current clock time), that is, *schedule* its reactivation for current clock time.
5. Allow interarrival period to elapse (via *delay*).
6. Return to step 1.

Step 4 provides the necessary event notice for the eventual continued execution of the server scenario algorithm *if* it becomes interrupted.
    Several questions remain unanswered. They include, for example,

1. How is the simulation started, stopped?
2. How can a statement in the arrival mechanism scenario algorithm (step 4) determine if the server scenario algorithm is discontinued as a result of *its* step 4 or step 6, that is, is it or is it not suspended? (It is obviously discontinued since the arrival scenario statements are being executed to make the determination.)
3. How might we implement the constructs associated with the delay and wait abstractions?
4. How do we identify scenarios?
5. What mechanism is used to generate the job data objects?

Questions from a related but somewhat different category include: How much effort must we expend to include two or more servers, two or more arrival streams, a different *queue discipline*?

In the next chapter we pursue these matters more vigorously. In this chapter we have attempted to introduce certain notions in an easy and informal manner. Next, however, we give a *semiformal* presentation* of the two scenarios. To do so we must assume the language constructs delay and wait, and control structures as found, for example, in ALGOL (see Ekman [1965]).

The scenario algorithm descriptions might then take the form

```
scenario server;³
generate queue named queue;
wait;
while true do
Begin
while queue ⌐ empty do
    Begin
    remove job from queue;
    draw service time for object job;
    delay service time;
    destroy job;
    end;
wait;
end;
end scenario description server;

scenario arrivals;
while true do
Begin
    draw interarrival time;
    generate job;
    place service time in job object, and job object in
    queue named queue;
    if server not represented in event list place notice for current
    time for it in event list (i.e., schedule its reactivation for current
    time); delay interarrival time as generated;
end;
end scenario description arrivals;
```

These descriptions, together with Figure 2.1, the description of event notices, and the event list, as well as the intended behavior of the delay and wait constructs give some insight into the concepts we

---

³ The semicolon delineates statements.

wish to support in a simulation language. We have pursued these matters in the belief that (see Houle et al. [1974]):

> The scenario approach for an element within a model localizes the attributes of the element necessary to represent its local state and protocol for interaction with other objects into a single structural entity. In this way the element state and actions are carried together as a natural partition of the total model.

PROCESSES AND PROCESS SYNCHRONIZATION

In the previous section we partially developed a model program for a single server queueing station consisting of two *interacting* scenario descriptions. The two descriptions were written so that a single processor could obey (execute) them in a piecemeal fashion giving attention first to one and then the other, such that each time processor attention is directed to one of the pair, execution is continued from the point of *last abandonment*. Further, as we have stated, the temporary abandonment may be for a specified or unspecified duration; the act of continuation is known as *reactivation,* and the first statement to be executed upon reactivation is called a *reactivation point.* The environment just described is one inhabited by *coroutines.* Thus, at an *operational level*, the scenario descriptions must be considered coroutines, a fact to remember when implementing a language to support our scenario view. Our tendency here, however, will be to consider the scenario descriptions not as coroutines but rather as *processes,* for reasons discussed next.

Let us reconsider the example of the last section. There the scenario descriptions were developed around (or from) the view of the server and arrival mechanisms. Alternately we could have developed the scenario around (or from) the view of the individual arriving units. Such is, in fact, the approach taken by GPSS. For the example, each view is viable and the important point is that the machinery we are developing will allow the choice. Notice further, that for the view developed, the server and arrival mechanism are *active* elements and the arriving units *passive* elements, whereas for the view now considered the reverse is true. A semiformal scenario model program with the arriving units as the active elements might take the following form.

scenario unit;
draw interarrival time and set into variable ia;
cause *next* unit to arrive at time given by current time + ia;
examine server;
if server busy then
    Begin
    join queue associated with server;
    wait;
    remove self from queue associated with server;
    end;
indicate that server is engaged by *this* unit;
Delay service time;
clear indicator set above;
examine queue'
if queue not empty then
place notice for activation of first unit in queue at current time;
end scenario description unit;

The scenario description is, of course, intended to serve as the behavior pattern for *all* units that enter the modeled system. Since a backlog (queue) of units may develop, we must expect the system to contain several units at any given moment. It is necessary to account for the state of each unit present in the modeled system. We can do so by specifying its status regarding the execution of the statements in the behavioral (scenario) description. We can make such an accounting by noting that the processor can at any moment be executing the scenario description statements on behalf of a single unit only. For the other units, the progress through the scenario must be suspended (as a result of wait or delay) or only about to begin as in the case of a new arrival. To distinguish between these alternatives, and at the same time provide a logical mechanism to account for units, we can assume that each has a unique copy of the scenario description associated with it, that creation of a unit implies generation of the copy, and that when the processor attempts to pass through the final end statement of a copy, the copy, and thus the unit, is cancelled and ceases to exist. We will assume further that each copy has a variable LSC associated with it (local sequence of control), which points (for suspended units) to the reactivation point statement, and for newly created units which have not yet received processor attention to the first statement of the scenario description. The construct we have sketched is generally known as a *process*. More formally, for the purposes of simulation, we may say that

> ... a process is a dynamic entity, a singularly occurring instance of execution of a set of logically related activities. Processes comprised of like sets of activities are considered to belong to the same *class*. At any point in time a number of such processes may exist in a system model, in varying stages of execution. Each is an instance or *object* of its class, uniquely identified among members of that class by certain attributes. The behavior of processes of the same class may be described by a single set of rules describing the activities of all processes from that class (the action statements) together with a set of attribute(s) values for each of the existing processes of that class (activation record). [MacDougall, 1973]

For the first variant of our model we observe that the *class* (scenario) declarations would ultimately support one process each, whereas from the second variant *class* declaration, several processes will spring.

The piecemeal execution by a *single* processor of the statements associated with the individual processes creates the *illusion* of parallel activity, and is thus termed *quasi-parallel processing*. Notice that a coroutine environment is necessary but not sufficient to support our simulations. In addition, we must support processes (multiple copies emanating from the same coroutine declaration) *and* certain *synchronizing primitives* to manipulate notices and thus activation and reactivation times.

Note further that our notion of process is essentially identical to the one associated with operating systems. In fact, a reader familiar with operating systems may find our development somewhat simplistic.

Here, as there, we are concerned with providing an adequate and convenient set of *synchronization* primitives. We define (see Hansen [1973]) synchronization as a general term implying a constraint on the order of operations in time. Since process objects must share resources and work cooperatively to mimic system behavior, we are particularly interested in synchronizations which provide mutual exclusion and a variety of cooperative process interactions. We define mutual exclusion as

> a mechanism whereby processes can acquire *exclusive* control of a *resource* for a period of time and then reliquish that control. Processes *competing* for the resource thus gain access to or control of the resource in *some* sequential order, the exact order being determined by the method of reassignment following release.

A mutual exclusion mechanism is necessary to manage the use of any *single capacity* resource which can be demanded by more than one object. Typical examples include the central processing unit in a computer system, a phone booth on a busy street, a shopping cart in a supermarket, and so on.

Requests for such resources must be made through the mutual exclusion device, where a record of unhonored requests is kept, so that when the resource is released by one process object, assignment to another is possible.

A mutual exclusion mechanism is precipitated by a competitive interaction among process objects. As our queuing example illustrates, scenario view simulation models also depend heavily on *cooperative* interactions among process objects. In variant one, for example, we can think of the arrival mechanism as *producing* units and the server as *consuming* them. The producer must restart the consumer if it has become idle, and the consumer must wait for arrival of additional units when its backlog becomes exhausted. For this situation, the arrival and service process objects must be aware of, and dependent upon, each other.

Frequently, situations occur wherein one set of process objects produces units of a commodity which are consumed by a second set of process objects. Synchronization is required so that objects of the second set do not attempt to consume nonexistent units of the commodity, and so that objects of the first set do not produce more than an allowed stockpile of the commodity. We refer to such constraints as producer/consumer synchronizations.

Finally, we consider a third situation wherein process objects require a certain partial or complete system state before their continuation is possible (denote the condition for the state by the Boolean B). Those objects that test and find that state does not prevail must be allowed to continue at the first epoch for which B becomes true. Potential epochs are those following all or a specified subset of system events. Following these events, each discontinued process object that might be effected (as determined by the nature of B and the event) must be allowed to recheck for a possible change in B. We refer to such synchronizations as *mass retrys* and consider them as a generalization of mutual exclusion and producer/consumer synchronizations.

In Chapter 5 we discuss these synchronizations further and provide simple realizations for each. Some readers will recognize that these synchronizations are simple variants of those associated with operating systems. A reader interested in pursuing these matters in that domain is referred to Hansen [1973].

CHAPTER 4

SIMULA: Providing the Tools

The use of processes as a method of realizing model programs was first proposed in the early 1960s by Knuth [1964] in the SOL language.[1] It is perhaps unfortunate that SOL did not receive the necessary support to bring it to common use. The SIMULA language, however, did. It was developed in Norway with the realization of model programs as the major (perhaps only) impetus. The original report can be found in Dahl [1966]. Like most languages it evolved and exists today in three versions. The original version [Dahl, 1966] remains available on UNIVAC equipment, whereas the second version can be found on most other computer systems. Definitive specification of the second version is given in Dahl et al. [1970]. Although there are important differences between the first and second versions, the second and third differ by the presence in the third of certain control structures not found in the second. A definitive report on this latest version may be found in Appendix A of Birtwhistle et al. [1973]. Our discussions will utilize the structures found in version two and, therefore, in the main version three as well.

SIMULA begins with ALGOL and extends the block concept to allow the generation and naming of blocks which can coexist as coroutines. Such blocks are known as *objects* and are generated from templates known as *class* declarations. We can, therefore, consider SIMULA to be ALGOL *plus* constructs necessary to

1. Specify class declarations
2. Generate coroutine objects from class declarations
3. Name generated objects and manipulate variables associated *with* named generated objects
4. *Concatenate* class declarations to realize a hierarchical structure of class declarations

---

[1] GPSS, as stated, also supports the process view, but in a more restrictive way because the active and passive elements are *predetermined*. GPSS dates from 1962.

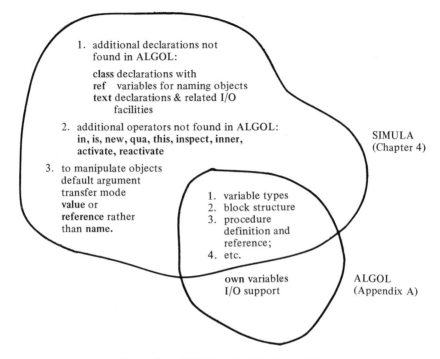

Figure 4.1   SIMULA ALGOL relationship

An understanding of SIMULA thus presupposes a familiarity with ALGOL, a summary of which is given in Appendix A. If we *add* a series of additional declaration forms and operators to ALGOL (to facilitate (1) through (4)) and *delete* those features of ALGOL which were poorly conceived, the result is SIMULA. The additions and deletions are summarized by Figure 4.1.

In this chapter we elaborate on the notions just introduced. In Chapter 5 we use these features to realize a flexible process oriented simulation system.

METALANGUAGE

A definitive statement of ALGOL exists in a document known as the ALGOL report.[2] The report gives a precise accounting of the

---

[2] The report may be found, for example, as an Appendix, in Bauman [1964].

language syntax and semantics. The precise syntax description is given via a metalanguage, a collection of symbols and definitions designed to describe the logical structure of a language. Because SIMULA is an extension of ALGOL, the same metalanguage should apply. It does, and in Bauman et al. [1964] and Birtwhistle et al. [1973] it is the device used to give a precise syntax description supplemented by an English language accounting of language semantics. Since we will make some use of the metalanguage, and since pursuit of SIMULA will eventually require reference to Dahl et al. [1970], we briefly consider its structure. To begin, we define certain metasymbols:

⟨a⟩ = an object from the collection of objects known as a

∷= = consists of

| = or

+ + = items enclosed within symbols are optional

{ } = a grouping device

The language syntax can be completely described by (possibly recursive) formulas using these symbols.

EXAMPLE 4.1   To demonstrate the use of these symbols we define ALGOL or SIMULA variable identifiers.
Syntax

⟨identifier⟩∷=⟨letter⟩|⟨identifier⟩⟨letter⟩|⟨identifier⟩⟨digit⟩

Semantics

identifiers serve to identify simple variables, arrays,
labels and procedures. They may be freely chosen.

Notice that identifiers must begin with a letter (the definition is *recursive*) and may be of any length. In this and the following chapter we freely use the metalanguage when it is felt that doing so contributes to the clarity of the presentation.

CLASS DECLARATIONS AND OBJECT GENERATION

As stated concisely by Dahl et al. [1972],

> ... a procedure which is capable of giving rise to block instances
> which survive its call is known as a class; and the instances will be
> known as objects of that class.

The declaration of a **class** has a form which parallels procedure
declarations, and is given by:

⟨class declaration⟩::= **class** ⟨class identifier⟩
              ⟨formal parameter part⟩;⟨specification part⟩;
              ⟨class body⟩
⟨class body⟩::=⟨statement⟩

As with procedures, the class body may be made considerable by
structuring and delineating it with **begin end** pairs. The formal
parameters, variables, and procedures declared within the body
constitute the *attributes* of that class.

Thus, considering the class body to be a *block,* we can view a
class declaration as having the following syntactic form and block
structure.

class $C_1(FP_1)$;
SP_1;
begin
    D_1;
    E_1;
end C_1;
	AP_1

	D_1
	E_1

C_1 = declaration syntax   object structure

where

      C_1 = class identifier
      FP_1 = formal parameters
      SP_1 = parameter specifications (parameter types and nondefault
            transfer modes)

AP_1 = actual parameters
D_1 = attribute declarations (includes variables and procedures)
E_1 = executable statements of *class* declaration, given via arbitrary block structuring.

EXAMPLE 4.2   To demonstrate, we specify a class declaration which characterizes a person's job. As input we give the hourly pay rate and years of service. The executable statements of the declaration calaculate the number of weeks of vacation earned, and the yearly salary excluding vacation pay. The declaration appears as:

```
class person (rate per hour, years of service);
real rate per hour; integer years of service;
begin
integer yearly salary, weeks of vacation;

weeks of vacation:= if years of service <5 then 1
                    else 2;

yearly salary:= (rate per hour)×40×(52-weeks of vacation);
end person;
```

Person objects have the attributes of rate per hour, years of service, yearly salary, and weeks of vacation, with *each person* object in possession of *private attribute* values. Thus each person object has *local* variables with the above named identifiers. New person objects are generated via expressions such as

```
new person(1.50, 2)
new person(2.00, 10)
```

Objects are generated by the functional designator *new* which returns as a value a *reference* (pointer) to the newly generated object. Formally we have that:

⟨object generator⟩::=**new**⟨class identifier⟩
                     ⟨actual parameter part⟩[3]

In order to subsequently refer to generated objects, the value

---

[3] The parameter transmission modes of SIMULA are summarized in Appendix B; an explanation of their meanings is given in Appendix C.

returned by the functional designator *new* must be retained. For this purpose a special variable type is necessary because the value is not of type **integer, real, Boolean,** and so on, but in reality a reference pointer to the object data structure. The special variables will have type **ref** and their declaration specifies (as a qualification) the class of objects to which the variable may refer. Formally

⟨reference variable declaration⟩::=
ref(⟨qualification⟩)⟨identifier list⟩
⟨qualification⟩::=⟨class identifier⟩

The qualification provides reference security (discussed later).
In addition we have three special operators:

:-	To denote reference assignments
= =	To denote reference quality (same object)
=/=	To denote reference inequality
is,in	explained later

and the reference value **none** which points to no object, and is *additionally* the initial value of all reference variables. Procedures may also be declared as type **ref**.

EXAMPLE 4.3   A functional procedure named, pick, which calculates and returns as its value a reference to a class ship object would have the header:

ref(ship) **procedure** pick;

EXAMPLE 4.4   To retain reference to generated class objects, the value returned by the functional designator must be assigned to a reference variable using the reference assignment operator. Thus if given

ref (ships) tug, boat, skow;

and the declaration

class ships;
.
.
.
end;

then

    Tug:-**new** ships;
    Boat:-**new** ships;

generates two ships objects and retains the references in the variables tug and boat. Further they refer to *different* objects so that the relational *expression*

    tug =/= boat

would be true. An object may be referenced by *several* variables, so that execution of

    skow:-tug;

would cause tug and skow to reference the same object. Further, reference variables can be subscripted and collected in arrays. Thus the declaration

    ref(ships) **array** fleet[1:50] ;

would provide for reference to fifty ships objects. A fleet of ships could then be generated (with retained references) via

    for i:=1 **step** 1 **until** 50 **do**
    fleet[i] :-**new** ships;

Once generated, an object may exist as a coroutine to be executed piecemeal. An object may cause its own execution to be abandoned, and that of another to be continued by executing

    Resume(x)

where x refers (i.e., x is a reference variable with value other than *none*) to the object or coroutine to be continued.

There remains one major difficulty. In the normal ALGOL-60 environment, block and procedure instances (or at least the activation records for them) are created when a block is entered, placed in a stack for execution, and removed from the stack and destroyed when execution passes through the end statement of the block or procedure.

In a real sense such block and procedure instances may be considered as attached to the immediate encompassing block or procedure. This situation is unsatisfactory for objects that are to survive when processor control passes from them. Further, since SIMULA is very much an extension of ALGOL-60, it is natural under SIMULA rules that an object created by another object be attached to that object. It is thus necessary and natural to provide a mechanism to break that bond. A mechanism to do so is provided by the statement

        detach;

which, when executed by the *attached* object, breaks the bond between it and its creator. Once broken, the lifespan of the offspring becomes independent of the lifespan of the parent. In reality, detach does slightly more. When an object is generated via *new,* the object data record is created and processor control passes immediately to execute the statements of the generated object. In this regard *new* bears a resemblance to normal procedure calls. Execution of detach *also returns* processor control to the creating object, and in particular to the *continued* execution of the statement which generated the object or its successor. The LSC variable (see Chapter 3) of the object is marked so that when the created object is next activated, its execution will continue from the statement following detach. The statement following detach is thus a reactivation point, and detach behaves as a kind of "return" statement. We could pursue this matter further by depicting the data structure (activation record) of the objects involved, and showing the ownership links, and so forth. At this point it does not seem crucial and thus we do not. The interested reader will find such material in Birtwhistle et al. [1973]. We summarize the situation in Figure 4.2 in which the arrows order the execution of statements. For the illusion of completeness we note that execution of detach by a detached object has the effect of resuming the encompassing block. Because this situation is seldom encountered, it is not of direct concern.

DISPOSITION OF DETACHED OBJECTS

We have not as yet completely accounted for the states in which objects may exist. Earlier we discussed the two states identified as

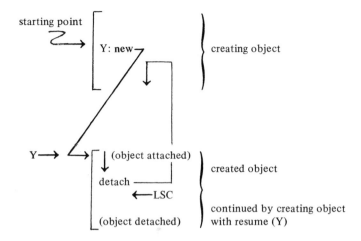

starting point

Y: new

creating object

Y⟶

(object attached)

detach

←LSC

(object detached)

created object

continued by creating object
with resume (Y)

Figure 4.2   Order of statement execution with new

active and suspended. To repeat, only one object may be active at a given moment. The active object is that one whose statements are being obeyed by the processor. Suspended objects are those which are to receive additional processor attention as a result of subsequent resumes on their behalf. It remains to account for the disposition of objects when processor control passes through the final *end* of its definition. The object disposition is then as follows.

1. If no references to the object exist, that object ceases to exist. This in essence implies that its activation record is destroyed. The memory space it occupied can then be reused by the SIMULA support system for the same or another purpose.
2. If a reference to the object exists, the object will continue to exist in a *terminated* state. A terminated object *may never* again be active. It will continue to exist as a data object (to be accessed by the remote access or *inspect* mechanisms).

A terminated object can be destroyed by setting all reference variables which refer to it to the value **none**. There must, of course, be at least one reference to a suspended object in order to insure its eventual continuation via resume (*). In other words, suspended objects are also destroyed if all references to them are cancelled. Finally, in case it is not now apparent, if a class declaration C does not contain resume statements nor a detach, then upon creation (i.e., as a result of **new** C), objects progress to the terminated state *without* interruption. This is the case in Example 4.2.

EXAMPLE 4.4   Imagine two objects named a and b. Object a has three executable statements identified by $a_1 a_2 a_3$, and object b has two executable statements identified by b_1 and b_2. We wish the statements to be executed *endlessly* in the order $a_1 b_1 a_2 b_2 a_3$. We can achieve the desired synchronization via resume and detach as shown by the program which follows.

```
Begin
ref(a0)a; ref(b0)b;

    class a0;                          numbers specify (partially)
    begin                             the order in which statements
    detach;              2.           are executed
L: a₁;                   6.    16.
    resume(b);           7.    17.
    a₂;                  10.    .
    resume(b);           11.    .
    a₃;                  14.    .
    goto L;              15.
    end a0;

    class b0;
    begin
    detach;              4.
L: b₁;                   8.    19.
    resume(a);           9.    20.
    b₂;                  12.    .
    resume(a);           13.    .
    goto L;              18.    .
    end b0;
 a:-new a0;              1.
 b:-new b0;              3.
    resume(a);           5.
end Block;
```

Note that the reference variables a and b are available to the objects even though not part of their declarations. By the ALGOL structure scoping rules, the reference to b in the a object and to a in the b

object is resolved by using the variables from the *encompassing* block in which they are defined.

REMOTE ACCESSING AND INSPECTION

An object whose statements are being obeyed by the processor is said to be *active*. For the moment, the state of all other existing objects must be considered *suspended* (and probably detached). Much convenience and flexibility can be achieved if the active object can base its behavior on the attributes of certain suspended objects. This capability requires special mechanisms because an object's attributes are generally accessible only by that object (when active). Two mechanisms are provided to facilitate such references. The first is known as remote access and has the general form

    object reference.attribute identifier in
            referenced object

For example, suppose an object has a *local* variable Y and is of *class* C. If we have

ref(C)X;

and X refers to the object in question, then a second object (of the same or different class) can manipulate the variable Y of the object referenced by X with access of the form

$X.Y$

The construct has the interpretation the Y belonging to the object referenced by X.

The construct is loosely spoken of as the "dot" notation. Such accesses can be cascaded so that, for example,

$X.Q.U.V.Z$

may be a legal access. Since expressions are evaluated from left to right, such expressions are meaningful only if X, Q, U, V are reference variables, whereas the type of Z is arbitrary but determines the type associated with the access.

Considerable use will be made of this feature throughout the rest of this text. One additional point should be made. Earlier, we characterized Y as a variable. The access remains legal, however, if Y is the identifier of a procedure defined within the *class* declaration C. By implication then

$X.Y$(actual parameters)

causes procedure Y associated with the object referenced by X to be executed.

EXAMPLE 4.5   Imagine an object w which generates person objects (Example 4.2) via

x:-**new** person(1.50,2);
y:-**new** person(2.00,10);

assuming that the declaration

ref(person)x,y;

has been made. Since the class person declaration does not use resume or detach, the objects are generated, their executable statements obeyed, and control returned to the w object. The w object can then reference the attributes of yearly salary of the object referenced by x with

x.yearly salary

and the yearly salary of the object referenced by y with

y.yearly salary,

thus making possible the *free use* of these values in the w object.

The dot notation provides, then, a limited or specific connection between objects. A more global connection is provided by *inspect* which, when executed by one object, allows it to reference *all* attributes of the inspected object without using the dot notation.

Formally, the mechanism has the form

⟨connection block1⟩::=⟨statement⟩
⟨connection block2⟩::=⟨statement⟩
⟨connection clause⟩::=**when**⟨class identifier⟩**do** ⟨connection block1⟩
⟨otherwise clause⟩::=⟨empty⟩|**otherwise** ⟨statement⟩

⟨connection part⟩::=⟨connection clause⟩|⟨connection part⟩
                      ⟨connection clause⟩

⟨connection statement⟩::= **inspect** ⟨reference expression⟩
                      do⟨connection block2⟩⟨otherwise clause⟩|
                      inspect⟨reference expression⟩⟨connection part⟩
                      ⟨otherwise clause⟩

Letting C_i denote class identifiers, X a reference expression, and S_i a statement, typical usages include

(a) **inspect** X **DO** S_1;
(b) **inspect** X **DO** S_1 otherwise S_2;
(c) **inspect** X when C_1 **DO** S_1 otherwise S_2;
(d) **inspect** X when C_1 **DO** S_1
              when C_2 **DO** S_2

              .

              .

              .

        when C_n **DO** S_n
        otherwise T;

where the otherwise clause is executed if the relational expression

$X = =$ **none**

is *true* or if X does not reference a class C_1, C_2 ... or C_n object. A void otherwise clause can be assumed if none is specified. When X is an object of *class* C_i, the statement S_i may freely contain accesses to attributes of objects of class C_i (as referenced by X) and obviates the remote access notation. Variables used in S_i which are not declared in C_i are taken from the block (or surrounding block) in which the reference is made using the normal ALGOL scoping rules.

CONCATENATION AND HIERARCHIES

The term *hierarchy* was originally used to denote a vertical authority structure in human organizations. In recent times the term has taken on a generalized meaning, particularly when used in connection with a description of complex systems. For the latter application its definition resembles a set of Chinese boxes. A set of Chinese boxes usually consists of a box enclosing a box which in turn encloses a third—the recursion continuing as long as the patience of the craftsman endures. Hierarchies can be likened to a variant of this pattern in which the opening of any box reveals not a single box but a small set of boxes—and again the recursion continues. The difference lies in the fact that the Chinese boxes require a complete ordering, whereas the variant is only a partial ordering which gives rise to a tree.

Such hierarchical systems are common in nature, and in fact it can be shown (see Pattee [1973]) that evaluation is speeded if *new* systems are built or evolve from stable subsystems rather than environmental constituent parts. A similar remark can obviously be made about the development of model programs; that is, we find utility in the ability to develop more elaborate program structures from simpler ones in a hierarchical fashion. SIMULA allows us to do so in a most convenient manner with the operation of *concatenation,* a binary operation defined between two class declarations C_1 and C_2 or a *class* C_1 and a block B, and produces as a *result* the declaration of a new *class* or block. The resulting class or block declaration is formed first by merging the attributes of *both* components, and then *combining* their action (executable) statements.

The operation of concatenation is specified by *prefixing* a block or class declaration with the name of a previously defined *class* name C. Suppose that C_1 has declaration as given on p. 32. Then a declaration of the form

```
C₁ class C₂(FP₂);
    SP₂;
    begin
      D₂;
      E₂;
    end C₂;
```

results in a class C_2 which has the *equivalent* declaration

```
class C₂(FP₁,FP₂);
SP₁;SP₂;
begin
D₁;D₂;
E₁;
E₂;
end C₂;
```

An object of *class* C_2 is considered a compound object. Furthermore, class C_2 is considered a subclass of class C_1, that is, the prefixed class is considered a subclass to the prefix class. A hierarchy of classes may be generated with declarations of the form

```
      class C₁;...;
C₁    class C₂;...;
      .

      .

      .
Cₙ₋₁  class Cₙ;...;
```

Then the entire list $C_1, \ldots C_{n-1}$ must be considered a prefix to C_n and its structure follows immediately by considering the single prefix case; that is, the nesting of D_i, E_i is continued. It is important to note that a single class may be used to prefix several different concatenated classes; that is, we can have, for example,

```
      class C₁;...;
C₁    class C₂;...;
C₁    class C₃;...;
```

Experience with concatenated classes teaches that the ability to better control the order in which the action statements are executed is desirable. In particular, it will be desirable to allow the body of the prefix class to be split. The prefix class body is split by use of the statement

```
inner;
```

and has the following effect. Let the definition of *class* C_2 be as given earlier, but change the definition of C_1 to

```
class C₁(FP₁)
SP₁;
Begin
D₁;
E₁₁;
inner;
E₁₂;
end;
```

For objects of **class** C_1, inner acts as a dummy statement and the order of execution is

$$E_{11};E_{12};$$

For objects of class C_2, however, the order of execution is

$$E_{11};E_2;E_{12};$$

which implies that *class* C_2 has the equivalent definition

```
class C₂(FP₁,FP₂);
SP₁;SP₂;
begin
  D₁;D₂;
  E₁₁;
  E₂;
  E₁₂;
end;
```

The split body feature is readily used to provide common initializing actions E_{11} and terminating actions E_{12}, to a variety of actions E_2.

Considerable use will be made of concatenation in the development of set and sequencing mechanisms necessary to simulation.

EXAMPLE 4.6   Imagine we are developing several class declarations, and we find that they have common initial and terminal sequences. We can write the initialization and termination sequences as a class declaration with form:

```
class common;
begin
⟨declarations⟩
⟨common initialization statements⟩
inner
⟨common termination conditions⟩
end;
```

and use it as a prefix to other class declarations via:

```
common class class name;
        begin
            .
            .
            .
        end class name;
```

so that each class has access to a *private* copy of the common initialization and termination declarations and actions. This feature is employed in Chapter 5 in the definition of *class* process.

As in ALGOL-60, a SIMULA block is delineated by a *begin end* pair. A block may be prefixed by a class identifier as stated earlier. A prefixed block formally has the syntax

```
⟨block⟩::= ┤⟨label⟩:┤...┤⟨block prefix⟩┤⟨block head⟩;
            ⟨compound tail⟩
⟨compound tail⟩::=⟨statement⟩end|⟨statement⟩;⟨compound tail⟩

⟨block prefix⟩::=⟨class identifier⟩⟨actual parameter part⟩
⟨block head⟩::= begin⟨declaration⟩|⟨block head⟩;⟨declaration⟩
```

The semantics is much the same as for prefixed class declarations, except that a prefixed block results in a block and not a class.

For completeness, a SIMULA program is given by

```
⟨program⟩::=┤⟨block prefix⟩┤⟨block head⟩;⟨compound tail⟩|
                    begin ⟨compound tail⟩
```

and is itself a block.

Next, we collect and present several miscellaneous but very useful *class* related operators included in the SIMULA definition.

LOCAL REFERENCE

The first provides a mechanism whereby an object can refer to itself (local reference) without access to a reference variable which refers to it. Local reference is made via the construct

> **this**⟨class identifier⟩

and has as a value a reference to the active object which must be of the class specified by the class identifier. Stated differently,

> **this** C_1

can be used only in the declaration of class C_1 or subclasses of C_1 .

RELATIONAL *IS* AND *IN*

The operators **is** and **in** test the class membership of a referenced object. Their usage syntax is

> ⟨reference expression⟩{**is**|**in**}⟨class identifier⟩

where a reference expression is any expression which designates an object reference. Their meanings are as follows:

1. X **is** C has value true if X refers to an object of *class* C, otherwise the value is *false.*
2. X **in** C has the value true if the value of X refers to an object of a class included in C, and is false otherwise. A class C_i is included by class C, if C appears directly or indirectly in the prefix to the declaration of class C_i. For example, on p. 43 C_1 *includes* C_2, ... , C_n. The operator **in** then connotes subclass.

For both operators, the relation is false if the value of X is none.

MORE ON REFERENCE QUALIFICATION

As we have stated, in the declarations of the form

ref(C)X;

the class name C is called the declared qualification of variable X. The qualification is included to provide reference security, that is, so that unintended attempts to use X to refer to objects from a class other than C can be detected (at compile time) and a diagnostic generated. Stated differently, such qualifications allow references to be resolved at compile time rather than execution time. Compound objects confuse this situation somewhat. Consider, for example,

$$\text{class } C_1 ;...;$$
$$C_1 \quad \text{class } C_2 ;...;$$

and

ref(C_1)X,W;
ref(C_2)Y,Z;

Then

Y:-**new** C_2; Z:-Y;

is legal, and so is

X:-**new** C_2;

or

X:-Y;

That is, a subclass reference may be assigned to a prefix *class* reference variable. Given a declaration ref $(C)X$, the reference variable X may *only* refer to objects of class C or its subclasses. Such usages are, in fact, resolved at compile time. For simulation purposes, in particular sequencing set manipulations, this capability is very necessary.

Reference assignments in the other direction, however, are illegal.

235716

That is, a reference variable X with the declared qualification C may not refer to an object belonging to a superclass of C (a class of which C is a subclass). Some of such illegal assignments are detectable at compile time; others have to be detected at run time. For example, consider again the declarations for classes C_1 and C_2 and variables X and Y as given above. With these declarations the assignment

   Y:-new C_1;

is illegal and detectable at compile time. On the other hand, the assignment

   Y:-X;

is legal at compile time and may be legal or illegal at run-time depending on the value of X. For example, the assignment in the sequence

   X:-new C_2;
   Y:-X;

is legal, whereas the same assignment in the sequence

   X:-new C_1;
   Y:-X;

constitutes a run-time error.

One further anomaly may arise with compound objects. Consider the partial declarations

          class C_1;
          begin real P,R;

             .

             .

             .
          end
     C_1 class C_2;
          begin Boolean P,Q;

             .

             .

             .
          end;

Together with

    ref(C_1)X; **ref**(C_2)Y;

and

    X:-Y:-**new** C_2;

Notice that the declared qualifications of X and Y are different; X is qualified by C_1, Y by C_2. The SIMULA rule is that

> An object reference has access to a concatenated object at its qualification level. The reference seeks for an attribute first at that level and then at outer levels in turn. The first encountered occurrence of the attribute is the one accessed.

According to this rule, for the example just constructed, $X.P$ accesses the real variable P, whereas $Y.P$ accesses the Boolean variable P. It would thus seem that certain accesses by X and certain accesses by Y. are forbidden. To eliminate the access restrictions and provide complete access freedom the operator

    qua

is provided. Usages take the form

    ⟨qualified reference⟩::=⟨reference expression⟩**qua**⟨class identifier⟩

If X is a reference expression with qualification C, then X **qua** D is legal only if D is C or a subclass of C. By using **qua**, any attribute of an object may be referenced. We summarize the cases, for the example, in the following table. This summary hopefully also tells the complete story.

Access Expression	Attribute Accessed {designated by giving type}
$X.P$	*real*
$Y.P$ or X**qua** $C_2.P$	*Boolean*
$X.R$ or $Y.R$	*real*;
$Y.Q$ or X**qua** $C_2.Q$	*Boolean*
Y **qua** $C_1.P$	*illegal qualification*

CHAPTER 5

SIMULA: Simulation Support

At this juncture it seems appropriate to recap and summarize our progress. In the earlier chapters we introduced the scenario approach to the development of model programs. We informally and then semiformally attempted to develop a scenario description of a simple queueing model in which we considered system behavior from the viewpoint of active components, and continued until all system behavioral aspects had been accounted for and all scenario interactions established. The impetus for the effort was the unsubstantiated claim that the scenario view of simulation is both natural and convenient in a wide variety of situations. It is unfortunate that this cliam can be accepted or rejected only by the experience gained by developing model programs.

In any case, pursuit of the scenario view precipitated the need for coroutines and the notion of processes (objects). It was at this point we set aside our modeling considerations and investigated the **class** concept of SIMULA, on the author's claim that it would be well suited to the development and realization of such model programs. We have thus considered all the important notions associated with the class concept, and can now use them to develop a simulation system. We proceed by developing a collection of class declarations which can be used as block and class prefixes and which provide a sufficient, convenient, and flexible set of constructs supportive of the process (scenario) view of simulation. These declarations fall into two major categories. Declarations of the first category, **class** SIMSET, support doubly linked circular lists. These lists are often called sets in the SIMULA literature, have objects as a membership, and form the basis for the realization of queues. Declarations in the second category, **class** SIMULATION, support scenario (process) descriptions, scheduling and synchronization constructs, and the time flow mechanism.

CLASS SIMSET: A LIST PROCESSING PACKAGE

Two-way lists (sets) can be used to realize the event list and all manner of queues. It is, therefore, appropriate to collect in a **class**

50

declaration definitions which provide such a capability. In order to name such sets we will associate with each a *head*.

The head provides a handle for the set and *points* to the first and last objects of its *membership*. Each object in the membership must have attributes succ and prede so that the integrity of the two-way list can be maintained (by pointing to successor and predecessor objects, respectively). Thus sets will have the structure depicted in Figure 5.1.

The operations associated with joining and leaving a set reduce to manipulation of the attributes, prede and succ, of the object joining or leaving the set, as well as those of its two current or intended neighbors. Notice (Figure 5.1) that both set members and the set head have the prede and succ attributes. It is natural, therefore, to provide head and member objectes with these attributes by specifying a **class** declaration which can be used as the prefix to the **class** declarations for head and member objects. Since the function of these attributes is *linkage* between head and number objects, we will give our class declaration that name. Similarly, we provide a class declaration which can give rise to head objects, and name it head.

Finally, because we want to specify set membership for a variety of objects, we specify a third **class** declaration which we may use as a prefix to other **class** declarations, the objects of which we should like to acquire set membership. We then collect these declarations in the declaration of **class** SIMSET, such that;

```
    class SIMSET;
    begin
        class linkage;...;
        linkage class head;...;
        linkage class link;...;
    end simset;
```

Since linkage is a prefix to head and link, we must define it first. We have

```
    class linkage;
    begin
    ref(linkage)succ,prede;
    ref(link)procedure suc;
        suc:-if succ in link then succ else none;
    ref(link)procedure pred;
        pred:-if prede in link then prede else none;
    end linkage;
```

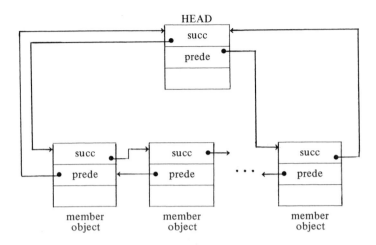

Figure 5.1   Set structure

In this chapter symbols set in italics are special in that they are protected. We will explain the implication later, and for now the reader may continue as though italics were regular (roman) type. The above class declaration consists of two declared attributes (succ and prede) and two procedures of **type ref** (suc and pred), each qualified by **class** identifier link. The procedures mask the circular nature of the set in that procedure suc and pred will return the value **none** if a member object is the last or first, respectively, of the membership.

Head objects are then generated from the following declaration. As a result of the prefix linkage, each head object will have the attributes prede and succ, and when a head object is generated, via *new* head, they are initialized to reflect an empty set.

```
linkage  class head;
         begin
         ref(link)procedure first;
         comment: returns the reference value of the first
                     object of the set;
         first:-suc;

         ref(link)procedure last;
         comment:  returns the reference value of the last
                     object of the set;
         last:-pred;
```

Boolean procedure empty;
comment: returns the value **true** if the set is empty;
empty:= *succ*= =**this** linkage;

integer procedure cardinal;
comment: returns the number of members of the set;
begin integer I; ref(linkage)x;
x:-**this** linkage;
for x:-x.*succ* **while** x=/=**this** head **do** I:=I+1;
cardinal:=I;
end cardinal;

procedure clear;
begin
comment: remove all objects from the set making it
empty;
    ref(link)x;
    for x:-first **while** x=/=**none do** x.out;[1]
end clear;

comment the body of the class declaration follows
and initializes the set by setting succ
and prede of the head object to refer to
itself;

succ:-prede:-**this** linkage;
end head;

We may think of the objects belonging to a set as ordered with the succ attribute of the head object referencing the first member object. The five procedures definitions contained in the declaration are included

1. to facilitate access to the first and last member objects
2. to easily determine if the set is void of member objects, i.e., empty
3. to determine the number of member objects
4. to void the set of its membership

---

[1] Out is a procedure of **class** link, given next. It removes the designated object from a set.

Logically we imagine each head object in possession of its private copy of these five routines. They are thus executed by a remote access of the form

    x.procedure name

where X references a head object.

EXAMPLE 5.1.

        If we have
        ref(head)X; **integer** Y;
        and in another object execute
        x:- **new** head;
        Then the remote reference
        Y:= X.cardinal;
        assigns Y the value zero.

We turn next to **class** link. Every object from a **class** declaration prefixed by link can acquire set membership.

The **class** link definition consists of four procedures and is given below.

```
linkage   class link;
          begin
          procedure out;
          comment   remove an object from a set and reestablish
                    proper links. If object is not the member
                    of a set, attempted removal is a dummy
                    statement;

          if succ=/=none then
            begin
            succ. prede:-prede;
            prede.succ:-succ;
            succ:-prede:-none;
          end out;

          procedure follow(x);
          ref(linkage)x;

          comment   insert object into set which contains X, at the
                    point following object referenced by x;
```

```
begin
    out;
    if x=/=none then
        begin
        if x.succ=/=none then
            begin
        prede:-x;
        succ:-x.succ;
        succ.prede:-x.succ:-this linkage;
            end;
        end;
end follow;


procedure precede(x);
ref(linkage)x;

comment insert object into set which contains x, at the
        point preceding object referenced by x;


begin
    out;
    if x=/=none then
        begin
        if x.succ=/=none then
            begin
        succ:-x;
            prede:-x.prede:
            prede.succ:-x.prede:-this linkage;
            end;
        end precede;


procedure into(s)
ref(head)s;
comment remove object from set to which it may be a
        member, if any, and insert as last object in
        set referenced by s;


begin
    out;
```

```
        if s=/=none then
          begin
          succ:-s;
          prede:-s.prede;
          prede.succ:-s.prede:-this linkage;
          end
        end into;
      end link;
```

Each object generated from a class declaration prefixed by link must be considered as in possession of a private copy of these procedures—procedures designed to facilitate the object's insertion into and removal from sets. Thus, the procedures of link objects (objects generated from class declarations prefixed by link) are referenced directly by an object on behalf of itself and remotely by one object on behalf of another. Thus an object referenced by A would execute

   into(z)

to place *itself* into the set referenced by z, whereas *another* object would execute

   A.into(z)

to achieve the same result. Finally, note that because the prefix linkage of link provides only one succ, prede attribute pair, objects of classes prefixed by link can at any point have membership in only a single set.

The **class** SIMSET declarations define a general list processing package. Its usage is best facilitated by prefixing the outermost block of a program by SIMSET, thus making the list processing package available to the entire program; that is, we write,

```
begin
    class simset;
    begin class linkage;...;
        linkage class head;...;
        linkage class link;...;
    end simset;

Simset begin   desired program which may contain class
               declarations prefixed by linkage, head,
               and link to provide list processing
          end program;
end;
```

SIMULA recognizes the futility of including the SIMSET declarations with each and every model program prepared. The situation is ameliorated in SIMULA because certain system class declarations are known to it. These system class declarations can be freely utilized in model programs by prefixing the outermost block of a model program with the system **class** name. Three such system class definitions are known to SIMULA. They are

SIMSET

SIMULATION (a subclass of SIMSET)

BASICIO (classes to facilitate input-output operations)

Certain attributes of system classes are not directly accessible in the body of block or class definitions which they prefix. This is done as a security measure; that is, the SIMULA compiler will recognize attempted usages of *safeguarded* attributes and generate diagnostic messages. Most safeguarded attributes can be accessed indirectly, through procedures, as for example, with the attributes prede and succ of class linkage. In this work we identify safeguarded attributes by identifying each appearance with italic type. Such protection can be avoided, and a different list processing package can be used, by redefining the system class SIMSET under a new identifier and then using the *new* definition identifier as a prefix instead of the old. In other words,

> the list processing and sequencing facilities provided are defined within the confines of the class concept and its operational mechanisms, and complete redefinition is possible, at the sacrifice of safeguarded attributes.

CLASS SIMULATION

The constructs of class simulation support the time flow mechanisms necessary for simulation. The declarations it contains may be grouped into three categories as depicted in Figure 5.2. The entries in the first category include the declaration for event notice objects and procedures to manipulate the sequencing set. The second category contains the declaration for class process, the definition of

```
simset  class simulation
        begin

            comment 1. declaration for event notices and
                         sequencing set manipulation procedures;

            link  class event notice (evtime,proc);
                  real evtime;ref(process)proc; Begin
                  procedure suc;...;
                  procedure pred;...;
                  procedure rank(before);
                  Boolean before;...;
                  end event notice;
            ref(head)SQS;
            ref(event notice)procedure firstev;
                  firstev:-SQS.first;

            ref(process)procedure current;
                  current:-firstev.proc;

            comment 2. scenario object class declaration prefix;

            link class process;...;

            comment 3. scheduling procedures used to
                         control process object behavior;

            real procedure time;time:=firstev.evtime;
            procedure hold(T);real T;...;
            procedure passivate;...;
            procedure wait;...;
            procedure cancel;...;
            procedure activate;...;
            procedure accum;...;

            comment     simulation initialization declarations
                         and statements;

            process class main program;begin L :detach;goto L;end;
            ref(main program)main;
            SQS:-new head;
            main:-new main program;
            main.event:-new event notice(0,main);
            main.event.into(SQS);
            end simulation;
```

Figure 5.2   The skeletal form of class simulation

which is the basis for the specification of scenario descriptions, by providing the bridge between the sequencing set and the resume construct available to class coroutine objects. The entries of the third category also manipulate the sequencing set by regulating the activation and reactivation times for process objects.

In summary, system class simulation provides the constructs which support the time aspects of simulation and includes definitions for:

1. Event notice generation, manipulation, and cancellation
2. The system clock
3. The sequencing set
4. Scheduling constructs
5. A link between the coroutines provided by **class** objects and the system clock and sequencing set

These provisions will be made via

1. Class event notice (EVTIME, process involved)
2. The attribute TIME (of class simulation)
3. The set SQS
4. Procedures such as hold, etc. (to be explained)
5. The declaration of

    link class process;

respectively. Further, as we shall see, the detach and resume constructs will play key roles in the specification of these constructs, but are seldom, if ever, used directly in model program scenario descriptions.

Class Event Notice and the Sequencing Set

The sequencing set with event notice objects as members is depicted in Figure 5.3, and, as can be seen, directly uses the set capabilities provided by SIMSET. Each notice contains a record of the simulated time at which an event is to occur, and a reference to the code segment (process object) which will affect the change of state. The notices are ordered in the set by increasing values of event time (evtime). The suc and pred procedures (see Figure 5.2) provide easy access to those event notices which precede and follow a given notice in SQS, and thus facilitate traversal of the set. Their

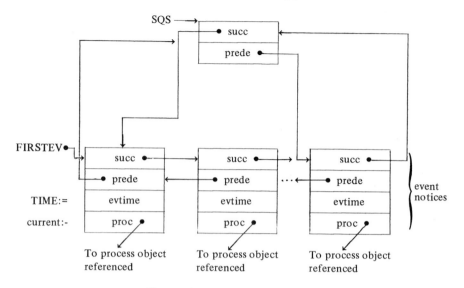

Figure 5.3   SQS and event notices

definitions are:

> **ref**(*event notice*)**procedure** suc;
>   suc:-**if** *succ* **is** *event notice* **then** *succ* **else none**;
> **ref**(*event notice*)**procedure** pred;
>   pred:-*prede*;

The procedure rank is used to determine notice *placement* and entry into SQS. It is defined by

> **procedure** *Rank* (*before*);
> **Boolean** *before*;
> **begin**
>   **ref**(*event notice*)*P*;
>   P:-*SQS*.last;
>   **for** P:-P **while** P.*evtime>evtime* **do** P:-P.pred;
>   **if** *before* **then**
>   **begin**
>   **for** P:-P **while** P.*evtime=evtime* **do** P:-P.pred
>   **end**;
>   follow(P);
>   **end** rank;

Observe that when entering a notice, SQS is searched in *reverse* order, that is, from the last notice toward the first (current), to determine the placement. This is done on the premise that the scheduled time is not near the current time. Notice also, that if the Boolean variable before is **true**, the new notice is entered, in SQS, preceding all those of equal event time.

Finally, as Figure 5.3 indicates, the procedure firstev provides a reference to the first notice in SQS, and current a reference to the *process* object associated with it. The *system clock* (current simulated time) is given by the procedure time and has the value associated with the event time of the first event notice. It is, therefore, the activation or reactivation time for the object (process) referenced by current.

Class Process and Scheduling Constructs

We must next link the activation and reactivation times of objects representing element scenario descriptions to event notices and thus the sequencing set. We do so by prefixing class scenario descriptions by the class identifier process defined below.

```
link class process
    begin

        comment reference variable for class object event notice;

        ref(event notice)event;
        Boolean terminated;

        Boolean procedure idle;
        comment object idle if no activation scheduled;
        idle:=event= =none;

        real   procedure evtime;
        if idle   then Error else evtime:=event.evtime ;
        Boolean   procedure terminated;

        terminated:=terminated;

        ref(process)procedure nextev;
        nextev:-if idle  then none
                    else if event.suc= =none then none
                    else event.suc.proc;.
```

```
detach;
comment concatenated scenario description placement;
inner;
terminated:=true;
passivate;
error;
end process;
```

Objects of class process are not viable by themselves, and as stated, the declaration is intended as a means of providing a preamble and postscript to scenario declarations. The intention is realized by concatenation and use of inner in the definition of class process.

EXAMPLE 5.2   If we write

```
process  class server;
         begin
         comment S represents a sequence of statements;
         S;
         end;
```

then server objects generated via **new** server have all the attributes of **class** process and **class** server, and the statements S given in the declaration of **class** server are placed at the point marked by inner in the **class** process declaration as guaranteed by the concatenation rules.

Earlier we characterized the state of an object as active, suspended, or terminated. For objects of class process (or objects of a class prefixed by process and referred to as process objects) we identify a fourth, the passive or *passivated* state. Thus, an object concatenated to the class process object may be

Active   Receiving processor attention and thus advancing through its action statements as given by the subclass declaration.

Suspended   Represented by an event notice in SQS and having, therefore, a scheduled activation or reactivation time (measured by the system clock). Such an object is active in the *simulation sense,* that is, it is delayed performing some activity. It is thus considered not idle. Notice that a process object may be represented by only one notice in SQS (again owing to the structure of linkage).

Passivated *Not* active, suspended, or terminated. Such an object has not exhausted its action statements but does not have a scheduled activation or reactivation time. In other words, its delay before continuation (as measured by the system clock) is of unknown duration. Its activation or reactivation must be scheduled by another object. A passivated object is considered idle.

Terminated As such it has exhausted its action statements and will continue to exist as data object as long as a reference to it exists (see Chapter 4). Notice by the declaration of **class** process that we may distinguish between passivated and terminated objects by the value of the Boolean variable terminated. An attempt to activate a terminated process object results in an error as shown.[2]

With these definitions, use of the *procedures* idle and terminated becomes obvious. *Procedure* evtime is provided so that other objects can access the event time of a suspended process object by remote access. *Procedure* nextev provides reference to the next process object in SQS. It may be used by a process object on behalf of itself or through remote access by any other object.

When a process object is generated as a result of new, it is immediately detached. It thus may be considered to exist in the passive state after generation. A mechanism must exist to generate an event notice and schedule the objects first active phase. This mechanism is provided by the constructs associated with **activate** and **reactivate** and the procedure *activate* to be discussed shortly. Before discussing those issues, we define the hold, passivate, cancel, and wait procedures, which are applicable to active or suspended objects, that is, to objects which are represented in SQS.

A realization of the delay construct, which we have discussed, is

---

[2] The procedure *error* is not directly accessible as indicated.

given by the *procedure* hold. Its definition is

```
procedure hold(T);
real T;
comment   via inspect we have attributes of the first
          event notice available directly, i.e. without
          remote access.
inspect  Firstev do
   begin
   if T ⩾ 0 then evtime:=evtime + T;
   if suc =/= none then
         begin
         if suc.evtime ⩽ evtime then
               begin
               out;
               Rank(false);
               resume (current);
               end;
         end;
   end hold;
```

When executed by the *active* process object, the implied reactivation time of the object, given by T + time, is compared with the event time of the next notice in SQS. If it is less than the time of the event time of the next notice, the active object is allowed to continue after the system clock is updated (updated as a result of changing the event time of the first notice—that of the active object). Otherwise the active object's notice is removed from SQS, reinserted at the proper point (by rank), and the object then referenced by current is activated (execution continued). Passivate, on the other hand, passivates the active object. Its definition is

```
procedure passivate;
begin
inspect current do
   begin
   event.out;event:-none
   end;
if SQS.empty then error
            else resume (current);
end passivate;
```

The procedure wait enters the active object into a named set and then passivates the object.

```
procedure wait(S);
ref (head)S;
```

begin
current.into(S);
passivate;
end wait;

The procedure cancel may be executed by the active object on behalf of itself or another object. Its definition is

procedure cancel(x);
ref(process)x;
if x= =current   **then** passivate
                else inspect x **do**
                        if *event*=/=**none then**

                        event.out;
    event:-**none**;
    end cancel;

Thus cancel (current) is equivalent to passivate. If the object referenced by *x* is suspended, it becomes passive, and if it is passive (or terminated), the procedure acts as a dummy statement.

As mentioned, these procedures move or destroy existing event notices but do not create them, and activation of a passive process object requires generation of a notice via

new *event notice*(,) .

The procedure *activate* performs this function, and we shall give its definition shortly. As the italic type indicates however, it is a protected (safeguarded) procedure and cannot be directly accessed in a model program. It may be accessed indirectly by the SIMULA scheduling statements **activate** and **reactivate**. Formally they have the form

⟨scheduling statement⟩::=⟨activation clause⟩⟨scheduling clause⟩
⟨activation clause⟩::={**activate**|**reactivate**}⟨reference expressions⟩
⟨scheduling clause⟩ ::={{**before**|**after**}⟨reference expression⟩|
            {**at**|**delay**}⟨arithmetic expression⟩ {**prior**}}

Since

reactivate x ⟨scheduling clause⟩;

where x is a reference to a process object, is equivalent to

cancel(x);
activate x ⟨scheduling clause⟩;

we need only discuss **activate**. From the metalanguage description, we find the allowable forms to be:

> **activate** x;
> **activate** x **at** T; or **activate** x **at** T **prior**;
> **activate** x **delay** T; or **activate** x **delay** T **prior**;
> **activate** x **after** y;
> **activate** x **before** y;

where x is a reference to a process object *not* represented in SQS, y is a reference to a process represented in SQS, and T is a real value with $T \geqslant 0$. The constructs have the meanings listed below. For

activate x after y;

An event notice for x is placed in SQS immediately following the notice for y. The *evtime* of the notice for x is set to the value found in the notice for y. Thus, object x is to be activated at the same simulated time as y.

activate x before y;

Same as above except notice for x is placed in SQS immediately before notice for y.

activate x delay T; or activate x delay T prior

Place notice for X in SQS with an event time (*evtime*) of current time $+ T$. Thus, object x is to be activated at simulated time T units in the future. Notice that **reactivate this** c **delay** T; is equivalent in function to hold (T) when executed by the currently active process on behalf of itself. When, however, the active process executes

Inspect x **when** c **do**
reactivate this c **delay**T;

on behalf of x, the effect is not the same as hold (T). The use of **prior** causes (see procedure activate) the notice to be placed (in SQS) preceding *all* others with an equal value of *evtime*.

activate x at T; or activate x at T prior;

Place notice for x in SQS with *evtime* equal to T. Notice that

activate x **delay** T;

is equivalent to

activate x **at** time$+$T;

The use of **prior** has the same effect as given above.

activate x;

Activate x immediately. That is, generate a notice for x, with *evtime*=time and place it in SQS preceding the notice for the currently active process. Note that all of the following are equivalent.

activate x;
activate x **delay** 0 **prior**;

activate x **at** time **prior**;
activate x **before** current;

These forms are known as *direct scheduling,* and have an effect much like a procedure call.

An activate statement has no effect if the object x is already represented in SQS (i.e., is active or suspended). All forms of **activate** or **reactivate** act as dummy statements if x refers to **none** or if x is a terminated object. With these remarks we may now define procedure *activate* which, via compiler-generated calls, carries out the scheduling requirements of **activate** and **reactivate**. The formal parameters of the procedure relate to the employed syntax of the **activate** or **reactivate** statement. Specifically,

REAC:=**if** the statement is **reactive then true else false**;
T:=value used, if given, 0 otherwise;
PRIOR:=**true** if **prior** employed, **false** otherwise;
X,Y are references to process objects as employed above;
CODE is a character string (delineated by quote marks) and is

'direct' if a scheduling clause is not employed
'at' if **at** employed
'delay' if **delay** employed
'before' if **before** employed
'after' if **after** employed

procedure *activate* (*reac,x,code,t,y,prior*);*value code*;
   ref (process) x,y;**Boolean** *reac, prior*;**text** *code*; **real** t;
   inspect x **do if** $\neg$ terminated **then**
   begin ref (process) z; **ref**(*event notice*)*ev*;
       if *reac* **then** *ev* :- *event*
       else if *event* =/= **none then go to** exit;

```
            z :- current;
            if code = 'direct' then
direct: begin event :- new event notice (time,x);
                event.precede (firstev)
            end direct
            else if code = 'delay' then
            begin t := t + time; go to at end delay
            else if code = 'at' then
at:         begin if t < time then t := time;
                if t = time ∧ prior then go to direct;
            event :- new event notice (t,x);
            event.rank (prior)
        end at
        else if(if y = = none then true else y.event = =none)
        then event :- none else
        begin event :- new event notice (y.event.evtime,x);
            if code  = 'before' then event.precede (y.event)
                            else event.follow (y.event)
        end before or after;
        if ev =/= none then
        begin ev.out; if SQS.empty then error end;
        if z =/= current then resume (current);
        exit: end activate;
```

In response to the execution of a scheduling statement, procedure activate generates an event notice (if activate rather than reactivate) and, using **procedure** *rank,* enters the notice into SQS at the proper point. By studying its definition the exact effect of each scheduling statement becomes known.

EXAMPLE 5.3   Suppose we execute

    activate x **delay** S;

on behalf of an object x represented in SQS i.e., a suspended object. From activate, we find the statement to be a dummy; thus, the previously scheduled activation time for object x remains in effect.

We now have a healthy complement of simulation support machinery. It is accessed in a manner analogous to SIMSET, that is, by prefixing a block by the **class** identifier simulation. Unlike SIMSET, however, simulation can be used at only one block level in a model program. A simple model program, then, may take the form simulation **begin**

⟨declaration of global variables⟩
⟨class declarations⟩
⟨executable statements to be concatenated with those
given in the **class** simulation declaration. We shall say
that these statements constitute the *main program*⟩
end;

The order of statement execution in the above program is as follows. First, the following sequence is executed from the body of the
class simulation. (See Figure 5.2.)

1. SQS:-**new** head;
2. main:-**new** main program;
3. main.*event*:-**new** *event notice* (0,main);
4. main. *event*. into (SQS);

Then the control is passed to the first executable statement of the
block prefixed by simulation, for example, the first statement of the
user main program.

The first statement in the above sequence establishes the sequencing set SQS. The remaining three statements, in conjunction
with the declaration of the process class main program (Figure 5.2),
enable the user main program to be treated as a process object. As we
shall see, there is some advantage to having the simulation block
(main program) enter into the simulation as a process. This is not,
however, directly possible because only class objects can be referenced, that is, blocks cannot. A simple artifice in the form of

process **class** main program;···;

as defined in **class** simulation (see Figure 5.2) does the job. Statement 2 in the above sequence creates an object from the dummy
process class main program, statement 3 generates an event notice
for the main program object, and statement 4 enters the notice into
SQS as the very first notice (thus making the main program the
current process). The declaration for **class** main program is simply

detach;

and the utility of the declaration can be clarified only by considering
the effect of using detach in concatenated objects (our earlier discus-

sion of detach preceded the notion of concatenated class declarations and compound objects). Specifically, when an object executes detach

1. control returns to the generating reference object (as described);
2. the effect of detach within a detached object is equivalent to a resume procedure for the associated prefixed block.

The net effect of these rules is to ensure that each time the main program is activated, a detach is executed and the statements of the block prefixed by simulation are continued. Further, because hold ( ), passivate, and so on, operate on current, they can by used directly in the simulation block. Although this satisfies our needs somewhat indirectly, it is effective. The net effect is that the simulation block can be treated as a process object, referenced by main, and can be active, suspended, or passive.

The simulation support machinery we developed is not tailored to a particular simulation application and thus is quite flexible, as we shall demonstrate here and in Chapters 6 and 7. Notice that our development has depended heavily on the constructs resume ( ) and detach, and although they are available for direct use, it will generally be sufficient to use them indirectly through class process objects and procedures such as hold and passivate.

EXAMPLE 5.4   The possible process object states, transitions, and transition directives are summarized in Figure 5.4.

OBJECT SYNCHRONIZATIONS

Before completing the model program for the queueing station begun in Chapter 3, we present realizations for typical object synchronizations, as discussed in Chapter 3. Here we concentrate on simple situations, and leave discussion of complex cases to Chapter 7.

Mutual Exclusion

Imagine the scenario for objects of class P to consist of three activities which we label A1, A2, and A3. During each activity one unit

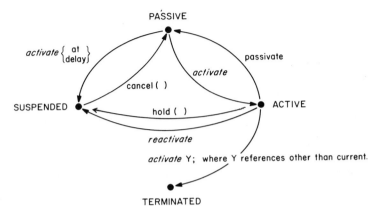

Figure 5.4   Possible process class object states

of one or more resources is required. Specifically,

A1   Requires one unit of resource R1,
A2   Requires one unit of resource R2,
A3   Requires one unit of resource R1.

A unit of resource R3 is required during the lifespan of each object. We initialize the variables AR1, AR2, and AR3 to reflect the initial number of available units of each resource. Next, to simplify our scenario description of **class** P objects, we declare the following procedure.

```
procedure waituntil(Boolean condition,queue);
name Boolean condition; Boolean Boolean condition;
ref(head)queue;
comment objects executing this procedure wait in a set
        named queue if Boolean condition is false;
begin
    into (queue);
retry:    if not Boolean condition then
                    begin
                    passivate; goto retry;
                    end;
            out;
end waituntil;
```

The activities of P objects are synchronized with respect to the resources (in the sense of mutual exclusion) as a result of the following scenario description.

```
process class P;
begin
A1:
    waituntil(AR1>0 and AR3>0, q1);
    AR1 :=AR1-1; AR3:=AR3-1;
    hold(activity 1 time);
    AR1:=AR1+1;
    comment attempt to activate P objects waiting for resources.
            P objects waiting to engage in A1 have priority for R1;
    activate q1.first; activate q3.first;
A2:
    waituntil(AR2>0, q2);
    AR2:=AR2-1;
    hold(activity 2 time);
    AR2:=AR2+1;
    comment attempt next to activate delayed P object;
    activate q2. first;
A3:
    waituntil(AR1>0, q3);
    AR1:=AR1-1;
    hold(activity 3 time);
    AR1:=AR1+1; AR3:=AR3+1;
    activate q1.first; activate q3.first;
end P scenario;
```

Producer/Consumer Relationship

Imagine that producer objects make "widgets" which are used by consumer objects. Imagine further that we may retain no more than max unused widgets in storage.

We can implement the proper synchronization between producers and consumers via the declarations:

```
        process class producers;
        begin
        comment w is a global variable giving the no of widgets in storage;
LOOP:   if w=max then passivate;
        hold(production time);
        w:=w+1;
```

```
    comment activate consumer if passive;
    activate consumer;
    goto LOOP;
    end producers;

    process class consumers;

LOOP:   if w=0 then passivate;
        w:=w−1;
        comment activate producer if passive;
        activate producer;
        hold(consumption time);
        goto LOOP;
        end consumers;
```

started off with the declarations

```
    ref(producers)producer; ref(consumers)consumer;    and
```

execution of
```
        producer:-new producers;
        consumer:-new consumers;
        activate producer delay 0;
        activate consumer delay 0;
```

Mass Retrys

Imagine a series of process objects, each of which executes procedure waituntil, as under "Mutual Exclusion," but with Boolean functions which are *not* all identical. Following a system change of state, certain of the blocked objects may be able to proceed (as their tested Boolean conditions will now be true), whereas others will remain blocked. Therefore, following each change of state which could conceivably alter the Boolean condition for one or more blocked objects, we must allow each to recheck to see if advance is possible. For each eligible change of state we would execute

```
    procedure checkall(q);
    ref(head)q;
    begin
    ref(process)P;
    for p:-q.last,p.pred while p =/= none do
    activate p after current;
```

      comment schedule activations (at current time) for all process
              objects in q before activating any of them;
    end checkall;

Since each member of the queue (set) is passive as a result of procedure waituntil, each will be given a choice to retest the Boolean condition which resulted in its blockage.

THE EXAMPLE COMPLETED

We are now in a position to realize the model programs for the two model variants introduced in Chapter 3. We give first the realizations, then a series of explanatory remarks. Several more examples follow.

For these and subsequent realizations no claim of optimality in coding is made. In fact, in some cases optimality was sacrificed so that the use of certain constructs could be demonstrated. In others the coding of individuals (other than the author) was used, particularly when their realizations seemed interesting or attractive. Having made these disclaimers we present the executable realization of the model programs we have been developing. For both variants, statements responsible for data collection have been purposely omitted, leaving only those responsible for the operational behavior of the modeled system. This was done so as not to obscure the structure, in this our first complete example. Further, collected statistics would have to be displayed, and that remains impossible because we have not broached the matter of input-output.

Variant 1:

```
simulation begin
          real lam,mu,simtime; ref(server)servs; integer u1,u2;
          comment  active   server and arrival mechanism;
          process class server;
          begin
          ref(head)queue;  ref(unit)job;
          queue:-new head;
          activate new arrivals(queue)delay 0;
          L1: passivate;
```

```
        for job:-queue. first while job =/= none do
          begin
              job.out;
              hold(job.servicetime);
          end
       goto L1;
       end server;
       process  class arrivals (Q);
                ref(head)Q;
                begin
          L1:   new unit.into(Q);
                if servs.idle then activate servs delay 0;
                Reactivate this arrivals delay negexp(lam,ul); goto L1;
                end arrivals;
       link class unit;
                begin
                comment passive units;
                real servicetime;
                servicetime:=negexp(mu,u2);
       end unit;
       comment next line is first executable statement in model program;
       simtime:=           ;
       mu:=                ;
       lam:=               ;
       ul=502;u2=320;
       servs:-new server;
       activate servs delay 0;
       hold(simtime); ⟨output stats when collected⟩;
  end;
```

Variant 2

```
simulation  begin
            comment active units;
            real lam,mu,simtime;     Boolean server busy;
            ref(head) Q;             integer ul,u2;

            process class unit;
            begin

            activate new unit at time+negexp(lam,ul);
```

```
if serverbusy then
    begin
    into(Q);
    passivate;
    out;
    end;
server busy:=true;
hold(negexp(mu,u2));
server busy:=false;
if ⌐Q. empty then activate Q.first after current;
end unit;
```

comment next line is first executable statement in model program;

```
simtime:=    ;
mu:=    ;
lam:=    ;
ul:=502; u2:=320;
Q:-new head;
activate new unit after current;
hold(simtime);⟨output stats when collected⟩;
end;
```

Remarks

1. Variant 2 is the more economical realization. Notice that there are *no* explicit references to unit objects in it. Unit objects continue to exist (via hold), because it causes a reference to the object to exist in SQS. Unit objects cease to exist after having executed their final statement.

2. Variant 1 could be improved by eliminating class unit objects and generating unit service times in the server scenario. This would easily be accomplished by replacing the *class* unit declaration by a *global* (global in the same way as lam, mu) variable, reflecting the number of units in a now *imaginary* queue. Class unit was included to demonstrate the use of objects that exist in a *terminated* state.

3. In variant 1 **reactivate** rather than **activate** is used because the object is scheduling its own next active phase.

4. The values given ul and u2 are somewhat arbitrary and simply determine or select a particular stream of values of exponential

variates for the interarrival and service times. The initial values given these variables form the *seeds* for the subsequent generations. Separate seeds are used to statistically uncouple the streams. A complete accounting of random drawing procedures is given in a later section.

5. For variant 1 you might ask why an *explicit* reference to the server object exists whereas an explicit reference to the arrivals object does not. The answer is again (see remark 1) a matter of reference and is precipitated by the use of passivate in the server object.

6. If the declaration of variable queue had been made global to both **class** declarations, it would not have been necessary to pass its value as an **argument** to the arrivals object. We have done so simply for demonstration.

7. For this example, we are not concerned with "proper" termination of model program execution. Here we have simply assumed the availability of a quantity, simtime, and allowed the program to continue until the system clock takes the value simtime, when the main program is reactivated. In our realizations this signals the end of the experiment. Subsequent examples contain variations on this procedure.

8. By the concatenation rules, the first executable statements of these realizations are

SQS:-**new** head

.
.
.

main.*event*.into(SQS);

(see Figure 5.2) followed by

simtime:=   ;

.
.
.

EXAMPLE 5.5   For the example variants, the synchronization of process objects is achieved by appropriate use of the scheduling constructs. To promote understanding, we reconsider variant 1 and trace (for a time) the contents of the sequencing set and the order in which statements are executed.

1. Initially, as can be ascertained from Figure 5.2 and remark 8, SQS contains a single notice (for the main program) scheduled for time zero. The situation is depicted in Figure 5.5, part (a). The main program then generates a server object (referenced by servs) and schedules its activation for time zero, thus leading to form (b).
2. The main program then executes hold(simtime) which alters SQS to form (c).
3. As a result, object serves (a server) is activated. It immediately generates an object arrivals and schedules its activation for the current time, producing form (d).
4. The object servs then passivates, leading to form (e).
5. The arrival object is activated next. It places a unit into the queue, and schedules reactivation for itself and the server object, so that SQS has form (f).
6. The server is now activated and begins its service on the first arrival. We cannot trace the flow further without knowledge of *actual* numbers drawn from the negative exponential distributions, as the server object now executes a hold ( ) operation to reflect a service activity. The next activation could be for (a) the arrival object, to reflect that next arrival or (b) the object referenced by servs to reflect a service completion.

All we can say is that from this point on SQS always contains a notice for the arrival object and the main program. It also contains one for the server object provided it finds units to serve.

INTERRUPTED ACTIVITY

The cancel ( ) and reactivate constructs are particularly useful for handling *interruptible activity*. In the Single Server Queueing System with a Preemptive Customer Example (Chapter 6) the server is preemptible by customers from a priority class, and a queue and the **reactivate** construct are employed to handle interrupted customers. Here, as an alternate example of interrupted activity, we consider a model program for the computer system depicted in Figure 5.6 and developed from a job's viewpoint.

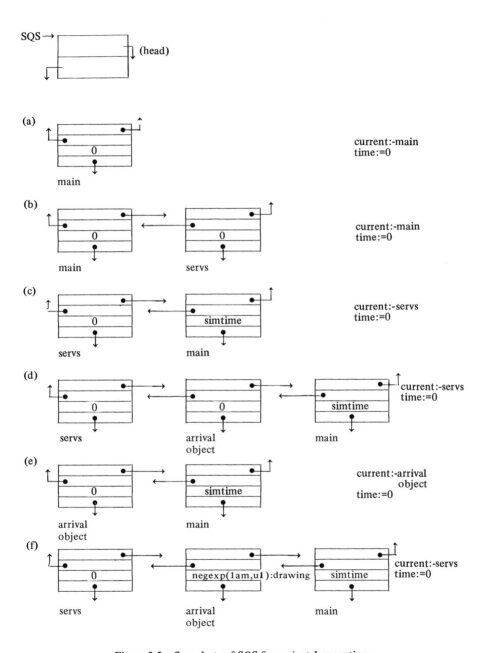

Figure 5.5 Snapshots of SQS for variant 1 execution

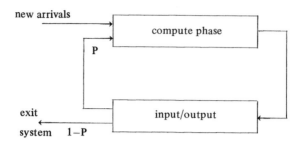

Figure 5.6 A job scenario

Jobs arrive at the system and cycle through computer input/output cycles. The number of cycles is determined by a Bernoulli trial following each input/output phase, such that with probability p, the job requests an additional compute phase, and with probability $1 - p$ leaves the system.

The job scenario is simply portrayed by

```
Process  class jobs(p);
         real p;
         begin
         integer i;
         for  i:=1, i+1 while draw(p,u)do
              begin
              compute (negexp (. . .));
              io(negexp(. . .));
              end;
         end job;
```

If we assume that new arrivals (to the processor) can preempt earlier arrivals at the compute stage, we have the potential for interrupted activity, and a job's service requirement may be fulfilled in *bursts*. We will account for this potentiality by associating with each job a record which contains a reference to it, and the job's remaining service time. We will associate two procedures, named suspend and start, with procedure compute. Suspend will be responsible for interrupting a job and placing the job's record at the bottom (last entry) of a queue generated via

```
ref(head)queue;
queue:-new head;
```

Procedure start restarts an interrupted compute burst. Formally, we have

```
procedure compute(t);real t;
begin
ref(record)x;
comment job receiving compute service is first member of queue;
x:-new record(t);
if ¬ queue.empty then suspend;
x.follow(queue);
comment attempt to perform complete service;
hold(t);
x.out;
start;
end compute;
procedure suspend;
comment  suspend compute phase for job holding the processor.
           Update job's record of remaining compute time;
begin ref(record)x;
x:-queue.first;
x.into(queue);
inspect x do begin
           t:=this record.job.evtime-time;
           cancel(job);
           end;
           end suspend;

procedure start;
comment restart first job in queue, if any;
if ¬ queue.empty then inspect queue.first qua record do

activate job delay t;

link   class record(t);real t;
       begin
       ref(jobs)job;
       job:-current;
       end record;
```

The use of helpers, suspend and start, is somewhat arbitrary because their definitions could easily be incorporated directly into compute's. They are included to promote readability.

The use of record objects is, however, less than arbitrary, because they separate the job scenario from the preemptive scheduling. As written, we have job's compute calls structurally independent from the way in which compute bursts are allocated.

AUXILIARY RECORDS AND PRIORITY QUEUES

Auxiliary records, as employed above, are handy constructs in a variety of situations.[3] Here we construct two procedures to realize a generalized priority queue; one enters *process objects* into a priority queue, whereas the other removes and returns a reference for the object with highest priority in a named priority queue. Additionally, the procedures are designed so that:

1. They work for any named queue designated (implicitly) as priority.
2. They allow any process object attribute to be used as *its* priority value. Members of a given priority queue may, in fact, be ordered on the basis of different attributes.
3. Process objects may be simultaneous members of several queues.

These qualifications are facilitated by *auxiliary records* defined by

```
link class record(0,p);
ref(process)0 ;real p;
```

and the procedures enter p queue and next pq out.

```
procedure enter p queue(object, priorityv,queue);
ref(process)object; real priorityv;ref(head)queue;
comment larger values of priorityv reflect lower priority;
begin
    ref(linkage)y; ref(record)z;
y:-queue;
if⌐queue.empty then
    begin
    if queue.last qua record.p≤priorityv
    then y:-queue.last
```

---

[3] Additional use of auxiliary records can be found at the end of Chapter 7.

```
    else for z:-y.suc while z.p≤priorityv do
            y:-z;
    end;
    new record(object,priorityv).follow(y);
    end enter p queue;

    ref(process)procedure next pq out (queue);
        ref(head) queue;
    begin
        ref(record)x;
    if queue.empty then next pq out:-none
    else begin
        x:-queue.first;
        x.out;
        next pq out:-x.0;
        end;
    end next pq out;
```

Notice that the active process object can place itself in such a queue by calling enter p queue with an actual first parameter of current or this process. Endless variants of these routines and ideas are possible. (The procedure rank declared in *class* event notice is one variant.)

PSEUDO RANDOM NUMBER STREAMS

The ability to generate streams of numbers uniformly distributed on $(0,1)$ is essential to stochastic simulation. More specifically, we require an algorithm to generate streams $U = \{u_0, u_1, u_2, \ldots\}$ such that the elements u_i are

(a) Independent (in the statistical sense) one of the other
(b) Uniformly distributed on $(0,1)$
(c) Dense on $(0,1)$

Further, a simulation may require many elements u_i, and so we require that

(d) The algorithm be efficient

Over the years a variety of algorithms have been proposed, and each has been judged by the criteria (a)–(d). From these proposals we find that the best algorithms are those based upon mathematical theory, and of those the most popular is the linear congruential.

The linear congruential method generates the integers z_i via

$$z_i = az_{i-1} + c \;(\text{mod } m) \tag{5.1}$$

form which u_i is formed by

$$u_i = z_i/m \tag{5.2}$$

The properties of congruential generators emerge from consideration of Equation (5.1). Equation (5.1) guarantees that $0, 1, \ldots, m-1$ are the only allowable values for z. Criteria (c), therefore, demands a large value of m. Further, once a z value is repeated, the entire sequence which follows it is repeated. The number of numbers P generated between repeats is the period or cycle of Equation (5.1), and we would like to have it as close to as possible its limiting value m. The period p can be theoretically linked (see Fishman [1973]) to $a, c, m,$ and z_0, the seed of the sequence. The theory is directed to providing criteria so that $a, c,$ and z_0 can be chosen, for m specified, to insure that p is as near m as is possible, criteria (c). Thus, theory allows evaluation of Equation (5.1) by criteria (c).

The form (5.1) disallows (a) in the strict sense, because each z_i is related to its predecessor and so to all z_j, $j = 0, 1, \ldots, i-1$. Amazingly, Equation (5.1) produces sequences satisfying (b) and (c), as determined by statistical tests[4] applied to the sequences produced. As a constant reminder of the inherent nonrandom nature of Equation (5.1), we call the sequences produced pseudorandom.

For the SIMULA system and a binary machine, we take $m = 2^n$, where n is the number of bits available to the coefficient in the floating point format. Theory dictates that $a = 5^{13}$ be used, yielding $p = 2^{n-2}$ if z_0 is odd.[5]

In the next section we often refer to the generation of u_i as a basic drawing. We cannot overemphasize the importance of good (by criteria a, b, c) streams U. A single bad stream can turn an otherwise carefully conducted simulation into a disaster.

---

[4] Complete discussions of the statistical tests employed can be found in Fishman [1973]. Since many are also useful to simulation input and output analysis, familiarity with them is recommended.

[5] On the Cyber 74 where $n = 48$, the cycle is long indeed.

VARIATE GENERATION

The ability to draw values for a random variable distributed according to an arbitrary distribution $F_x(x)$, is known as variate generation. There are two basic techniques for performing such drawings, and both rely on the availability of a random number stream U. One approach, the inverse transformation method, is based upon the following observation. Let U be uniformly distributed on (0, 1), then for x distributed according to $F_x(x)$, we have

$$\Pr\{x \leqslant a\} = F_x(a) = \Pr\{U \leqslant F_x(a)\} = \Pr\{F_x^{-1}(U) \leqslant a\}.$$

From this relationship we see that x and $F_x^{-1}(U)$ are identically distributed. Thus, a mechanism for drawing values of $F_x^{-1}(U)$ gives a mechanism for drawing values of x. Since we have a mechanism for drawing values of U, we have a method for generating values x, applicable to those functions $F_x(x)$ for which the inverse $F_x^{-1}(U)$ can be determined. Our procedure then, to draw a value of x, consists of obtaining a basic drawing, say μ from the stream U, evaluating $F_x^{-1}(\mu)$, and then setting $x = F_x^{-1}(\mu)$.

The classic application of the method is to the exponential distribution $F_x(t) = 1 - e^{-\lambda t}$, $\lambda > 0$, which yields $x = -\ln(1 - U)/\lambda = -\ln(U)/\lambda$, since U and $1 - U$ have identical distributions. The method is, however, applicable to continuous or discrete distributions defined on a finite or infinite range.

The second approach is applicable primarily to continuous distributions defined on a finite range. In essence, it consists of repeatedly performing a sampling experiment until a specified condition is met. The nature of the condition and experiment determine the distribution from which values will be drawn. To illustrate the method, consider $f_x(x)$ defined for $R = a \leqslant x \leqslant b$. Select a constant c so that $f(x) \leqslant c$, $x \in R$.

The rejection method dictates that we:

1. Generate U_1 and U_2.
2. Form $Y = a + (b - a)U_1$.
3. Accept $X = Y$ as the drawn value of X if $U_2 \leqslant f(x)/c$.
4. Otherwise reject Y, and return to step 1.

It is a simple matter to verify that the x values drawn are distributed according to $f_x(x)$. To do so note first that Y is uniformly distributed on (a, b) so that

$$\Pr(Y = x) = dx/(b - a) \qquad a \leqslant x \leqslant b.$$

Further, since U_2 is uniform on $(0, 1)$, we have

$$\Pr\left(U_2 \leqslant \frac{f(x)}{c} \mid Y = x\right) = \frac{f(x)}{c} \qquad (5.3)$$

so that

$$\Pr\left(U_2 \leqslant \frac{f(x)}{c}\right) = \int_a^b \Pr\left(U_2 \leqslant \frac{f(x)}{c} \mid Y = x\right) \cdot \frac{dx}{(b-a)}$$

$$= \frac{1}{c(b-a)} \int_a^b f(x) = \frac{1}{c(b-a)}. \qquad (5.4)$$

Finally, steps 1 and 2 and the definition of conditional probability together yield

$$\Pr\left(Y = x \mid U_2 \leqslant \frac{f(x)}{c}\right) = \frac{\Pr(U_2 \leqslant f(x)/c \mid Y = x)dx/(b-a)}{\Pr(U_2 \leqslant f(x)/c)}$$

which, after substitution of Equations (5.3) and (5.4), gives

$$\Pr\left(Y = x \mid U_2 \leqslant \frac{f(x)}{c}\right) = f(x)dx \qquad (5.5)$$

Notice that Equation (5.4) gives, for a given trial, the probability of generating an acceptable X value. Since the trials are independent, the generation of an acceptable X requires n trials with probability $q(1 - q)^{n-1}$, where $q = 1/[c(b - a)]$. The expected number of trials necessary to the generation of an X is, therefore, inversely proportional to $c(b - a)$. The method is especially attractive when it is difficult to obtain an expression for $F_x^{-1}(x)$.

All variate generation algorithms are based on these two general approaches, and many are quite ingenious. The particulars for a variety of functions $F_x(x)$ can be found in Fishman [1973].

Simula provides a battery of drawing procedures. All require basic drawings from a stream U, and have the side effect of advancing the stream U by one or more values. We list their headings and summarize their purpose.

1. **Boolean procedure** draw (a, U); **name** U; **real** a; **integer** U; The value is **true** with probability a, **false** with probability $1 - a$. It is always **true** if $a \geqslant 1$, always **false** if $a \leqslant 0$.

2. **Integer procedure** randint (a, b, U); **name** U; **integer** a, b, U; The value is one of the integers $a, a + 1, ..., b - 1, b$ with equal probability. It is assumed that $b \geqslant a$.

3. **Real procedure** uniform (a, b, U); **name** U; **real** a, b; **integer** u; The value is uniformly distributed in the interval $[a, b]$. It is assumed that $b > a$.

4. **Real procedure** normal (a, b, U); **name** U; **real** a, b; **integer** U; The value is normally distributed with mean a and standard deviation b.

5. **Real procedure** psnorm (a, b, c, U); **name** U; **real** a, b; **integer** c, U; The value is approximately normal, and is formed as the sum of c basic drawings, transformed according to:

$$a + b \left(\sum_{i=1}^{c} u_i - c/2 \right) \sqrt{12/c}$$

and is based on the central limit theorem. This procedure is faster but less accurate than the preceding one; c is assumed $\leqslant 12$.

6. **Real procedure** negexp (a, U); **name** U; **real** a; **integer** U; The value is a drawing from the negative exponential distribution with mean $1/a$.

7. **Integer procedure** Poisson (a, U); **name** U; **real** a; **integer** U; The value is a drawing from the Poisson distribution with parameter a. Several basic drawings may be required. When the parameter a is greater than 20.0, the value is approximated by integer (normal $(a, \text{sqrt}(a), u)$) or when this is negative, by zero.

8. **Real procedure** Erlang (a, b, U); **name** U; **value** a, b; **real** a, b; **integer** U;

   The value is a drawing from the Erlang (Gamma) distribution with mean $1/a$ and standard deviation $1/(a\sqrt{b})$. It requires b basic drawings u_i, if b is an integer value, and $c + 1$ basic drawings u_i otherwise, where c = entier (b). Both a and b must be greater than zero.

9. **Integer procedure** discrete (A, U); **name** U; **array** A; **integer** U;
The one-dimensional array A, augmented by the element 1 to the right, is interpreted as a step function of the subscript, defining a discrete (cumulative) distribution function. The array is assumed to be of type *real*.

    The function value is an integer in the range [lsb, usb + 1], where lsb and usb are the lower and upper subscript bounds of the array. It is defined as the smallest i such that $A[i] > u$, where u is a basic drawing and $A[\text{usb} + 1] = 1$.

10. **Real procedure** linear (A, B, U); **name** U; **array** A, B; **integer** U
The value is a drawing from a (cumulative) distribution function $F_x(x)$, which is obtained by linear interpolation in a nonequidistant table defined by A and B, such that $A[i] = F_x(B[i])$.

    It is assumed that A and B are one-dimensional real arrays of the same length, that the first and last elements of A are equal to 0 and 1, respectively, and that $A[i] \geqslant A[j]$ and $B[i] \geqslant B[j]$ for $i > j$.

11. **Integer procedure** histd (A, U); **name** U; **array** A; **integer** U;
The value is an integer in the range [lsb, usb] where lsb and usb are the lower and upper subscript bounds of the one-dimensional array A. The latter is interpreted as a histogram defining the relative frequencies of the values.

    This procedure is more time-consuming than the procedure discrete, where the cumulative distribution function is given but is more useful if the frequency histogram is updated at run run time.

The Computer System Reliability Study Example of Chapter 6 employs several of these procedures in response to the requirements of Table 6.4. The generators are collected and selected by *procedure* variate. Note that the required chi-squared generator is not among our procedures. This omission offers no difficulty because a chi-squared random variable X^2 with $E(X^2) = n$, $V(X^2) = 2n$ is given by

$$X^2 = \sum_{i=1}^{n} N_i{}^2$$

with the N_i distributed standard normally. Thus, variates for entry three of the table are easily obtained by summing the square of ten standard normal variates. Many useful relationships of this kind exist. One, for example, relates Erlangian random variables with integral parameter b to exponentially distributed variables. If E_r is an Erlangian random variable with $E[E_r] = 1/a, V[E_r] = 1/(a^2 b)$. Then

$$E_r = \sum_{j=1}^{b} e_i$$

where the e_i are exponentially distributed with $E(e_i) = 1/(ba)$.

For demonstration this relationship has been used to generate variates of entry 4 of Table 6.4, the Computer System Reliability Study Example (Chapter 6). Additional generators are used in other examples.

Finally, note that in procedure variate in the Computer System Reliability Study Example, we have assigned a separate stream U to each random variable used. This is generally a good policy and helps to insure a proper comparison of companion relizations emanating from two or more runs of the same model with different parameters and/or seeds.

UTILITY PROCEDURES

Data collection is an integral part of the simulation process. Often simple data collection mechanisms such as the discrete time integral and the histogram mechanisms are adequate. The first provides estimates of the mean of a simulation response variable, the second an approximation to its distributional form.

Discrete Time Integral

Use of the discrete time integral is usually associated with occupancy calculations and we will explain it in that context. Suppose that a component (e.g., a queue and server) can be occupied by n units, $n \geqslant 0$ and we wish to calculate the mean number of units which occupy the component during the simulation. For discrete event simulation, the occupancy changes at discrete time points, say t_i, and is occupied by n_i units after the change. If N changes occur during the course of the simulation, then

$$I = \sum_{j=0}^{N-1} n_j(t_{j+1} - t_j) \qquad (5.6)$$

defines the time integral I. Generally $t_0 \geqslant 0$, and marks the beginning of the data collection interval, and t_N is T the length of the simulation run.

Average occupancy is then given by I/T, and from Little's formula, the average occupancy time per unit is given by I/M, with M a count of the number of units that occupied the component, during $(t_N - t_0)$.

During the simulation, I of Equation (5.6) is easily maintained. When y units are added to the occupancy of the component, we execute

        I:=I + Nx(time-TL);
        N:=N + y;
        TL:=time;
        M:=M + 1;

and when y units vacate (leave) the component we execute

        I:= I + Nx(time-TL);
        N:= N - y;
        TL:= time;

Assuming that TL is initialized to t_0, I and M to zero, the N to an appropriate value.

SIMULA supplies a globally available procedure, named ACCUM, to perform these manipulations. Its definition is:

```
procedure accum(i,t1,n,y);
name i,t1,n; real i,t1,n,y,;
begin
    i:=i + nx(time-t1);
    t1:=time; n:=n+y;
end accum;
```

Notice that if n_i has only the values zero (for idle) or one (for busy), then i gives an estimate of component utilization.

A somewhat different use can also be made of the procedure. For the queueing system of the Finite Source Queueing Model Example, for instance, we are interested in estimating the steady-state probabilities, p_n, n = 0, 1, ..., N of there being n customers in the system. Estimates of p_n *can* be obtained by maintaining N discrete time integrals, one for each allowable state. The integral assigned to state n records the total time the system is in state n. The N integrals are declared by

real array p[o:n] ; real lastime, one; integer insystem;

in an appropriate block. Then for an arrival, and assuming ONE has the value 1, we can execute

accum (p[insystem] , lastime, one, 0);
insystem:=insystem +1;

and for a departure

accum (p[insystem] , lasttime, one, 0);
insystem:=insystem-1;

The desired estimates are then given by the values

p[i] /time i=0,1,. . .,n

and can be calculated at the close of the simulation run. For this usage, note that the procedure call

accum(p[insystem] , lastime, one, 0);

is simply equivalent to

p [insystem] :=p[insystem] + (time-lastime);
lastime:=time;

We can also plot the p_n, as a function of n, to obtain a pictorial of the state distribution. Such a display is known as a histogram, and a second utility procedure is provided to directly collect data for histograms.

Histograms

During a simulation we can monitor the frequency with which a given variable assumes each of a finite set of values, or the frequency with which its value falls within specified subranges of its range of definition. From such data the histogram is constructed, and, for example, provides approximation to the frequency or distribution function for a stochastic output variate. SIMULA provides the procedure histo to facilitate the data collection and display process. Its head is given by

> **procedure** histo (a,b,c,d,)
> **array** a,b; **real** c,d;

and operates as follows.

A reference to histo updates, the vector array a of frequency counts by an amount d, as determined by the subrange into which the observation c falls. The subrange's boundaries are given by the vector array b. Specifically, $a[lba + i]$ is increased by d, where i is the smallest integer such that $c \leqslant b[lbb + i]$, and lba, lbb are, respectively, the lower subscript bounds of the arrays a and b. It is assumed that the cardinality of a exceeds that of b by one, and that the last element of a is used to record the frequency of observations that exceed in value the last element of b. The Computer System Reliability Study Example uses histo to obtain data on the distribution of time between failures for the system studied. The updates are performed in line 59 with vector b initialized in lines 78–79. Reduction of the data to fractional frequencies requires maintenance of an additional variable, say k, which is incremented by one at each update. Alternatively, the value of k could be found at the end of the simulation run by summing up all components of the array a. The fractional frequencies are then given by $a[i]/k$.

BASICIO

The input-output system supported by SIMULA is *file directed,* where a file is a collection of related information organized in chunks called *records*. The system **class** BASICIO supports elaborate machinery designed to facilitate file manipulation. The mechanisms provided differ significantly, however, from those found in most ALGOL systems and are built upon the concept of a **text**. A text is a string of characters and as such may be considered an object. Text *objects* are referenced by identifiers declared by

> **text** ⟨identifier list⟩;

Special procedures exist to create and manipulate text objects. Here, we will not consider the details of these manipulatory mechanisms, because our sole interest in them stems from the fact that they form the basis for SIMULA input-output, and in that connection we associate text objects with file records.

For output we construct a text object which is to correspond to a file record and then direct that the text object *value* be appended to a named file as a record. For input we direct that a record be transferred from a file and become the value associated with a referenced text object. Data items are then pulled from the text object (remember the text object value is a character string). The routines which allow for the composition and decomposition of text objects are known as text *editing* and *de-editing* procedures. They are quite powerful, and available at all class and block levels. The class declarations INFILE, OUTFILE, and PRINTFILE make extensive use of these procedures in their direct support of the input-output activity. In turn, these class declarations are a part of the class BASICIO which we may assume to prefix the block which encompasses our entire model *program.* INFILE, OUTFILE, and PRINTFILE contain the definitions for a series of procedures which allow us to first manipulate a text object, referenced by *image,* and also to transfer the value of image from and to files.

Because we can go a long way toward satisfying our input-output requirements with these procedures, we will not pursue text editing or file **class** declarations further than to specify the *use* of these routines. They will then be used freely in future model programs. In the Computer System Memory Conflict Study Example (Chapter 6) we examine the input-output constructs of file *class* declarations more closely. The reader interested in pursuing these matters further is thus directed to that Example, or Birtwhistle [1973a].

In INFILE we have:

(a) **integer procedure** inint;

which *scans* past blank characters in the current and subsequent input image (card) values and decodes an integer numeric value, utilizing all character positions in those image values until a blank is encountered. The current position within an image value is recorded in a character position pointer.

EXAMPLE 5.6   Before inint is executed we have:

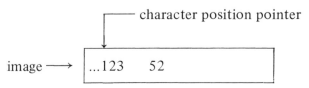

then

    I:=inint;

results in *I* taking the value 123 and alters image pointers to:

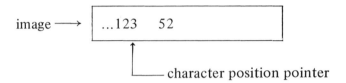

image   ⟶   ...123   52

                └── character position pointer

    (b) **real procedure** inreal;

does the same as inint except for real values. The allowable forms of real numbers are as produced by outreal or outfix (see below).

    In OUTFILE we have

    (a) **procedure** outint(i,w);**integer** i,w;. . .;

which uses w character positions to record in the image with an output file the value of i; that is, the output format is Iw.[6] The image character pointer is updated by w.

    (b) **procedure** outfix(*r, n, w*);**real** *r*;**integer** *n,w*;. . .;

The real value r is placed in the image value, using w character positions, n of which follow the decimal point; that is, the output is $Fw.n$. The character pointer is updated.

    (c) **procedure** outreal(r,n,w);**real** r;**integer** n,w;. . .;

The output is $Ew.(n-1)$. The character pointer is updated.

    (d) **procedure** outimage;

Transfers the value referenced by image to the file as a record. The image value is cleared to blanks and the character pointer set to one.

    (e) **procedure** outtext(T);**text** T;. . .;

––––––––––

[6] In the Fortran sense.

A copy of the character sequence represented by the actual argument is placed into the image value. Following the insertion the character pointer is updated. The easiest way to use this procedure is via a text value given as an actual argument, for example,

outtext("characters");

where " " denote and delineate an actual text object (rather than a referenced text object).

Since these procedures are declared in the class declarations of INFILE and OUTFILE, to be useful, objects must be generated from those classes. In this regard we may assume that two such objects are generated automatically by the SIMULA system, one for card input, the other line printer output. For the latter the object is generated from *class* PRINTFILE, which is prefixed by OUTFILE. The *class* PRINTFILE contains additional useful formatting procedures. Among them are

(a) **procedure** spacing(N);**integer** N;. . .;

Normally the spacing value is 1 and successive images are placed (printed) on successive lines. A call

spacing(m);

will alter this normal setting and cause $m - 1$ blank lines to appear between successive lines of output. An m value of 0 results in over-printing, and $m < 0$ an error.

(b) **procedure** eject(N);**integer** N;

can be used to skip to a designated line on a page. That is

eject(m);

will skip to line m of the current page if not passed, otherwise to line m of the next page. The next image output then appears on line m. Usually the number of lines per page is between 60 and 65.

We have not come close to indicating the generality or flexibility of the SIMULA input-output structure, because, as indicated, our needs are handily served in most cases with card input, line printer output, and the simple formatting procedures given. As stated, the

Computer System Memory Conflict Study Example (Chapter 6) has a more elaborate input requirement and uses several features not yet discussed.

At this point we are in a position to examine the Examples of Chapter 6. They may be examined in any order because they are in a real sense independent one of the other.

CHAPTER 6

Tactical Considerations and Complete Examples

In the preceding chapters we first developed a general machinery (Chapter 4), and then, using that machinery as building blocks, developed next a process or *scenario-oriented* simulation system (Chapter 5). We would be remiss if we did not at this point include a series of examples to clarify, amplify, and generally demonstrate use of the system. Such a presentation is the primary purpose of this chapter, and six systems are discussed and modeled. Five of the six examples explore very simple systems. We have purposely made them so as our objectives are didactical in nature and not directed to the reporting of case studies. We do not, therefore, (except for the Computer System Memory Conflict Study Example) dwell on the verification or validation of the systems modeled, nor for that matter account for our interest in the system itself. However, lest the reader think the simulation system suitable only to very simple models, in the last example we report on an actual application.

To avoid errors in presentation, the model programs are displayed via listings produced by the language compiler.[1] To become acquainted with the format, we present listings for model variants 1 and 2, developed earlier. As can be seen, due to the limitations of most input-output devices, keyword symbols are represented by a string of characters enclosed by a special *escape* character. A full accounting of the allowable representations of keywords and symbols is given in Appendix D. As is also evident, the compiler conveniently numbers statements of the model program in the left margin. This is done to provide a mechanism for associating diagnostic messages with the lines in error (diagnostics are generally given following the model program listing). For our purposes, these numbers provide a mechanism whereby we may refer to individual lines of the model program. For all listings given, we mark the boundaries of major segments by lines consisting of asterisks (e.g., lines 30 and 36) and

---

[1] All examples were run on a Cyber-74.

judiciously provide annotation for readability. For variants 1 and 2, to verify that the model programs are viable, we have included statements in each to collect data for (line 13 in variant 1 and line 18 in variant 2), then calculate (line 47 in 1 and 34 in 2), and display (lines 48–50 in 1 and 35–37 in 2) an estimate of server utilization. The last two lines of each variant listing signal end of input to the compiler, and appear at the end of every model program displayed.

As Figure 1.4 and its accompanying text indicate, simulation is more than a model program. In Chapter 1 we characterized simulation by saying that

> the methodology of simulation involves a representational approach
> to phenomena.

MODEL PROGRAMS

Variant 1

```
0       SIMULATION #BEGIN#
0                   #COMMENT#   ACTIVE SERVER AND ACTIVE SOURCE#
1       #REAL# LAM,MU,SIMTIME#  #REF#(SERVER) SERVS#
3       #INTEGER# U1,U2#
4       #REAL# BUSYTIME#
5
5
5       PROCESS #CLASS# SERVER#
6       #BEGIN#
6                   #REF#(HEAD) QUEUE#  #REF#(UNIT) JOB#
8       QUEUE:- #NEW# HEAD#
9       #ACTIVATE# #NEW# ARRIVALS(QUEUE) #DELAY# 0#
10      L1:     PASSIVATE#
11      #FOR# JOB :- QUEUE.FIRST #WHILE# JOB=/= #NONE# #DO#
12                  #BEGIN#
12                  JOB.OUT#
13                  BUSYTIME := BUSYTIME+JOB.SERVICETIME#
14                  HOLD(JOB.SERVICETIME)#
15                  #END#
18      #GO TO# L1#
19      #END# SERVER
20      ************************************************************ #
22
22      PROCESS #CLASS# ARRIVALS(Q)#
23                  #REF#(HEAD) Q#
24      #BEGIN#
24      L1:     #NEW# UNIT.INTO(Q)#
25      #IF# SERVS.IDLE #THEN# #ACTIVATE# SERVS #DELAY# 0#
27      #REACTIVATE# #THIS# ARRIVALS #DELAY# NEGEXP(LAM,U1)#
28      #GO TO# L1#
29      #END# ARRIVALS
30      ************************************************************ #
32
32      LINK #CLASS# UNIT#
33      #BEGIN#
33                  #REAL# SERVICETIME#
34      SERVICETIME:=NEGEXP(MU,U2)#
35      #END# UNIT
36      ************************************************************ #
```

```
38
38                 #COMMENT#  MAIN PROGRAM:  ;
39
39      SIMTIME:=10000;
40      MU:=1;
41      LAM:= .5;
42      U1:=502;   U2:=320;
44      SERVS:- #NEW# SERVER;
45      #ACTIVATE# SERVS #DELAY# 0;
46      HOLD(SIMTIME);
47      BUSYTIME:=BUSYTIME/TIME;
48      OUTTEXT(#UTILIZATION =#);   OUTFIX(BUSYTIME,5,8);
50      OUTIMAGE;
51      #END# SIMULATION;
51                 #EOP#
51                 FINIS
```

UTILIZATION = 0.50037

Variant 2

```
0       SIMULATION #BEGIN#
0                 #COMMENT# ACTIVE UNITS;
1                 #REAL# LAM,MU,SIMTIME;   #BOOLEAN# SERVER BUSY;
3                 #REF#(HEAD) Q;
4                 #REAL# T,BUSYTIME;
5                 #INTEGER# U1,U2;
6
6
6       PROCESS #CLASS# UNIT;
7       #BEGIN#
7       #ACTIVATE# #NEW# UNIT #AT# TIME+NEGEXP(LAM,U1);
8       #IF# SERVER BUSY #THEN#
9                 #BEGIN#
9                 WAIT(Q);
10                OUT;         #COMMENT# REMOVE SELF FROM Q;
12                #END#;
15      SERVERBUSY := #TRUE#;
16      T:=TIME;
17      HOLD(NEGEXP(MU,U2));
18      BUSYTIME:= BUSYTIME+(TIME-T);
19      SERVERBUSY:= #FALSE#;
20      #IF# #NOT# Q.EMPTY #THEN# #ACTIVATE# Q.FIRST #AFTER# CURRENT;
22      #END# UNIT
23      ****************************************************** ;
25
25                #COMMENT#  MAIN PROGRAM:  ;
26
26      SIMTIME:=10000;
27      MU:=1;
28      LAM:= .5;
29      U1:=502;   U2:=320;
31      Q:- #NEW# HEAD;
32      #ACTIVATE# #NEW# UNIT #AFTER# CURRENT;
33      HOLD(SIMTIME);
34      BUSYTIME:=BUSYTIME/TIME.
35      OUTTEXT(#UTILIZATION =#);   OUTFIX(BUSYTIME,5,8);
37      OUTIMAGE;
38      #END# SIMULATION;
38                #EOP#
38                FINIS
```

UTILIZATION = 0.50037

We thus emphasized those aspects germane to the identification of components and the development of scenario descriptions of their behavior patterns and interactions (synchronizations). Alternately [Kleijnen, 1974], we may characterize it by defining

> simulation as experimentation with a (stochastic) abstract model over time.

This formulation emphasizes that simulation is a sampling experiment requiring attention to statistical decision and analysis.

To this author's view, simulation is in reality an amalgam of both characterizations, each being equally important. Before proceeding to our examples we amplify somewhat on each of these views.

MORE ON MODEL PROGRAM DEVELOPMENT

As we pointed out earlier, the form of a simulation model is much influenced by the machinery that will ultimately be used to realize it. That is, in one way or another, computer language confines the modeler to some kind of conceptual framework in which the model program (and hence the model) must be developed. General purpose languages provide too scant or improper a framework and support system, whereas some simulation languages are overly restrictive and provide little latitude in model or model program development.

Our major contention has been that a model consisting of inter-acting component scenarios (processes) is natural to a wide variety of situations. It was, in fact, on the basis of this single assumption that the *class* concept of SIMULA was developed, and it is from this single but fundamental concept that the compact yet flexible and powerful system of Chapter 5 sprang. That system offered complete flexibility in the selection of active and passive components, and the remote reference features provided very general mechanisms for altering system state, that is, component attributes. Further, the synchronization (scheduling constructs) are sufficiently general and powerful to implement complex resource allocation rules giving a latitude not offered by many systems. Additionally, one often finds that the quickest way to fully understand the features of a simulation language is to examine the algorithms and code of which it is made. Thus, it is more than a happy curiosity that the entire SIMULA simulation system is realized quite compactly *within* the language itself. It is also important to note that the system is extendable and modifiable (Chapter 7). In fact, in a very real sense, the SIMULA system *incorporates* or includes the features of most simulation language systems. Specifically, it can be used to realize models that employ not only the scenario scanning approach but also the activity scanning or event sequencing schemes (see Chapter 7). A unit time advance mechanism can also be had.

Many persons engaged in simulations would consider the SIMULA system weak because it does not automatically perform data collection, analysis, and display. Even so, we remain unconvinced that the omission represents a weakness. We believe that, in general, it is better to provide the tools, as SIMULA does, which allow data collection and display to be tailored to the case at hand. As a case in point, it would be reasonably difficult to use the regenerative data collection scheme (see next section) in many extant simulation systems. With SIMULA it is as easy (or difficult) as using any other. Further, the idea of incorporating data analysis machinery into a simulation system may well be inappropriate. Most computer systems have a library of powerful statistical data analysis packages that are convenient to use.[2] When complex analyses are required, it seems more appropriate to have the simulation system, that is, the model program, merely record the observations for subsequent input to these "canned" routines.[3] For simple analyses, as in our examples, a few statements in the model program quickly tailor it in the desired way while providing complete control over what data is collected.

Finally, we believe that the scenario descriptions are consistent with the notions of structured programming, in that action and attribute sequences are localized (see Chapter 3), thus facilitating readability and program correctness.

STATISTICAL ASPECTS

Design: Strategic Planning

As pointed out earlier, simulation is a statistical experiment and as such requires both design and analysis. Design is concerned with

---

[2] For example, IMSL library, International Mathematical and Statistical Libraries Inc.

[3] In this regard, simulation systems with a checkpoint continue (restart) capability are highly desirable. GPSS comes close to providing such a feature.

determining which runs should be made, that is, what parameter settings should be used for runs and the order in which the runs are made, in order to obtain as much information as possible, with the fewest runs and least human effort.

In statistical parlance, each input variable (including distribution and transformational rule) is called a *factor* and the values, forms, and relationships which they may assume are considered *levels*. Simulation experiments are concerned with recording, via selected *performance measures,* the effects of one or more factors at one or more levels. Further, we usually distinguish between *qualitative* and *quantitative* factors. Quantitative factors can be considered at a potentially infinite number of levels, whereas qualitative factors can be considered only at a very limited number of levels. Under this dichotomy, transformational rules and policies would be considered qualitative and numerically measurable attributes quantitative.

EXAMPLE 6.1   For the queueing system discussed in Example 1.3, k, the number of servers, as well as λ and μ would be considered quantitative, whereas the implied first-come-first-served queue selection discipline would be a qualitative factor.

To investigate k factors, each factor at L_i, $i = 1, \ldots, k$, levels, requires

$$T = \prod_{i=1}^{k} L_i$$

runs. Quite obviously, T can become large quite rapidly, and as it does, the cost of the *simulation study* becomes more and more unreasonable. Put simply then, *experimental design* attempts to *limit* the number of levels that need be examined in a simulation experiment and does so by identifying those levels most relevant to the questions the simulation study is designed to answer. There are many standard designs for various k, L_i, and so on, which have proven useful. Excellent discussions of these matters are given in Fishman [1973] and Kleijnen [1974], so we will not further pursue the matter.

EXAMPLE 6.2   A more common situation requires that the effect of different policies (e.g., resource allocation rules) be compared or that the optimum value (i.e., the value which optimizes certain performance measures) of a quantitative factor be found.

In a sense, experimental design is concerned with the *strategic* planning of the simulation study; that is, it is more concerned with *what* experiments (what simulation runs and at what levels) should be performed than with *how* the runs should be performed. How a simulation run should be conducted is the concern of the *tactical* planning of the experiments.[4] Before discussing tactical planning, however, we insert a word about input data analysis.

Input Analysis

As mentioned in Chapter 1, during the synthesis stage of model development, we expect that "real world" data will be collected to facilitate the parameterization of the model. As pointed out in Kleijnen [1974], collected data can be used to support simulation as model program input in any of three ways. Namely:

1. Collected data can be used to select a *theoretical* distribution. The model program then uses the data *indirectly* by drawing variates from the selected theoretical distribution.
2. Collected data can be used to construct an empirical distribution from which the model program can draw variates (see Fishman [1973], p. 232 for the procedure).
3. Collected data can be used *directly* by the model program. Model programs making this use of data are generally termed *trace driven* (data trace); that is, unlike the use in 1 and 2 above, the collected values are assigned as necessary to a model program variable.

With option one, the following procedure is used. First, select *candidate* distribution forms, perhaps by visual comparison of theoretical forms with the histogram display of the collected data. In Schmidt [1970], a lovely collection of forms is displayed to facilitate the selection process. Next, parameterize the form (again using the collected data) and perform *goodness-of-fit* tests to select from among the candidate forms. Procedures such as

---

[4] The terms *tactical* and *strategic* were originally used in this context in Conway [1963].

the Chi-squared and Kolomogorov-Smirnov tests are generally used. A basic discussion of these techniques is found in Schmidt [1970], whereas more advanced presentations on these and related matters can be found in Knuth [1971] and Fishman [1973]. For a discussion of efficient computational procedures for the Kolomogorov-Smirnov test see Gonzalez [1976].

It is generally easiest to use the data in the third way. Kleijnen suggests (and we agree) that the third alternative may be used to facilitate validation, but that the first alternative is more appropriate for purposes of experimentation.

Finally, note that the goodness-of-fit tests mentioned above are also applicable to the analysis of simulation outputs, that is, to determine the distributional form of variables from data collected during simulation (see a Computer System Reliability Study Example).

Tactical Planning: Output Analysis

During the initial stages of model development (particularly the zeroth and first of Figure 1.4) the measures of interest are identified, and data collection, analysis, and display methodologies are selected. The selection of collection and analysis methodologies is guided at least in part by the type of information (transient or steady-state) that the model is intended to provide. If information about the transient state is desired, then time-series analysis or autoregressive moving average methods are more appropriate than other methods (see Box [1970], Mihram [1972], or Fishman [1973]). This type of situation is encountered when we are more concerned about how a system performs from *startup,* or after a drastic augmentation or change in its inputs, than we are in its long-run or steady-state behavior. Although these methods are also applicable to simulations designed to investigate steady-state behavior, other simpler but adequate schemes are often used. Because most simulations (including our examples) are designed to investigate behavior under steady-state conditions, the remainder of this section is devoted to a discussion of the simpler data collection and analysis methods to which we alluded.

To proceed, let us assume that the simulation produces observations $x_1, x_2, \ldots, x_n$ for a stochastic output variable $X,$ where X may be a single component in a vector of response variables. Further, let us assume that the simulation is designed to produce the estimator $\hat{E}(X)$[5] of $E(X)$, the expected value of the variable. The estimator

$$\bar{X} = \hat{E}(X) = \frac{1}{n} \sum_{i=1}^{n} X_i \qquad (6.1)$$

is generally used because it is simple and unbiased, that is, $E[\hat{E}(X)] = E(X)$. Assuming for the moment that the observations are *independent*, we also have the *sample variance*

$$s^2 = \hat{\sigma}_X{}^2 = \frac{1}{n-1} \sum_{i=1}^{n} (x_i - \bar{x})^2 \qquad (6.2)$$

as an unbiased estimator of the variance, $\sigma_X{}^2$, of X. Further, we have that the variance of $\bar{X}$ is given by

$$\sigma_{\bar{x}}^2 = \frac{\sigma_x{}^2}{n} \qquad (6.3)$$

which can be estimated by

$$\hat{\sigma}_{\bar{x}}^2 = \frac{\hat{\sigma}_x{}^2}{n} = \frac{s^2}{n} \qquad (6.4)$$

Additionally, on the basis of the central limit theorem, we have that the quantity

$$\frac{\bar{X} - E(X)}{\sigma_{\bar{X}}} \qquad (6.5)$$

assumes a standard normal distribution in the limit, as n, the number of observations, becomes unbounded. Further, the limiting distribution of Equation (6.5) still obtains when $\sigma_{\bar{X}}$ is replaced by s. If the observations x_i are normally distributed, the quantity

$$\frac{\bar{X} - E(X)}{\hat{\sigma}_{\bar{X}}} = \frac{\bar{X} - E(X)}{s/\sqrt{n}} \qquad (6.6)$$

has a t-distribution with $(n - 1)$ degrees of freedom. Under these conditions, expression (6.6) allows us, to seek that value $t_{n-1,1-\alpha/2}$ for which

$$\Pr\left[\bar{X} - (s \cdot t_{n-1,1-\alpha/2})/\sqrt{n} < E(X) < \bar{X} + (s \cdot t_{n-1,1-\alpha/2})/\sqrt{n}\right] = 1 - \alpha$$
$$\text{for } 0 < \alpha < 1 \qquad (6.7)$$

---

[5] We shall denote the estimator of a parameter by a hat, that is, $\hat{\theta}$ is an estimate of the parameter θ.

and which implies that out of all those *intervals* with endpoints

$$I = \bar{X} \pm (s \cdot t_{n-1,1-\alpha/2})/\sqrt{n} \qquad (6.8)$$

approximately $100 \cdot (1 - \alpha)$ percent of them will contain the parameter $E(X)$. The interval I, given by Equation (6.8), is known as the confidence interval for $E(X)$ at the $1 - \alpha$ *significance level*. Since for $n > 30$, the t-distribution has for practical purposes assumed the form of the normal, we can for $n > 30$, confidently replace the value $t_{n-1,1-\alpha/2}$ from the t-distribution by its corresponding value (designated by $Z_{1-\alpha/2}$ and *independent* of n) from the normal. Furthermore, even when the observations x_i are not normally distributed, Equation (6.7) results in (usually) a relatively small error when used to estimate the confidence interval of $E[X]$. The distribution of Equation (6.6) converges to normal in any case, so that Equation (6.7) can be comfortably used with $t_{n-1,1-\alpha/2}$ replaced by $Z_{1-\alpha/2}$, as n, the number of observations, becomes large (large may be as small as 30). The procedure given in Appendix F can be used to calculate the points $Z_{1-\alpha/2}$. Alternately, they can be determined from tables (e.g., the tables in the Appendix of Mihram [1972].[6] We can, therefore, use either the confidence interval (6.8) or the variance estimate (6.4) to specify the *reliability* of the estimator (6.1).

The problem with these procedures is that they presuppose that the observations $x_1, \ldots, x_n$ are independent. In reality, observations emanating from simulation runs are usually *correlated* (generally positively). For correlated observations, (6.1) continues to hold, but (6.3) and (6.4) do not. For correlated observations, we define the *autocovariances* R_k of the observations by

$$R_k = E\{(X_i - E(X))(X_{i+k} - E(X))\} \qquad (6.9)$$

and estimate the quantities by

$$\hat{R}_k = \frac{1}{n-k} \sum_{i=1}^{n-k} (X_i - \bar{X})(X_{i+k} - \bar{X}) \qquad (6.10)$$

where, of course, $R_0 = \sigma_X^2$ and $\hat{R}_0 \doteq s^2$. Further, we define the

---

[6] For derivations and further discussion of these results, see Fishman [1973] or Mihram [1972].

autocorrelation function, $\rho(k)$, to be given by

$$\rho(k) = \frac{R_K}{R_0} \tag{6.11}$$

and estimated by

$$\hat{\rho}(k) = \frac{\hat{R}_k}{\hat{R}_0}. \tag{6.12}$$

Then, it is easily shown (see, e.g., Mihram [1972]) for correlated observations that

$$\hat{\sigma}_{\bar{X}}^2 = \frac{s^2}{n}\left\{1 + 2\sum_{k=1}^{n-1}\left(1 - \frac{k}{n}\right)\hat{\rho}(k)\right\} \tag{6.13}$$

or alternately that

$$\hat{\sigma}_{\bar{X}}^2 = \frac{1}{n}\left\{\hat{R}_0 + 2\sum_{k=1}^{n-1}\left(1 - \frac{k}{n}\right)\hat{R}_K\right\} \tag{6.14}$$

As Equation (6.13) reveals, Equation (6.4) underestimates $\sigma_{\bar{X}}^2$ if the $\hat{\rho}(k)$ are nonzero and positive.

We consider Equation (6.14) to be a *direct* method of handling correlated observations; it is the method used in the Batch Arrival System Example which follows. Other *direct* methods include those provided by the time series techniques mentioned earlier. There are also several *indirect* methods which we discuss next, all of which were conceived as methods which produce independent observations. Three such methods are common and are known as:

1. Method of replication,
2. Method of subruns (or independent blocks),
3. Regenerative method.

We discuss each in turn.

Method of Replication

This method consists of making k *independent* runs (or *replications*) and obtaining m observations from each. The runs are made independent by using different seeds for the variate generators used in the model. Let $\bar{X}_i$ be the average response obtained from the ith run by using Equation (6.1) with n equal to m. As a result of the seeding procedure, the $\bar{X}_i$'s $i = 1, \ldots, k$ are independent, and if the same initial conditions are employed for each run (which we now assume), they are also identically distributed. Since the $\bar{X}_i$'s are independent and identically distributed (iid), we can use them in Equations (6.1) and (6.2) with $n = k$ to obtain estimates $\bar{X}$ and s^2 for $E(X)$ and $\sigma_X{}^2$, respectively. They can, therefore, also be used in Equation (6.4) with $n = k$. Further, because the $\bar{X}_i$ are at least *approximately* normal, they can be used in Equation (6.7) with $n = k$ to produce an approximate confidence interval for $E(X)$. The validity of the approximation improves, of course, with increasing k.

Since the $\bar{X}_i$ are only approximately normal, the confidence interval calculation must also be considered approximate. Additionally, since the X_i in any replication are positively correlated, as pointed out earlier, the $\bar{X}_i$ can be *influenced* or *biased* by the initial or startup conditions employed, particularly if they are not representative of steady-state conditions.

To eliminate bias, it is desirable to avoid data collection during the transient phase, or to avoid its use in Equation (6.1) if it must be collected during that phase (usually the simpler alternative). Either course of action requires that we estimate the duration of the transient phase. If our estimate is too short, nonrepresentative observations will be used in Equation (6.1). If our estimate is too long, valuable observations will be discarded. The first error biases the results; the second increases the cost of the simulation (in computer time) and/or decreases the number of observations used in Equation (6.1).

It is unfortunate that *no* effective quantitative procedure exists to estimate the length of the transient phase. The best procedures seem to be based on educated guesses and a variety of rule of thumb approaches are reported in Emhoff [1970]. The viability of these rules, which is low, is discussed by Gafarian et al. [1977].

EXAMPLE 6.3 Consider again the system in Example 1.2. If operation of the system is begun with $P_0(0) = 1$, $P_1(0) = 0$, then a transient phase must be passed over before steady-state conditions are realized (approximately). For general systems where equations

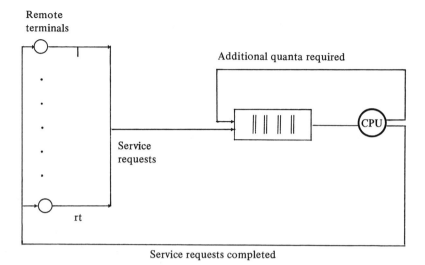

Figure 6.1 Model of a time-shared computer system

such as (1.1) and (1.2) are not available, it is difficult to estimate the duration of the transient phase, but for the system in Example 1.2, observations collected during that phase may not be representative of steady-state behavior which, as we discussed in Chapter 1, is independent of initial conditions.

EXAMPLE 6.4 To demonstrate and compare data collection strategies, we will later report results on the simulation of the time-shared computer *system model* depicted in Figure 6.1. The system model consists of rt remote terminals connected to a computer processor (CPU) which services requests according to a *round robin scheduling discipline.*[7] The terminals generate processor service requests (jobs) which join the queue, and are eventually satisfied. Once satisfied, a new request is not generated until a time—the think-time—has elapsed.

For the model, we assume that think-times are exponentially distributed with parameter λ_1, that total service requests are exponentially distributed with parameter λ_2, that the quantum size

---

[7] A round robin discipline is one in which jobs are selected from the front of a queue, given at most a small fixed size amount of server (CPU) time, known as a quantum, and returned to the end of the queue if its total service request remains unsatisfied.

is q, and that in switching from one job to another, the CPU suffers an overhead time of length τ. We imagine the measure of interest to be the mean $E(T_R)$ of the time T_R which elapses between a terminal's submission of a service request (job) and the completion of that service (the elapsed period being known as the response time). This model has been analyzed analytically in Adiri [1969] and we will use certain analytically obtained results for comparative purposes. This model should also be compared with the one in the Finite Source Queueing Model Example.

EXAMPLE 6.5[8] A convenient and effective means of estimating the transient is given by simulating the system and *periodically* using Equation (6.1) to produce estimates based on the number of observations available to that time. If the results are plotted, a visual estimate of the duration of the transient can be made. To illustrate, consider simulation of the model of Example 6.4, with $1/\lambda_1 = 25$, $1/\lambda_2 = 0.8$, $\tau = 0.015$, $q = 0.1$, and rt set first to 25 and then 35. In Figure 6.2 we have plotted estimates (estimates were produced after every 20 observations) of the mean response time $E(T_R)$ as a function of n, the number of observations. Plotted for each value of rt are three replications numbered (1), (2), and (3). From these plots we observe that

1. The *transient response* may converge to the steady-state response from *above* or *below*.
2. The system with the heavier load converges more slowly (this is generally true and has theoretical support).
3. The *transient response* (*not* period) is ended (approximately) after 200 to 300 observations for rt = 25 and after 500 to 600 observations when rt = 35.

The method of replication can lead to biased estimators and, additionally, can be expensive if it is necessary to delete a large number of observations (i.e., if the transient response is long) from the beginning of *each* of the k replications. It is natural, therefore, to seek alternative data collection strategies. The method of replications has its place, however. In particular, some systems cannot be

---

[8] The simulation results reported in Examples 6.5, 6.6, and 6.9 were obtained by Sargent and reported in Sargent [1976].

$1/\lambda_1 = 25$ $1/\lambda_2 = 0.8$ $q = 0.1$ $\tau = 0.015$

initial conditions: all terminals begin in think state

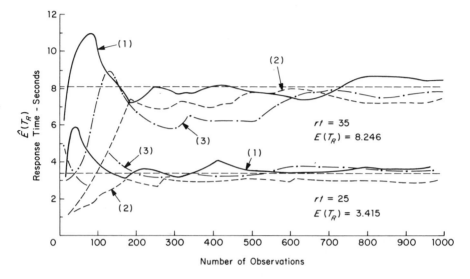

Figure 6.2   Transient responses

simulated for an arbitrarily long period of time because a specified critical event *must* be used to terminate the run. For such systems, the method of replications is natural. For systems which can be run for an arbitrary time, the method of subruns is generally preferable.

Method of Subruns

For this method, we make one continued run from which observations contributing to the transient response are not used. The observations from this *single* long run are divided into k subruns. Thus, if the run contains km observations (after deletion of transient observations), each subrun contains m observations. Using Equation (6.1) with $n = m$, we compute $\bar{X}_i$, $i = 1, \ldots, k$ as for replications. If m is of reasonable size, the $\bar{X}_i$ are uncorrelated[9] and are usually assumed independent as well. Further, for reasonable m, the $\bar{X}_i$ are

---

[9] Estimates of correlation can be made using Equation (6.12) with $X_i = \bar{X}_i$ and $n = k$.

also *approximately* normally distributed. With these observations, a point estimate of $E(X)$ can be obtained by using the $\bar{X}_i$'s in Equation (6.1) (with $n = k$), and a confidence interval obtained from Equation (6.8) with $n = k$. If Equation (6.12) shows the $\bar{X}_i$'s to be correlated, then Equation (6.14) can be used instead of Equation (6.8).

The method of subruns is preferable to replications because only a single transient period need be considered. For either method, however, initial conditions representative of steady state should be used if available, because using them shortens the transient and lowers the cost of the simulation. Such conditions are usually unknown, although *pilot* runs may be used to estimate them. Either method—replication or subruns—may be applied to most of the examples that follow. For the last method to be considered—the regenerative method—a determination of the transient phase is unnecessary.

EXAMPLE 6.6   In Tables 6.1 and 6.2, we present simulation results for the model described in Example 6.4 with parameter values as given in Example 6.5 with rt = 25. For these parameter values, we have from Adiri [1969] that $E[T_R]$, the expected response time, is 3.415. For the simulation results reported, n represents the total number of observations generated and d represents the number deleted from the beginning of each run. We let k represent the number of replications or subruns (as appropriate) and designate by m the number of *usable* observations in each run or subrun. We, therefore, have $n = k(d + m)$ for the method of replications, and $n = d + km$ for the method of subruns. For each method, results are reported for two independent experiments (different seeds) labeled 1 and 2 in Tables 6.1 and 6.2.

Confidence intervals are reported by recording I_2, the confidence interval half-width [i.e., the confidence interval is given by $\bar{X} \pm I_2$, as given in Equation (6.8)] and are reported at the 90 percent level (i.e., $i - \alpha = 0.9$)

The results are indicative of what can be expected from simulation. Observe the variability in the point estimates produced by the two experiments, and also that they converge, as expected, as n is increased.[10]

---

[10] We recommend the simulation of systems for which analytic solutions are known as a method of becoming familiar with simulation methodology and its limitations.

Table 6.1
Replication Method Data

		k	5		10		20		40	
n	d	Exp	1	2	1	2	1	2	1	2
1000	0	$\bar{x}$	2.634	3.423	2.857	3.597	2.744	2.975	2.646	2.606
		$S_{\bar{X}_i}^2$	0.237	0.595	0.437	2.786	0.161	3.276	1.994	2.066
		I_2	0.464ᵃ	0.736	0.383ᵃ	0.968	0.490ᵃ	0.700	0.375ᵃ	0.383ᵃ
	50	$\bar{x}$	2.672	3.659	2.962	3.939				
		$S_{\bar{X}_i}^2$	0.127	0.641	1.371	1.825				
		I_2	0.340ᵃ	0.764	0.679	0.783				
2000	0	$\bar{x}$	3.228	3.493	2.798	3.538	2.934	3.352	2.881	3.068
		$S_{\bar{X}_i}^2$	0.355	0.237	0.334	0.825	0.474	2.346	1.637	2.150
		I_2	0.568	0.465	0.334ᵃ	0.526	0.266ᵃ	0.592	0.341ᵃ	0.391
	50	$\bar{x}$	3.330	3.605	2.813	3.633	3.125	3.728		
		$S_{\bar{X}_i}^2$	0.317	0.284	0.194	0.445	1.482	2.160		
		I_2	0.537	0.509	0.255ᵃ	0.387	0.471	0.568		
	100	$\bar{x}$	3.408	3.555	2.738	3.480				
		$S_{\bar{X}_i}^2$	0.524	0.323	0.956	0.596				
		I_2	0.690	0.542	0.567ᵃ	0.448				
	200	$\bar{x}$	3.823	3.564						
		$S_{\bar{X}_i}^2$	1.141	0.406						
		I_2	1.019	0.608						
ᵇ	200	m	160	360	80	180	40	90		
		$\bar{x}$	3.674	3.442	3.690	3.284	2.782	3.686		
		$S_{\bar{X}_i}^2$	1.341	0.060	1.702	0.432	1.115	1.274		
		I_2	1.104	0.233	0.756	0.381	0.408ᵃ	0.436		

ᵃ Confidence interval does not contain the mean 3.415.
ᵇ For this block of the table, m rather than n is given.

The difference between the estimates of $\bar{X}$ in the two experiments is indicative of the *variability* that can be expected from runs based on different seeds. Note that in certain cases (indicated in Tables 6.1 and 6.2), the theoretic mean does *not* lie within the confidence interval calculated.

Regenerative Method

The regenerative method is relatively new. It was formally introduced in Crane [1974], and is the most flexible of the methods

Table 6.2
Batch Method Data

n	d		k = 5		10		20		40		x	
		Exp	1	2	1	2	1	2	1	2	1	2
1000	0	$S_{\bar{X}_i}^2$	1.026	0.319	1.575	0.517	2.421	1.150	3.785	1.791	3.597	2.943
		I_2	0.966	0.538	0.727	0.417[a]	0.602	0.414[a]	0.518	0.357[a]		
	200	$S_{\bar{X}_i}^2$	0.167	0.214	1.086	0.631	3.385	1.489	4.656	2.881	3.679	2.977
		I_2	0.390	0.441	0.604	0.460	0.711	0.472	0.575	0.452		
2000	0	$S_{\bar{X}_i}^2$	0.333	0.343	0.752	0.441	1.409	0.943	2.080	1.677	3.298	3.344
		I_2	0.550	0.559	0.503	0.385	0.459	0.375	0.384	0.345		
	200	$S_{\bar{X}_i}^2$	0.307	0.376	0.486	0.391	0.929	1.028	2.093	2.430	3.301	3.404
		I_2	0.529	0.585	0.404	0.362	0.373	0.392	0.385	0.415		
4000	0	$S_{\bar{X}_i}^2$	0.083		0.209		0.471		1.017		3.377	
		I_2	0.274		0.265		0.265		0.269			

[a] Confidence interval does not contain the mean 3.415.

presented. It is applicable to those stochastic simulations which are *regenerative,* that is, to simulations (*processes*) which statistically and literally start over at an increasing sequence of regeneration times $\{\beta_i : i \geqslant 1\}$.[11] That is, between any two consecutive regeneration times, say β_i and β_{i+1}, the output variables of the process are independent and identically distributed replicates of those produced between any other two consecutive regeneration times.

EXAMPLE 6.7   Typically, a regeneration time β_i is signaled by the entrance of the model (or component) to a specified state. For a queueing station model, for example, each entry to the *empty* and *idle* state serves to identify a regeneration time, because upon entering this state, the model's development proceeds in a manner independent of its past history. For queueing stations, the conditions under which the empty and idle state will infinitely reoccur are well known. A summary may be found in Crane [1974]. Further, for some models, we may be able to identify *several* states which identify regeneration times.

The regenerative method is flexible in that it affords a mechanism to estimate the expected value of arbitrary real-values functions $f(\cdot)$ of the output variable X, or vector of variables X. To facilitate the discussion that follows, we let $E\{f(X)\} \equiv r$, let $\alpha_i = \beta_{i+1} - \beta_i$, assume that $E(\alpha_i) < \infty$, and refer to the interval $[\beta_i, \beta_{i+1}]$ as the *i*th *cycle* (of the process). Let

$$Y_i = \int_{\beta_i}^{\beta_{i+1}} f[X(t)]\,dt \qquad i \geqslant 1. \qquad (6.15)^{12}$$

Then, it has been shown [Crane, 1975b] that

$$E\{f(X)\} = E[Y_1]/E[\alpha_1] \equiv r \qquad (6.16)$$

and the object of the regenerative method is the estimation of the middle term of Equation (6.16).

EXAMPLE 6.8   To give some indication of the generality of Equation (6.15) we present several possible functions.

(a) Suppose we are interested in the probability (for a queueing

---

[11] Our notation is consistent with that used in the majority of papers published on the regenerative method.

[12] Note the similarity between the construct of Equation (6.15) and the notion of a discrete time integral as given earlier.

system) of finding an idle server. Then (for the ith cycle) let

$$X = \begin{cases} 1 \text{ if the server is idle} \\ 0 \text{ otherwise} \end{cases}$$

and $f \equiv X$. Then Y_i is the *length* of time the server is idle (in the ith cycle), and α_i is the length of the cycle. The fraction of idle time is then given by Equation (6.16).

(b) Suppose we are interested in estimating (again for a queueing system) the mean number of customers in the queue. Let $X = i$ when there are i customers in the queue, and let $f \equiv X$. If Y_i is given by Equation (6.15) and α_i given as in (a), then the expected number in queue is given by Equation (6.16). The Finite Source Queueing System Model Example uses a generalization of this idea.

(c) In (a) and (b), Y_i was given by the integral (6.15), and α_i was given by the integral

$$\alpha_i = \int_{\beta_i}^{\beta_{i+1}} dt$$

That is, both Y_i and α_i were given by the *continuous accumulation* of the appropriate function. In some cases, certain *discrete* analogs are appropriate. For these latter instances, Y_i is usually a *sum* of observations and α_i is a *count* related to the number of elements in the sum Y_i. Suppose, for example, that we are interested (for a queueing system) in the expected time a customer spends in queue. If we let Y_i be the sum of customer waiting times, and let α_i be a count of the number of customers served during the ith cycle, then the expected waiting time is given by Equation (6.16).

(d) If we let

$$f(x) = \begin{cases} 0 \ x < 5 \\ 1 \ x \geqslant 5 \end{cases}$$

with $X = W$, the waiting time of a customer, and α_i as in (c), a count of the number of customers served in the ith cycle, then Equation (6.16) produces

$$E\{f(W)\} = \Pr\{W > 5\}$$

if Y_i is given by the sum of the $f(x)$ values for the customers served in the cycle.

Additional examples and commentary may be found in Iglehart [1975c].

In summary then, the regenerative method employs the *values* $Y_1, \ldots, Y_n$ and $\alpha_1, \ldots, \alpha_n$ from n cycles to estimate the middle term of Equation (6.16). Additionally, as the pairs (Y_i, α_i) are *independent* and *identically distributed,* a confidence interval can also be given as is shown next. Specifically, let

$$\bar{Y} = \frac{1}{n} \sum_{i=1}^{n} Y_i \qquad (6.17)$$

and

$$\bar{\alpha} = \frac{1}{n} \sum_{i=1}^{n} \alpha_i. \qquad (6.18)$$

Also, let

$$\hat{\sigma}_{11}^2 = s_{11} = \frac{1}{n-1} \sum_{i=1}^{n} (Y_i - \bar{Y})^2, \qquad (6.19)$$

$$\hat{\sigma}_{22}^2 = s_{22} = \frac{1}{n-1} \sum_{i=1}^{n} (\alpha_i - \bar{\alpha})^2 \qquad (6.20)$$

and

$$\hat{\sigma}_{12}^2 = s_{12} = \frac{1}{n-1} \sum_{i=1}^{n} (Y_i - \bar{Y})(\alpha_i - \bar{\alpha}). \qquad (6.21)$$

The classical estimator for r (see Equation 6.16) is then given by

$$\hat{r}_c(n) = \frac{\bar{Y}}{\bar{\alpha}} \qquad (6.22)$$

A confidence interval for this quantity may be found as follows. Let $D_i = Y_i - r\alpha_i$. By our assumptions on the pairs (Y_i, α_i), the D_i are independent and identically distributed. Also $E(D_i) = 0$ and

$$\text{Var}\,(D_i) = \sigma^2 = \sigma_{11} - 2r\sigma_{12} + r^2\sigma_{22}. \qquad (6.23)$$

By the central limit theorem we have that

$$\frac{\dfrac{1}{n}\displaystyle\sum_{i=1}^{n} D_i}{\sigma\sqrt{n}} \tag{6.24}$$

(σ from Equation 6.23) approaches a standard normal variable as $n \to \infty$. Then, using the fact that $D_i = Y_i - r\alpha_i$, we can rewrite Equation (6.24) as

$$\frac{\dfrac{1}{n}\displaystyle\sum_{i=1}^{n} Y_i - r\dfrac{1}{n}\displaystyle\sum_{i=1}^{n}\alpha_i}{\sigma\sqrt{n}} = \frac{\sqrt{n}(\hat{r}_c - r)}{(\sigma/\bar{\alpha})}, \tag{6.25}$$

which by implication must also become standard normal as $n \to \infty$. If we estimate σ by

$$\hat{\sigma}_c = (s_{11} - 2\hat{r}_c s_{12} + \hat{r}_c s_{22})^{1/2}, \tag{6.26}$$

then we have *approximately* that

$$\Pr\left\{-Z_{1-\alpha/2} \leqslant \frac{\sqrt{n}(\hat{r}_c - r)}{(\hat{\sigma}/\bar{\alpha})} \leqslant Z_{1-\alpha/2}\right\} = 1 - \alpha \tag{6.27}$$

from which [in a manner analogous to Equation (6.8)] we find the confidence interval

$$I_c = \hat{r}_c \pm \frac{Z_{1-\alpha/2}\hat{\sigma}_c}{\sqrt{n}\bar{\alpha}} \tag{6.28}$$

We refer to the interval I_c as the *classical confidence interval*. Alternately, if Equation (6.26) in Equation (6.27) is replaced by[13]

$$\hat{\sigma}_f = (s_{11} - 2rs_{12} + r^2 s_{22})^{1/2}, \tag{6.29}$$

we are confronted by the inequality

$$\frac{\left|\dfrac{\bar{Y}}{\bar{\alpha}} - r\right|}{\hat{\sigma}_f} \leqslant Z_{1-\alpha/2}\bar{\alpha}/\sqrt{n} \tag{6.30}$$

---

[13] The subscript f is in deference to E. C. Fieller who originally proposed Equation (6.32).

which, when solved for r yields

$$r = \frac{\overline{Y\alpha} - ks_{12}}{(\overline{\alpha}^2 - ks_{22})} \pm \frac{\sqrt{(ks_{12} - \overline{Y\alpha})^2 - (\overline{\alpha}^2 - ks_{22})(\overline{Y}^2 - ks_{11})}}{(\overline{\alpha}^2 - ks_{22})} \qquad (6.31)$$

with $k = (Z_{1-\alpha/2})^2/n$. The quantity (6.31) has the form

$$I_f = \hat{r}_f \pm \frac{\sqrt{(ks_{12} - \overline{Y\alpha})^2 - (\overline{\alpha}^2 - ks_{22})(\overline{Y}^2 - ks_{11})}}{(\overline{\alpha}^2 - ks_{22})} \qquad (6.32)$$

with

$$\hat{r}_f = \frac{\overline{Y\alpha} - ks_{12}}{\overline{\alpha}^2 - ks_{22}} \qquad (6.33)$$

Thus, $\hat{r}_f$ can be used as a point estimator for Equation (6.16) with Equation (6.32) as its associated confidence interval. Our interest in Equation (6.32) stems from the fact that it is used in many of the papers which report on the regenerative method, Crane [1974] in particular. As dicussed in Iglehart [1975a], however, Equation (6.22) is generally preferable to Equation (6.33) in that Equation (6.22) produces *less* biased estimates then does Equation (6.33).

A still better estimate is produced by the jackknife estimator

$$\hat{r}_j = \frac{1}{n} \sum_{i=1}^{n} \theta_i \qquad (6.34)$$

where

$$\theta_i = n(\overline{Y}/\overline{\alpha}) - (n-1)\left(\sum_{j \neq i} Y_j \bigg/ \sum_{j \neq i} \alpha_j\right) \qquad (6.35)$$

It can be shown, Iglehart [1975c], that Equation (6.34) together with

$$\hat{s}_j = \left\{\sum_{i=1}^{n} [\theta_i - r_j]^2/(n-1)\right\}^{1/2} \qquad (6.36)$$

can be used to yield (approximately) the $100(1 - \alpha)$ percent confidence interval

$$I_j = \hat{r}_j \pm Z_{1-\alpha/2}\hat{s}_j/\sqrt{n} \qquad (6.37)$$

On the basis of experiments (see Iglehart [1975a]), Equations (6.34) and (6.37) are preferable, in terms of bias and converge properties, to Equations (6.22), (6.28), (6.33), and (6.32). Its form, however, is more difficult to program and requires *more* storage than the others because the observations must be saved. This extra storage requirement is especially important when we remember that the central limit theorem was used in the derivation of these confidence interval *estimates,* and their application requires, therefore, relatively large samples. The preferable second choice is given by the classical estimators of Equations (6.22) and (6.28). For large samples, the performance of all pairs is very comparable (see Iglehart [1975a] for examples and supporting *evidence*).

The regenerative method is attractive if a sequence of regeneration points can be identified, since we need no longer give special attention to observations collected during the transient phase. For systems (models) where such points cannot be identified, an approximation technique can be applied (see Crane [1975a]).

The regenerative method can also be used in conjunction with a *sequential sampling* plan so that the simulation can be terminated after a sufficient number of cycles has been obtained. Specifically, we can simulate until the confidence interval half-width I_2 is within 100δ percent of r. For this criterion, the number of cycles is given by that smallest n for which

$$\frac{Z_{1-\alpha/2}\,\sigma}{E(\alpha)\sqrt{n}} \leqslant \delta r$$

or for which

$$n \geqslant \left(\frac{Z_{1-\alpha/2}}{\delta}\right)^2 \left(\frac{\sigma}{rE(\alpha)}\right)^2 \qquad (6.38)$$

Because the quantities σ, r, $E(\alpha)$ are *unknown*, the sampling plan is to continue to observe cycles until Equation (6.38) is satisfied, that is, until a number m of cycles has been observed for which

$$\left(\frac{\hat{\sigma}(m)}{\hat{r}(m)\overline{\alpha}(m)}\right)^2 \left(\frac{Z_{1-\alpha/2}}{\delta}\right)^2 \leqslant m \qquad (6.39)$$

This scheme is particularly simple to implement when Equation (6.39) is used with Equations (6.22) and (6.28).

A general discussion of these and other matters is found in Iglehart [1975c]. A slightly different view is given in Lavenberg [1975a], and additional examples of simulations that employ the method have been reported in Lavenberg [1975b] and Halachmi [1976].

EXAMPLE 6.9 In Table 6.3 we present results using Equation (6.28) for the model presented in Example 6.4, with parameters as given in Example 6.5, using the empty and idle state to identify regenerative points. As with the other methods, certain of the confidence intervals calculated fail to contain the parameter being estimated. The Batch Arrival System Example also uses the regenerative method, but uses $\hat{r}_c$ together with $\hat{I}_f$.

While the regenerative technique is attractive, its use is limited to situations where regeneration points (or suitable approximate regeneration points) can be identified, and the length of a cycle $\beta_{i+1} - \beta_i$ is reasonable. For situations where these requirements are not realized, the method of subruns is an attractive *alternative* since only a single transient phase need be suffered.

Before leaving the subject, we note that the "state-time approach" employed in Fishman [1973] (section 10.16), is essentially the

Table 6.3
Regenerative Method Data

Experiment 1				Experiment 2			
No. of Cycles	No. of Observations	$\hat{r}$	I_2	No. of Cycles	No. of Observations	$\hat{r}$	I_2
5	72	4.883	1.588	5	10	0.985	0.488[a]
10	78	4.546	1.588	10	19	0.851	0.302[a]
20	128	3.582	1.469	20	39	1.120	0.521[a]
40	173	3.148	1.228	40	181	2.896	0.851
80	336	3.464	0.876	80	363	2.905	0.747
160	780	3.681	0.648	160	728	2.938	0.469[a]
164	784	3.669	0.647	191	793	2.817	0.450[a]
219	988	3.604	0.561	226	975	2.887	0.386[a]
320	1451	3.496	0.453	320	1431	3.126	0.351
361	1584	3.378	0.433	351	1598	3.208	0.365
402	1796	3.355	0.395	396	1800	3.264	0.353
450	1988	3.301	0.367	418	1987	3.333	0.341

[a] Confidence interval does not contain the mean 3.415.

regenerative method. There, however, the construction of a confidence interval is based on yet another approach. Specifically, in section 10.16 of Fishman [1973], *estimates* of $E(\overline{Y}/\overline{\alpha})$ and $\text{Var}(\overline{Y}/\overline{\alpha})$ are used to construct a confidence interval.

EXAMPLE 6.10   Consider random variables X and Y with $E(X) = \mu_1$, $E(Y) = \mu_2$ $\text{Var}(X) = \sigma_X{}^2$, $\text{Var}(Y) = \sigma_Y{}^2$. Write these variables in the form

$$X = \mu_1 + \epsilon_1$$

$$Y = \mu_2 + \epsilon_2$$

for *new* random variables ϵ_1, ϵ_2. Consider the quantity

$$\frac{1}{Y} = \frac{1}{\mu_2 + \epsilon_2}$$

and expand the right-hand side in a Taylor's series about the point μ_2 producing,

$$\frac{1}{Y} = \frac{1}{\mu_2} - \frac{1}{\mu_2{}^2}\,\epsilon_2 + \frac{1}{\mu_2{}^3}\,\epsilon_2{}^2 + R$$

with R representing higher order terms. Then

$$\frac{X}{Y} = \frac{(\mu_1 + \epsilon_1)}{\mu_2}\left[1 - \frac{\epsilon_2}{\mu_2} + \frac{\epsilon_2{}^2}{\mu_2{}^2} + R\right]$$

$$\doteq \frac{\mu_1}{\mu_2} - \frac{\mu_1 \epsilon_2}{\mu_2{}^2} + \frac{\mu_1}{\mu_2{}^3}\epsilon_2{}^2 + \frac{\epsilon_1}{\mu_2} - \frac{\epsilon_1 \epsilon_2}{\mu_2{}^2} + \frac{\epsilon_1{}^2 \epsilon_2}{\mu_2{}^3} + \cdots$$

From this expansion, we have

$$E\left(\frac{X}{Y}\right) \doteq \frac{\mu_1}{\mu_2} \tag{6.40}$$

using terms to first order in ϵ_i, $i = 1, 2$, as $E(\epsilon_i) = 0$ by necessity. A more accurate approximation is obtained by using terms through second order, and doing so yields the approximation

$$E(X/Y) \doteq \frac{\mu_1}{\mu_2} + \frac{\mu_1}{\mu_2{}^3}\,V(Y) - \frac{\text{cov}(X,\,Y)}{\mu_2{}^2} \tag{6.41}$$

$$= \frac{\mu_1}{\mu_2}\left[1 + \frac{V(Y)}{\mu_2{}^2} - \frac{\text{cov}(X,\,Y)}{\mu_1 \mu_2}\right]$$

as $V(\epsilon_1) = V(X)$ and $V(\epsilon_2) = V(Y)$, and so on, by necessity. Next, using Equation (6.40) and only first-order terms for X/Y, we approximate $V(X/Y)$ by

$$V(X/Y) \doteq E\left\{\left(\frac{\epsilon_1}{\mu_2} - \frac{\mu_1}{\mu_2^2}\epsilon_2\right)\right\}^2$$

which expands to

$$= E\left\{\frac{\epsilon_1^2}{\mu_2^2} - \frac{2\mu_1}{\mu_2^3}\epsilon_1\epsilon_2 + \frac{\mu_1^2}{\mu_2^4}\epsilon_2^2\right\}$$

$$= \frac{V(X)}{\mu_2^2} + \frac{\mu_1^2}{\mu_2^4}V(Y) - \frac{2\mu_1}{\mu_2^3}\operatorname{cov}(X, Y)$$

or

$$V\left(\frac{X}{Y}\right) \doteq \frac{\mu_1^2}{\mu_2^2}\left[\frac{V(X)}{\mu_1^2} + \frac{V(Y)}{\mu_2^2} - \frac{2}{\mu_1\mu_2}\operatorname{cov}(X,Y)\right] \quad (6.42)$$

as $\operatorname{cov}(X, Y) = \operatorname{cov}(\epsilon_1, \epsilon_2)$.

The estimator (6.41) is obviously biased, but it, together with Equation (6.42), can be used to establish an approximate confidence interval for $E(X/Y)$.

In Fishman [1973], section 10.16, Equations (6.41) and (6.42) are used with X given by Equation (6.17) and Y by Equation (6.18), that is, the associations

$$X \equiv \bar{Y} = \frac{1}{n}\sum_{i=1}^{n} Y_i$$

$$Y \equiv \bar{\alpha} = \frac{1}{n}\sum_{i=1}^{n} \alpha_i$$

are made, which when used in Equation (6.41), yields

$$E\left[\frac{\bar{Y}}{\bar{\alpha}}\right] \doteq \frac{E(Y)}{E(\alpha)}\left[1 + \frac{1}{n}\underbrace{\left\{\frac{\sigma_\alpha^2}{E^2(\alpha)} - \frac{\sigma_{\alpha,Y}^2}{E(Y)E(\alpha)}\right\}}_{\theta_1}\right]$$

and when used in Equation (6.42), results in

$$
V\left[\frac{\overline{Y}}{\overline{\alpha}}\right] \doteq \left[\frac{E(Y)}{E(\alpha)}\right]^2 \cdot \frac{1}{n}\underbrace{\left[\frac{\sigma_Y{}^2}{E^2(Y)} + \frac{\sigma_\alpha{}^2}{E^2(\alpha)} - \frac{2\sigma_{Y,\alpha}{}^2}{E(Y)E(\alpha)}\right]}_{\theta_2}
$$

Then, treating $\overline{Y}/\overline{\alpha}$ as a normal variable, we can write approximately that[14]

$$
\Pr\left[\left|\frac{\overline{Y}}{\overline{\alpha}} - \frac{E(Y)}{E(\alpha)}\left[1 + \frac{\hat{\theta}_1}{n}\right]\right| \leqslant Z_{1-\alpha/2}\frac{E(Y)}{E(\alpha)}\sqrt{\frac{\hat{\theta}_2}{n}}\right] = 1 - \alpha
$$

The expression on the left can be solved for $E(Y)/E(\alpha)$ to produce the approximate confidence interval

$$
\frac{\overline{Y}/\overline{\alpha}}{1 + \dfrac{\hat{\theta}_1}{n} + Z_{1-\alpha/2}\sqrt{\dfrac{\hat{\theta}_2}{n}}} \leqslant \frac{E(Y)}{E(\alpha)} \leqslant \frac{\overline{Y}/\overline{\alpha}}{1 + \dfrac{\hat{\theta}_1}{n} - Z_{1-\alpha/2}\sqrt{\dfrac{\hat{\theta}_2}{n}}}
$$

Notice that Equation (6.41) is a biased estimate and also that the accuracy of the approach is much influenced by the *rate* at which $\overline{Y}/\overline{\alpha}$ coverges to normality. The original source may be consulted for further information on this approach.

We reiterate that the material presented is but a sampling of the statistical material available, and that the material we have included was selected for its simplicity and wide applicability. For additional information, including material on *variance reduction* techniques, the reader is referred to Fishman [1973], Mihram [1972b] and Kleijnen [1974].

We now turn to the primary purpose of this chapter, namely, a series of sample model programs. Recall that our intent is to demonstrate use of the material presented so far, and especially to demonstrate use of the system developed in Chapter 5.

---

14 $\hat{\theta}_1$, $\hat{\theta}_2$ are estimates of θ_1, θ_2 obtained by using Equations (6.19), (6.20), and (6.21).

A BATCH ARRIVAL SINGLE SERVER QUEUE SYSTEM EXAMPLE[15]

System Description

Consider the system depicted in Figure 6.3, consisting of a single server queueing system, with a batch (bulk) arrival input mechanism. We assume that arrivals, that is, a batch of customers of size k, occur at unit time increments. The number of customers in a batch is assumed to be 0, 1, 2, 3 with probability 0.6, 0.2, 0.1, and 0.1, respectively. Arrivals join the queue and are served in a first-come-first-served order, with the service time per customer being one time unit. The initial ordering of the customers within a nonempty batch is arbitrary since the average wait time (in queue) per customer is the measure of interest.

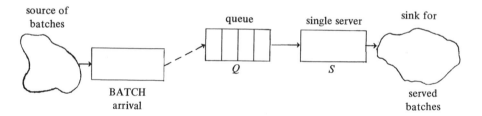

Figure 6.3   Batch arrival system

Model Realization

For this, our first example, we proceed more slowly by paying more attention to detail than we will subsequently. The essence of the model is given by the scenarios for the arrival mechanism and the server. The first executable statement (of the model program) is line 65. Lines 65–80 establish certain constants, read in the batch size probabilities (lines 69–72), and establish the input vector for the drawing procedure named discrete (see Chapter 5). Then objects are

---

[15] For analytic treatment of this example, see Franta [1974].

created for the queue (line 77), server (line 78), and arrival mechanism (line 79). A reference to the server object is passed to the arrival object as an argument and is done solely for demonstration since the global reference variable named S could have served directly.

After scheduling an activation for the arrival object, the main program becomes passive to await the termination of the simulation, at which time it again becomes active (as a result of line 58) to process and display the data collected during simulation (lines 84–130).

The arrival mechanism (lines 16–30) regulates the arrival of batches which are processed by the server (the server scenario is given by lines 33–61).

Batches of jobs are represented by objects of class delcaration batch (lines 8–13). A batch object is generated at each arrival epoch (line 19). As a result of that generation, a batch object *completely* e cecutes its action statements (lines 11–12) [as its prefix (line 8) is link rather than process, thus allowing batch objects to become members of sets, but depriving them of the piecemeal execution capability provided by prefix process], and becomes a (terminated) *data object.*

The arrival object scenario examines the size of the generated batch (line 20) and places the batch object into the queue (line 22) if its size is nonzero. Next, it alerts the server, if idle, to the availability of a batch (line 23). Finally, it delays a batch interarrival time (line 28) and repeats the process. Note that a batch has two attributes, namely, arrival time and size, and that these attributes are freely accessed by the arrival object through the "dot" notation.

The server scenario (lines 36–60) removes batches from the queue (lines 39–40), determines their size (line 43), and executes a delay (line 56) to represent service on behalf of each member of the batch. The sequence is repeated (line 60) as long as the queue contains batches. Should the queue become empty, the server becomes passive, that is, idle (line 36), and awaits notification by the arrival object (line 23) of the arrival of a batch. The simulation is performed for a fixed number of batches as controlled by lines 45 and 58. The server object collects the raw data (lines 46–53) for later display by the main program (lines 83–130). The individual observations, that is, the time each customer spends in queue, are given by the difference between the current time and the arrival time of the batch in which it was contained, plus an add on to account for its position in that batch (line 51). The observations are saved so that a variance for the mean wait can be calculated [see Equation (6.14)]. Additionally, while the sum for the calculation of the mean wait [see Equation (6.1)] is being formed (line 52), so are certain other summary counts (lines 44, 45, 50).

When the simulation is terminated, that is, when the requisite number of batches has been served, certain summary statistics are first calculated and reported (see lines 84–97). Next, the point estimate for the mean customer (job) time in queue is reported (lines 95, 101–106). The remaining lines (lines 107–130) calculate and display an estimate of the variance of the mean wait time estimator. For this example, the correlations between observations are handled directly by Equation (6.14). That is, the variance of the estimated mean wiat is given by

$$V\left(\begin{array}{c}\text{estimated}\\\text{mean wait}\end{array}\right) = \frac{1}{n}\left[R_0 + 2\sum_{j=1}^{n-1}\left(1 - \frac{j}{n}\right)R_j\right] \qquad (6.43)$$

with the R_j given by Equation (6.9). We estimate R_j by $\hat{R}_j$ with $\hat{R}_j$ given by

$$\hat{R}_j = \frac{1}{n-1-j}\sum_{i=1}^{n-j}(x_i - \bar{x})(x_{i+j} - \bar{x}) \qquad (6.44)$$

rather than Equation (6.10), where the x_i are the waiting times of individual customers and $\bar{x}$ is the mean of the x_i. Instead of estimating all $n - 1$ values of R_j for Equation (6.43), we choose to include only those for which $|\hat{\rho}_j| = |R_j/R_0| > 0.01$, on the assumption that accuracy is not sacrificed by omitting terms beyond that level.

The terms (6.44) are calculated directly (lines 112–114) and added to a running sum (line 117), which forms the terms of Equation (6.43). The estimator of Equation (6.43) is then calculated by line 125, which assumes its form as a result of the fact that $\hat{R}_0$ was also included in the running sum.

The only drawback of Equation (6.44) is that when used directly we are obliged to *save all* the observations x_i until the end of the simulation, since $\bar{x}$ must be calculated from Equation (6.1) before it can be used.[16] Alternately, we can expand Equation (6.44) to obtain

$$\hat{R}_j = \frac{1}{n-1-j}\left\{ \sum_{i=1}^{n-1} x_i x_{i+j} - \bar{x}\sum_{i=1}^{n-j} x_i - \bar{x}\sum_{i=j+1}^{n} x_i + (n-j)\bar{x}^2 \right\} \quad (6.45)$$

Then, if $j \ll n$, the middle terms are each approximately equal to $(n-j)\bar{x}$ so that Equation (6.45) becomes approximately

$$\hat{R}_j \approx \frac{1}{n-1-j}\left\{ \sum_{i=1}^{n-j} x_i x_{i+j} - (n-j)\bar{x}^2 \right\} \quad (6.46)$$

For the example $j \ll n$ the effect of using Equation (6.46) rather than Equation (6.44) is seen in the second reported output. This output was obtained via the model program with lines 113–114 changed to the form shown in Figure 6.4.

As can be seen, the sacrifice in substituting Equation (6.46) for (6.44) is minimal. The appeal of Equation (6.46) is that it does not require that *all* observations be saved, but rather allows the sums Σx_i and $\Sigma x_i x_{i+j}$ to be updated as observations x_i becomes available.

It is well known, however, (see Fishman [1973]) that formulas such as (6.46) can be computationally unstable. An attempt to avoid instability, while at the same time obviating the need to retain all observations until run termination, is given by the computational scheme reported in Hanson [1975].

```
111          ‡BEGIN‡
111          COVJ:=0;
112          ‡FOR‡ I:=1 ‡STEP‡ 1 ‡UNTIL‡ NJOB-J  ‡DO‡
113              COVJ := COVJ + X[I]*X[I+J];
114          COVJ := (COVJ-(NJOB-J)*AJOBWAIT∆2) / (NJOB-1-J);
115          ‡IF‡ J=0  ‡THEN‡ COV0:=COVJ;
117          VARJOBW := VARJOBW + (1-J/NJOB)*COVJ;
118          OUTINT(J,2);
119          OUTREAL(COVJ,5,15);
120          OUTFIX(COVJ/COV0,5,15);   OUTIMAGE;
122          ‡END‡;
125      VARJOBW := (2*VARJOBW-COV0)/NJOB;
126      OUTIMAGE;
127      OUTTEXT(#VARIANCE OF THE MEAN = #);
128      OUTFIX(VARJOBW,6,10);  OUTIMAGE;
130      ‡END‡ SIMULATION;
```

Figure 6.4   Altered statistics calculation scheme

---

[16] If a priori, we determine a value of k such that only the terms R_j, $j \le k$, are to be included in Equation (6.43), then Equation (6.46) requires only that we save the last k observations.

In summary then, in this example we have examined

1. The use of link as a class prefix
2. The computational consequences of correlated observations
3. The organization and purpose of the individual model statements.

Model Program

```
 0     SIMULATION ‡BEGIN‡         ‡COMMENT‡ BATCH ARRIVAL MODEL;
 1         ‡INTEGER‡ U,BATCHLIM,NBATCH,NJOB,J,I;
 2         ‡REAL‡ INTERARR,ABATCHW,AJOBWAIT,VARJOBW,COV0,COVJ;
 3         ‡ARRAY‡ SIZE DIST, SIZE HIST [0:3];
 4         ‡REAL‡ ‡ARRAY‡ X[0:6000];
 5         ‡REF‡ (HEAD) Q;
 6         ‡REF‡ (ARRIVE) A;  ‡REF‡ (SERVE) S;
 8
 8
 8     LINK ‡CLASS‡ BATCH;
 9     ‡BEGIN‡
 9         ‡INTEGER‡ SIZE;  ‡REAL‡ ARTIME;
11     ARTIME:=TIME;
12     SIZE:=DISCRETE(SIZEDIST,U);
13     ‡END‡ BATCH
14     ***********************************************************  ;
16
16     PROCESS ‡CLASS‡ ARRIVE(R);
17         ‡REF‡ (SERVE) R;
18     ‡BEGIN‡
18         ‡REF‡ (BATCH) B;
19     LOOP: B:-‡NEW‡ BATCH;
20     ‡IF‡ B.SIZE=0 ‡THEN‡ B:- ‡NONE‡  ‡ELSE‡
22         ‡BEGIN‡
22         B.INTO(Q);
23         ‡IF‡ R.IDLE ‡THEN‡ ‡ACTIVATE‡ R ‡AFTER‡ CURRENT;
25         ‡END‡;
28     HOLD(INTERARR);
29     ‡GOTO‡ LOOP;
30     ‡END‡ ARRIVE
31     ***********************************************************  ;
33
33     PROCESS ‡CLASS‡ SERVE;
34     ‡BEGIN‡
34         ‡REF‡(BATCH) B;  ‡INTEGER‡ BSIZE,JOB;
36     START:  ‡IF‡ Q.EMPTY ‡THEN‡ PASSIVATE;
38         ‡COMMENT‡ WILL BE AWAKEN BY ARRIVAL;
39     B:- Q.FIRST;     ‡COMMENT‡ PICK UP FIRST BATCH ;
41     B.OUT;           ‡COMMENT‡ TAKE IT OUT OF THE Q;
43     BSIZE:= B.SIZE;
44     SIZEHIST[BSIZE]:=SIZEHIST[BSIZE]+1;
45     NBATCH:=NBATCH+1;
46     ABATCHW:=ABATCHW+(TIME-B.ARTIME);
47         ‡COMMENT‡ ACCUMULATIVE BATCH WAIT-TIME IN THE Q;
48     ‡FOR‡ JOB:=1 ‡STEP‡ 1 ‡UNTIL‡ BSIZE ‡DO‡
49         ‡BEGIN‡    ‡COMMENT‡  X IS JOB WAIT IN THE Q;
50         NJOB:=NJOB+1;
51         X[NJOB]:=(TIME-B.ARTIME)+(JOB-1);
52         AJOBWAIT:=AJOBWAIT+X[NJOB];
53         ‡END‡;
56     HOLD(BSIZE);      ‡COMMENT‡ SERVICE TIME FOR THE ENTIRE BATCH;
58     ‡IF‡ NBATCH=BATCHLIM ‡THEN‡ ‡ACTIVATE‡ MAIN ;
60     ‡GOTO‡ START;
61     ‡END‡ SERVE
62     ***********************************************************  ;
```

```
64            ‡COMMENT‡ ************ MAIN PROGRAM ************ ,
65
65      BATCHLIM:=3000;
66      U:=555;
67      INTERARR:=1;         ‡COMMENT‡ TIME BETWEEN BATCH ARRIVALS;
69      SIZEDIST[0]:=INREAL;    ‡COMMENT‡ READ IN BATCH SIZE DISTRIBUTION;
71      ‡FOR‡ J:=1 ‡STEP‡ 1 ‡UNTIL‡ 3 ‡DO‡
72              SIZEDIST[J]:=INREAL+SIZEDIST[J-1];
73      OUTTEXT(#BATCH SIZE DISTRIBUTION (0,1,2,3): #);
74      ‡FOR‡ J:=0 ‡STEP‡ 1 ‡UNTIL‡ 3 ‡DO‡ OUTFIX(SIZEDIST[J],3,7);
76      OUTIMAGE;
77      Q:- ‡NEW‡ HEAD;
78      S:- ‡NEW‡ SERVE;
79      A:- ‡NEW‡ ARRIVE(S);
80      ‡ACTIVATE‡ A ‡AFTER‡ CURRENT;
81      PASSIVATE;
82              ‡COMMENT‡ RUN THE SIMULATION FOR A FIXED NUMBER OF BATCHES;
83
83              ‡COMMENT‡ REPORT STATISTICS;
84      OUTTEXT(#SIZE-HISTOGRAM FOR SERVICED BATCHES#);
85      ‡FOR‡ J:=0 ‡STEP‡ 1 ‡UNTIL‡ 3 ‡DO‡  OUTINT(SIZEHIST[J],7),
87      OUTIMAGE;
88      OUTTEXT(#NUMBER OF BATCHES SERVICED =#);
89      OUTINT(NBATCH,6); OUTIMAGE;
91      OUTTEXT(#NUMBER OF JOBS =#);
92      OUTINT(NJOB,6); OUTIMAGE;
94      ABATCHW:=ABATCHW/NBATCH;
95      AJOBWAIT:=AJOBWAIT/NJOB;
96      OUTTEXT(#E(BATCH WAIT)=#);
97      OUTFIX(ABATCHW,5,10);  OUTIMAGE;  OUTIMAGE;
100
100             ‡COMMENT‡ ESTIMATE VARIANCE OF THE MEAN OF JOB WAIT-TIME;
101     OUTTEXT(#JOB WAIT-TIME STATISTICS:#);  OUTIMAGE;
103     OUTTEXT(#     MEAN =#);  OUTFIX(AJOBWAIT,5,10);  OUTIMAGE;
106     OUTIMAGE;
107     OUTTEXT(# J    AUTOCOVARIANCE  AUTOCORRELATION#); OUTIMAGE,
109     OUTIMAGE;
110     ‡FOR‡ J:=0, J+1 ‡WHILE‡ ABS(COVJ/COV0) ‡GREATER‡ 0.01   ‡DO‡
111             ‡BEGIN‡
111             COVJ:=0;
112             ‡FOR‡ I:=1 ‡STEP‡ 1 ‡UNTIL‡ NJOB-J  ‡DO‡
113                 COVJ := COVJ + (X[I]-AJOBWAIT)*(X[I+J]-AJOBWAIT);
114             COVJ := COVJ/(NJOB-1-J);
115             ‡IF‡ J=0  ‡THEN‡ COV0:=COVJ;
117             VARJOBW := VARJOBW + (1-J/NJOB)*COVJ;
118             OUTINT(J,2);
119             OUTREAL(COVJ,5,15);
120             OUTFIX(COVJ/COV0,5,15);  OUTIMAGE;
122             ‡END‡;
125     VARJOBW := (2*VARJOBW-COV0)/NJOB;
126     OUTIMAGE;
127     OUTTEXT(#VARIANCE OF THE MEAN = #);
128     OUTFIX(VARJOBW,6,10);  OUTIMAGE;
130     ‡END‡ SIMULATION;
130             ‡EOP‡
130             FINIS
```

Program output using the exact method (6.44) for calculation of $\hat{R}_j$

```
BATCH SIZE DISTRIBUTION (0,1,2,3):   0.600  0.800  0.900  1.000
SIZE-HISTOGRAM FOR SERVICED BATCHES     0   1519    761    720
NUMBER OF BATCHES SERVICED =  3000
NUMBER OF JOBS =  5201
E(BATCH WAIT)=   1.32533
```

```
JOB WAIT-TIME STATISTICS:
    MEAN =   1.90098

 J    AUTOCOVARIANCE    AUTOCORRELATION

 0     4.8685‡+000         1.00000
 1     4.1966‡+000         0.86200
 2     3.7915‡+000         0.77879
 3     3.5881‡+000         0.73701
 4     3.3228‡+000         0.68252
 5     3.0829‡+000         0.63323
 6     2.8944‡+000         0.59452
 7     2.7026‡+000         0.55512
 8     2.5284‡+000         0.51935
 9     2.3571‡+000         0.48415
10     2.2115‡+000         0.45425
11     2.0740‡+000         0.42601
12     1.9484‡+000         0.40021
13     1.8388‡+000         0.37769
14     1.7306‡+000         0.35548
15     1.6159‡+000         0.33191
16     1.5121‡+ ¯00        0.31059
17     1.4074‡+000         0.28910
18     1.3242‡+000         0.27199
19     1.2384‡+000         0.25437
20     1.1449‡+000         0.23516
21     1.0579‡+000         0.21729
22     9.8607‡-001         0.20254
23     8.7945‡-001         0.18064
24     7.9790‡-001         0.16389
25     7.4903‡-001         0.15385
26     6.7673‡-001         0.13900
27     6.2082‡-001         0.12752
28     5.8343‡-001         0.11984
29     5.3136‡-001         0.10914
30     4.6489‡-001         0.09549
31     3.9301‡-001         0.08073
32     3.1648‡-001         0.06501
33     2.6335‡-001         0.05409
34     1.9261‡-001         0.03956
35     1.2817‡-001         0.02633
36     7.1243‡-002         0.01463
37     3.6605‡-002         0.00752

VARIANCE OF THE MEAN =     0.022140
```

Program output using the approximate form (6.46) for calculating R_j

```
BATCH SIZE DISTRIBUTION (0,1,2,3):    0.600  0.800  0.900  1.000
SIZE-HISTOGRAM FOR SERVICED BATCHES      0   1519    761    720
NUMBER OF BATCHES SERVICED =  3000
NUMBER OF JOBS =  5201
E(BATCH WAIT)=   1.32533

JOB WAIT-TIME STATISTICS:
    MEAN =   1.90098

 J    AUTOCOVARIANCE    AUTOCORRELATION

 0     4.8685‡+000         1.00000
 1     4.1969‡+000         0.86206
 2     3.7925‡+000         0.77899
 3     3.5890‡+000         0.73719
```

4	3.3240#+000	0.68276
5	3.0847#+000	0.63361
6	2.8958#+000	0.59480
7	2.7039#+000	0.55539
8	2.5300#+000	0.51968
9	2.3590#+000	0.48455
10	2.2141#+000	0.45478
11	2.0776#+000	0.42675
12	1.9530#+000	0.40116
13	1.8444#+000	0.37885
14	1.7377#+000	0.35693
15	1.6243#+000	0.33365
16	1.5216#+000	0.31254
17	1.4172#+000	0.29110
18	1.3342#+000	0.27406
19	1.2491#+000	0.25657
20	1.1566#+000	0.23757
21	1.0706#+000	0.21992
22	9.9952#-001	0.20530
23	8.9320#-001	0.18347
24	8.1158#-001	0.16670
25	7.6374#-001	0.15667
26	6.9211#-001	0.14216
27	6.3649#-001	0.13074
28	5.9903#-001	0.12304
29	5.4763#-001	0.11249
30	4.8035#-001	0.09867
31	4.0840#-001	0.08389
32	3.3217#-001	0.06823
33	2.7971#-001	0.05745
34	2.1000#-001	0.04314
35	1.4550#-001	0.02989
36	8.8129#-002	0.01810
37	5.3789#-002	0.01105
38	1.8273#-002	0.00375

VARIANCE OF THE MEAN =   0.022284

A COMPUTER SYSTEM RELIABILITY STUDY EXAMPLE[17]

System Description

A computer system is composed of ten units, five of which are tape units of the same manufacturing series; each tape unit has a random operating time T between successive maintenance requirements (failures). The distribution of each of these five random variables is presumed to be $f_1(t)$, as given in Table 6.4 The remaining five units in the computer system have random interfailure times T_i, with the density function $f_i(t)$, $i = 2, 3, 4, 5$, and 6, respectively.

Whenever any one of the ten units fails, repair is presumed to begin immediately requiring exactly 1 hour. System users require that at least two of the five tape units, and all of the five nontape units,

---

[17] This example was originally discussed in Mihram [1972b, p. 284].

Table 6.4
Computer system interfailure time distributions

i	Family	$E(T_i)$	Var (t_i)	$f_i(t)$
1	Exponential	2	$2^2 = 4$	$\frac{1}{2}e^{-t/2}$
2	Normal	9	2	$(2\pi)^{-1/2}e^{-(t-9)^2}/4$
3	Chi-squared	$(2)(5) = 10$	$2^2 \times 5 = 20$	$t^{5-1}e^{-t/2}/(2^5 \cdot 4!)$
4	Gamma	$6^{-1} \times 9 = 1.5$	$6^{-2} \times 9 = 0.25$	$6^9 t^{9-1}e^{-6t}/8!$
5	Normal	6	1	$(2\pi)^{-1/2}e^{-(t-6)^2}/2$
6	Gamma	10	10	$t^{10-1}e^{-t}/9!$

be operational in order to have an operational system. Otherwise, the system is considered "down" (or "to have failed") until the necessary repairs are completed. Therefore, once the system has (by definition) failed, each operating unit in the system is left running until the system itself is returned to the operational state, at which time each such unit continues to operate for the time remaining until its failure.

Model Realization

The essence of the model program is given by the procedure variate, the procedure system, and the simple component scenario.

The procedure variate provides values for the component interfailure times according to the distributional forms of Table 6.4. When a component (line 68) references the procedure, it passes its designated index as a parameter so that (line 9) the correct variate generator can be selected.

Note, as discussed in Chapter 5, that a variate generator for Chi-square variables is not directly provided but is easily obtained by recalling that a Chi-squared variable is the sum of squared normal variables. Further, although a Gamma (Erlangian) generator is available, it was not used for case four, but instead (for demonstration) the variates are obtained by summing exponential variates. Relationships such as those between random variables can be very useful. Also as suggested earlier, observe that a separate random number stream is associated with each variate generator.

The component scenario is easily ascertained from a reading of lines 64–74. We assume the simulation is conducted to collect information on the distribution of system "up" time, that is, the distribution of *system interfailure* times. For the output shown, the simulation was run for a 2-month period (actually 60 consecutive 24-hour days), during which time procedure system references maintained a system status and collected data to display a sample distribution of system interrepair times.

The sample distribution is displayed (line 101) by the procedure plot histo defined in Appendix E. The asymmetric shape of the plot is as expected, because there is evidence to suggest (see Mihram [1972b]) that the minimum of a sample of variates drawn from positive-valued random variables is distributed according to the Weibull distribution defined by

$$f_w(y) = by^{b-1} \exp\left[-(y/a)^b\right]/a^b \qquad y \geqslant 0, \qquad (6.47)$$

where a, b are positive-valued parameters. The shape of the histogram is suggestive of a Weibull distribution with shape parameter $b < 1$. To determine more reliably the verisimilitude between the sample histogram and Equation (6.47), one would employ techniques such as the Chi-square and Smirnov-Kolomogorov tests (see Fishman [1973]).

In summary then, we have presented this example to

1. Demonstrate a battery of variate generators
2. Demonstrate use of the procedure histogram and the procedure plot histogram.
3. Broach the possible distributional form of the minimum of a set of positive-valued random variables, because such forms are nearly as common to simulation results as is the normal.

Model Program

```
0      SIMULATION #BEGIN#        #COMMENT# COMPUTER SYSTEM MAINTENANCE#
1           #REAL# #ARRAY# A[1:17], B[1:16];
2           #INTEGER# #ARRAY# SEED[1:6];
3           #INTEGER# I,U,
4           #INTEGER# TAPE,OTHER;   #REAL# TC;
6           #BOOLEAN# SUP;
7
7
7      #REAL# #PROCEDURE#  VARIATE(I);
8           #INTEGER# I;
```

```
 9      ≠BEGIN≠
 9          ≠SWITCH≠   TAG := ONE,TWO,THREE,FOUR,FIVE,SIX;
10          ≠INTEGER≠ U,J;   ≠REAL≠ V;
12      ≠IF≠ 1 ≠LESS≠ 6 ≠THEN≠ I:=1 ≠ELSE≠ I:=I-4;
15      U:=SEED[I];
16          ≠GOTO≠ TAG[I];
17
17      ONE:  V:=NEGEXP(0.5,U);     ≠GOTO≠ R;
19
19      TWO:  V:=ABS(NORMAL(9.0,SQRT(2.0),U));   ≠GOTO≠ R;
21
21      THREE: V:=0; ≠FOR≠ J:=1 ≠STEP≠ 1 ≠UNTIL≠ 10 ≠DO≠
23          V:=V+NORMAL(0,1.0,U)∧2;   ≠GO TO≠ R;
25              ≠COMMENT≠ CHI-SQUAR WITH 10 DEGREES OF FREEDOM;
26
26      FOUR: V:=0; ≠FOR≠ J:=1 ≠STEP≠ 1 ≠UNTIL≠ 9 ≠DO≠
28          V := V+NEGEXP(6.0,U);       ≠GO TO≠ R;
30              ≠COMMENT≠ ERLANG WITH 9 DEGREES OF FREEDOM;
31
31      FIVE: V:=ABS(NORMAL(6.0,1.0,U));   ≠GOTO≠ R;
33
33      SIX:  V:=ERLANG(0.1,10,U);
34
34      R: VARIATE:=V;   SEED[I]:=U;
36      ≠END≠ VARIATE
37      ************************************************************ ;
39
39      ≠PROCEDURE≠ SYSTEM (U,UP);
40          ≠INTEGER≠ U;  ≠BOOLEAN≠ UP;
42      ≠COMMENT≠ INVOKED WHEN COMPONENT[U] CHANGES STATE;
43      ≠BEGIN≠
43          ≠BOOLEAN≠ DSTATE;  ≠INTEGER≠ ADD;
45      ADD:= ≠IF≠ UP ≠THEN≠ 1 ≠ELSE≠ -1;
48      ≠IF≠ U ≠GREATER≠ 5 ≠THEN≠ OTHER:=OTHER+ADD ≠ELSE≠ TAPE:=TAPE+ADD;
51      DSTATE:= ≠IF≠ TAPE ≠GREATER≠ 1 ≠AND≠ OTHER=5
51          ≠THEN≠ ≠TRUE≠ ≠ELSE≠ ≠FALSE≠;
54          ≠COMMENT≠ SUP=OLD STATE, DSTATE=NEW STATE OF THE SYSTEM;
55      ≠IF≠ DSTATE ≠AND≠ ≠NOT≠ SUP  ≠THEN≠ TC:=TIME
56      ≠ELSE≠
57      ≠IF≠ ≠NOT≠ DSTATE ≠AND≠ SUP  ≠THEN≠ HISTO(A,B,TIME-TC,1.0);
59          ≠COMMENT≠ IF GOING DOWN, RECORD HOW LONG THE UNIT WAS UP;
60      SUP:=DSTATE;
61      ≠END≠ SYSTEM
62      ************************************************************ ;
64
64
64      PROCESS ≠CLASS≠ COMPONENT(I);
65          ≠INTEGER≠ I;
66      ≠BEGIN≠
66      L:  SYSTEM(1,≠TRUE≠);          ≠COMMENT≠ REPORT GOING UP;
68      ≠REACTIVATE≠ ≠THIS≠ COMPONENT ≠AT≠ TIME+VARIATE(I);
69      SYSTEM(1,≠FALSE≠);             ≠COMMENT≠ REPORT GOING DOWN;
71      HOLD(1);                        ≠COMMENT≠ REPAIR TIME;
73      ≠GOTO≠ L;
74      ≠END≠ COMPONENT
75      ************************************************************ ;
77
77
77          ≠COMMENT≠ ************* MAIN PROGRAM: ************* ;
78
78      B[1]:=0.2;
79      ≠FOR≠ I:=2 ≠STEP≠ 1 ≠UNTIL≠ 16 ≠DO≠ B[I]:=B[I-1]+0.2;
81          ≠COMMENT≠ HISTOGRAM INTERVALS;
82      U:=501;
83      ≠FOR≠ I:=1 ≠STEP≠ 1 ≠UNTIL≠ 6 ≠DO≠ SEED[I]:=2*RANDINT(1,500,U)+1;
85          ≠COMMENT≠ INITIALIZE RANDOM STREAMS WITH RANDOM ODD VALUES;
86      ≠FOR≠ I:=1 ≠STEP≠ 1 ≠UNTIL≠ 10 ≠DO≠
```

```
R7              ≠ACTIVATE≠ ≠NEW≠ COMPONENT(1);
R8       HOLD(1440);
R9
R9       OUTTEXT(#HISTOGRAM FOR SYSTEM UP-TIME #);   OUTIMAGE;
91       OUTIMAGE;
92       ≠FOR≠ I:=1 ≠STEP≠ 1 ≠UNTIL≠ 17 ≠DO≠
93          ≠BEGIN≠
93          ≠IF≠ I ≠LESS≠ 17 ≠THEN≠ OUTFIX(H[1],3,5)  ≠ELSE≠ SETPOS(6);
96          OUTINT(A[1],10);
97          OUTIMAGE;
98          ≠END≠;
101      PLOT HISTO (A,B,17,30,75);
102      ≠END≠ SIMULATION;
102                ≠EOP≠
102                FINIS
```

HISTOGRAM FOR SYSTEM UP-TIME

```
0.200        141
0.400        116
0.600         81
0.800         80
1.000         71
1.200         64
1.400         45
1.600         43
1.800         29
2.000         15
2.200          8
2.400          4
2.600          3
2.800          0
3.000          0
3.200          0
              0
```

```
140. ******
135.      *
130.      *
125.      *
120.      *
115.      ****
110.      *   *
105.      *   *
100.      *   *
 95.      *   *
 90.      *   *
 85.      *   * ****
 80.      * **** *
 75.      * *  * *
 70.      * *  * ****
 65.      * *  * * ****
 60.      * *  * * * *
 55.      * *  * * * *
 50.      * *  * * * *
 45.      * *  * * * *******
 40.      * *  * * * * * *
 35.      * *  * * * * * *
 30.      * *  * * * * * ****
 25.      * *  * * * * * * *
 20.      * *  * * * * * * *
 15.      * *  * * * * * * ****
 10.      * *  * * * * * * * ****
  5.      * *  * * * * * * * * *******
     ---------------------------------------------------------
       0.200      0.800      1.400      2.000      2.600      3.200
          0.400      1.000      1.600      2.200      2.800
             0.600      1.200      1.800      2.400      3.000
```

LIMITS: HISTOGRAM:

	141.	116.	81.	86.	71.	64.
1.200#+000	45.	43.	29.	15.	8.	4.
2.400#+000	3.	0.	0.	0.	0.	

FILAMENT CAPPING EXAMPLE[18]

System Description

Imagine a bulb capping system as depicted in Figure 6.5.

Uncapped bulbs move on a conveyer belt which moves for $2T$ time units, and then is still for $6T$ time units. Opposite each stopping position is a picker-capper pair which puts bulbs on uncapped filaments.

Capping takes $3T$ time units after which the "capper" gets a new bulb from its "picker" partner if the picker has one available; otherwise it waits until its partner has one.

A picker takes 7–11 time units (the actual value being uniformly distributed in the range given) to retrieve a bulb, orient it, and move to the transfer position. The transfer of a bulb from picker to capper is instantaneous. The objective of the simulation is assumed to be obtaining information on how many filaments go uncapped with N picker-capper machines.

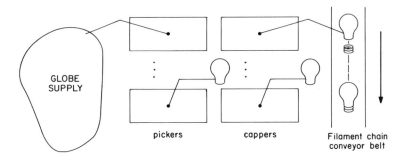

Figure 6.5   Capping system

---

[18] This example was originally examined by Dr. R. Dietvorst, Eindhoven, Holland, and is discussed in Birtwhistle [1972].

Discussion of Realization

We can realize the system by modeling a moving filament chain and a number of picker and capper pairs. We proceed, therefore, by developing scenarios for pickers, cappers, and the filament chain.

The pickers obey the following scenario:

```
arm   class picker;
        begin
nextbulb:
        delay(time to pick a globe from supply);
        ⟨set status to indicate to capper
        partner that a globe is available⟩;
        if partner is waiting for a globe then
            begin
            ⟨transfer globe to partner⟩;
            ⟨activate passive partner⟩;
            end
                            else
            begin
            ⟨become passive⟩;
            ⟨transfer globe to partner⟩;
            end;
        ⟨set status to indicate globe not available⟩;
            goto nextbulb;
        end picker scenario description;
```

In the model program, the status of a picker is given by the Boolean attribute full, declared in the class arm declaration which is used as a prefix to the class picker declaration. Since each capper must also have a status attribute, arm is also a prefix to the class capper declaration. The class arm objects also provide the attribute through which each member of a picker-capper pair can reference (synchronize with) its partner. The scenario for a picker's-capper partner is, then, as follows.

```
arm class capper;
        begin
nexttry:
        while conditions for capping not fulfilled do ⟨become passive⟩;
        ⟨cap filament logically⟩;
        delay(capping time);
```

> **if** partner is ready with a globe **then**
> ⟨notify partner that transfer can occur⟩;
> **goto** nexttry;
> **end** capper scenario description;

For capping, we must have

1. The belt stopped and sufficient time left to complete capping before the belt starts to move
2. The globeless filament occupying the position opposite the capper on the belt
3. A globe for the capper

as determined by line 61 of the capper scenario.

The filament chain is modeled as a Boolean array (line 8). Position zero of the array *always* contains an uncapped filament and is used as a source from which new filaments can be moved onto the chain (lines 22–23). Position $N + 1$, on the other hand, is the inspection position for filaments exiting the chain. The chain is moved, stopped, and maintained by the filament chain scenario given next.

> process   **class** filament chain;
>   **begin**
> Nextcycle:
>   ⟨turn on "ok to cap" signal⟩;
>   **for** each capper **do**
>   **if** uncapped filament at stopping
>   station adjacent capper **then**
>   ⟨notify capper⟩;
>   delay (stopping time-capping time);
>   ⟨turn off "ok to cap" signal⟩;
>   ⟨move the filament chain⟩;
>   delay (moving time + capping time);
>   **goto** nextcycle;
>   **end** filament chain scenario;

We include the output from two *pilot runs,* one with one picker-capper pair, the other with two, used *only* to investigate the *rectitude* of the model program and *precede* experiments to determine the steady-state behavior of the system. We have included this example to provide additional exposure to scenario development, while demonstrating (very simply) the use of a prefix class, and interobject reference.

For *actual* experiments, we suggest that line 41 be changed so that *each* picker uses a different random stream.

Model Program

```
 U    ≠BEGIN≠                        ≠COMMENT≠  FILAMENT CAPPING;
 1         ≠INTEGER≠ N;        ≠COMMENT≠ NUMBER OF MACHINES;
 3         ;REAL≠ MOVING TIME, STILL TIME, CAPPING TIME;
 4    MOVING TIME:=2.0;
 5    STILL TIME:=6.0;
 6    CAPPING TIME:=3.0;
 7
 7
 7    ≠FOR≠ N:=1,2  ≠DO≠
 8    SIMULATION ≠BEGIN≠
 8         ≠BOOLEAN≠ ≠ARRAY≠ FILAMENT WITHOUT BULB [0:N+1];
 9         ≠REF≠(PICKER) ≠ARRAY≠ P[1:N];
10         ≠REF≠(CAPPER) ≠ARRAY≠ C[1:N];
11         ≠INTEGER≠ NEW FILAMENTS, UNCAPPED, I;
12         ≠BOOLEAN≠ OK TO CAP;
13
13
13    PROCESS ≠CLASS≠ FILAMENT CHAIN;
14    ≠BEGIN≠
14         ≠INTEGER≠ I;
15    NEXT CYCLE:
15    OK TO CAP := ≠TRUE≠;
16    ≠FOR≠ I:=1 ≠STEP≠ 1 ≠UNTIL≠ N ≠DO≠
17         ≠IF≠ FILAMENT WITHOUT BULB[I] ≠THEN≠ ≠ACTIVATE≠ C[I];
19    HOLD(STILL TIME - CAPPING TIME);
20    OK TO CAP := ≠FALSE≠;
21    NEW FILAMENTS := NEW FILAMENTS +1;
22    ≠FOR≠ I:=N+1 ≠STEP≠ -1 ≠UNTIL≠ 1 ≠DO≠
23         FILAMENT WITHOUT BULB[I] := FILAMENT WITHOUT BULB[I-1];
24    ≠IF≠ FILAMENT WITHOUT BULB[N+1] ≠THEN≠ UNCAPPED:=UNCAPPED+1;
26    HOLD (MOVING TIME + CAPPING TIME);
27    ≠GO TO≠ NEXT CYCLE;
28    ≠END≠ FILAMEN CHAIN
29    ***************************************************** ;
31
31    PROCESS ≠CLASS≠ ARM(I);        ≠INTEGER≠ I;
33    ≠BEGIN≠
33         ≠COMMENT≠ PROVIDES ATTRIBUTES FOR PICKERS AND CAPPERS;
34         ≠BOOLEAN≠ FULL;
35         ≠REF≠(ARM) PARTNER;
36    ≠END≠ ARM
37    ***************************************************** ;
39
39    ARM ≠CLASS≠ PICKER;
40    ≠BEGIN≠
40         ≠INTEGER≠ U;
41         U:=501;     ≠COMMENT≠ SEED FOR RANDOM STREAM;
43    NEXT BULB:
43    FULL:= ≠FALSE≠;
44    HOLD (UNIFORM(7,11,U));           ≠COMMENT≠ PICKING TIME;
46    FULL:= ≠TRUE≠;
47    ≠IF≠ PARTNER.FULL ≠THEN≠ PASSIVATE ≠ELSE≠
49         ≠BEGIN≠
49         PARTNER.FULL := ≠TRUE≠;
50         ≠ACTIVATE≠ PARTNER ≠AT≠ TIME;
51         ≠END≠;
54    ≠GO TO≠ NEXT BULB;
55    ≠END≠ PICKER
56    ***************************************************** ;
```

```
58
58        ARM #CLASS# CAPPER#
59        #BEGIN#
59              #INTEGER# CAPPED,DUMMY#
60        FULL:= #TRUE##
61        NEXT TRY:
61        #FOR# DUMMY:=DUMMY
61        #WHILE# #NOT# (OK TO CAP #AND# FULL #AND#
61                                        FILAMENT WITHOUT BULB[I]) #DO#
62              PASSIVATE#
63        FILAMENT WITHOUT BULB[I] := #FALSE##
64        CAPPED:=CAPPED+1#
65        HOLD (CAPPING TIME)#
66        FULL := PARTNER.FULL#   #COMMENT# GET THE BULB FROM PICKER#
68        #IF# PARTNER.FULL #THEN# #ACTIVATE# PARTNER #AT# TIME#
70        #GOTO# NEXT TRY#
71        #END# CAPPER
72        ************************************************************** #
74
74        #COMMENT#    ********** MAIN PROGRAM ********** #
75
75        FILAMENT WITHOUT BULB[0] := #TRUE##
76        #FOR# I:=1 #STEP# 1 #UNTIL# N #DO#
77              #BEGIN#
77              C[I] :- #NEW# CAPPER(1)#
78              P[I] :- #NEW# PICKER(1)/
79              C[I].PARTNER :- P[I]#
80              P[I].PARTNER :- C[I]#
81              #ACTIVATE# C[I]#
82              #ACTIVATE# P[I]#
83              #END##
86        #ACTIVATE# #NEW# FILAMENT CHAIN#
87        HOLD(20000).
88              #COMMENT# SIMULATION TIME#
89
89
89        SPACING(2)#
90        #IF# LINE #GREATER# 50 #THEN# EJECT(6)  #ELSE# EJECT(LINE+6)#
93        OUTTEXT(#***** N =#)#   OUTINT(N,2)#   OUTIMAGE#
96        OUTTEXT(#CAPPER  CAPPED#)#   OUTIMAGE#
98        #FOR# I:=1 #STEP# 1 #UNTIL# N #DO#
99              #BEGIN#
99              OUTINT(I,6)#
100             OUTINT (C[I].CAPPED,8)#
101             OUTIMAGE#
102             #END##
105       OUTINT(UNCAPPED,6)#
106       OUTTEXT(#  FILAMENTS GOT THROUGH UNCAPPED#)#   OUTIMAGE#
108       OUTINT(NEWFILAMENTS,6)#
109       OUTTEXT(#  WAS THE TOTAL OF NEW FILAMENTS.#)#   OUTIMAGE#
111       #END# SIMULATION BLOCK#
114       #END# PROGRAM BLOCK#
114             #EOP#
114             FINIS
```

```
***** N = 1
CAPPER  CAPPED
    1     2223
  276  FILAMENTS GOT THROUGH UNCAPPED
 2500  WAS THE TOTAL OF NEW FILAMENTS.

***** N = 2
CAPPER  CAPPED
    1     2223
    2      276
    0  FILAMENTS GOT THROUGH UNCAPPED
 2500  WAS THE TOTAL OF NEW FILAMENTS.
```

A SINGLE SERVER QUEUE SYSTEM
WITH A PREEMPTIVE CUSTOMER EXAMPLE

System Description

The queueing system depicted in Figure 6.6 consists of a single server which services two classes of customers designated as ordinary and priority types. The interarrival times for ordinary customers are drawn from a 2-phase hyperexponential distribution, that is, from a distribution with

$$f_x(y) = \begin{cases} \lambda_{21} e^{-\lambda_{21} y} & \text{with prob } p \\ \lambda_{22} e^{-\lambda_{22} y} & \text{with prob } (1 - p) \end{cases} \tag{6.48}$$

or equivalently with

$$f_x(y) = p \lambda_{21} e^{-\lambda_{21} y} + (1 - p) \lambda_{22} e^{-\lambda_{22} y}. \tag{6.49}$$

From Equation (6.49) we easily find the mean interarrival time to be given by $p/\lambda_{21} + (1 - p)/\lambda_{22}$. Service times for ordinary customers are taken as the absolute value of standard normal drawings. The mean service time is, therefore, given by

$$\frac{2}{\sqrt{2\pi}} \int_0^\infty x e^{-x^2/2} \, dx = \frac{\sqrt{2}}{\sqrt{\pi}} \tag{6.50}$$

There is a *single* priority customer. Whenever this customer arrives (at the server), he is given immediate service (service times drawn from a 2-phase Gamma distribution) even if service of an ordinary customer must be preempted (a *preempt resume* discipline is assumed). Following service, the priority customer returns to a holding area where he remains before making a subsequent request for service. The priority customer remains in the holding area for a time drawn from a negative exponential distribution. The situation is summarized by Table 6.5.

For this system, owing to the presence of the priority customer, analysis (as discussed in Chapter 1) is reasonably difficult. Server utilization ρ, for example, is still related to the steady-state probability P_0 of an empty queue and idle servers by $P_0 = 1 - \rho$, but it is difficult to express ρ directly as was done in Equation (1.5). Equations such as (1.9) are even more difficult to obtain for the P_n.

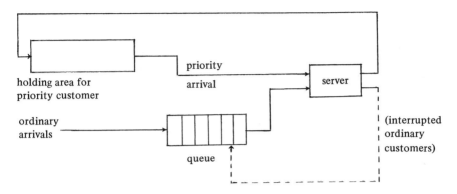

Figure 6.6 Preemptive priority system

It is therefore natural to simulate the system when knowledge of such measures is required. We assume here that ρ alone is required.[19]

As was made apparent in Chapter 1, analytic forms for P_n, and so on, are highly dependent on interarrival and service time distributional forms. Some relationships, for example Little's formula (1.6), are not. For the case at hand, an invariant can be found which is useful. Specifically, let us find an expression for $E[C]$, the steady-state average time which elapses when an ordinary customer begins and completes service (including delays due to preemption). Because

Table 6.5
Summary of Customer Characteristics

Customer Class	Family	Parameters
Priority		
Holding times	Exponential	$\lambda_1 = 1$
Service times	2-phase Erlangian	$E(S_1) = \text{mean} = 1/2$
Ordinary		
Interarrival times	2-phase hyper-exponential	$\lambda_2 = 1/(P/\lambda_{21} + (1 - P)/\lambda_{22})$
		Mean = $1/\lambda_2$
Service times	Absolute value of standard normal	$E(S_2) = \text{mean} = \sqrt{2/\pi}$
		See Equation (6.50)

---

[19] In point of fact, an analytic expression can be obtained for ρ, although we assume otherwise. In any case, unavailability of such an expression suggests that simulation be used.

the arrival mechanism that governs the priority customer is *exponential*, and because it is in effect only when the priority customer is *not* in service, any ordinary customer will experience on the average $\lambda_1 E[S_2]$ preemptions (i.e., the *net effect* is that of a Poisson source). Each preemption requires $E[S_1]$ time units on the average. Therefore, the average value of C is given by

$$E[C] = E[S_2] + E(S_1)\lambda_1 E(S_2). \qquad (6.51)$$

This expression can be used directly in Equation (1.6) to give

$$\rho' = \lambda_2 E[C],$$

the expected utilization of the server by ordinary customers and those priority customers arriving during the service of an ordinary customer. Therefore, $\rho' < \rho$, and we have a lower bound on ρ.

We will use Equation (6.51) as an aid in obtaining valid steady-state results. Specifically, we will use the model program to estimate $E[C]$ (see lines 48, 56, 57, 118). Additionally, an estimate $\hat{\rho}$ for ρ (lines 58, 122) will be calculated.

Assuming that *both* estimates converge at about the same rate (a not unreasonable assumption), we can compare $\hat{E}[C]$ with $E(C)$ to obtain information on the merits of $\hat{\rho}$ (realize also that $\rho' < \rho < 1$, so that $\hat{\rho}$ must also be in this range). Turning to the output, we find that $\hat{E}(C)$ differs from $E(C)$ by about 0.02. On the basis of our assumption, we expect $\hat{\rho}$ to be a reasonable estimate of ρ (the exact value is $\rho = 0.488$), and we are reasonably confident that the model has been operating in steady state for some time. Similar usage can be made of $E(C)$ and so on, should $\hat{P}_n$ be desired, although for this latter case, we doubt the compatibility of the convergence rates, and the regenerative methodology becomes more appropriate.

Model Realization

The operational essence of the model program is given by the priority source, ordinary arrival, and server scenarios. The priority source or customer cycles endlessly through service and holding times. When the priority customer arrives for service, it preempts the ordinary customer in service (*if any*) by returning it to the *front* of the queue (line 15) after having calculated its remaining service time (line 14). It then engages the server on behalf of itself by *rescheduling* the server's next activation time (line 21).

Ordinary customers simply arrive (are created as process objects), join the queue (line 35), and notify the server of their existence if it is idle (line 36). Each ordinary customer schedules the arrival of its successor (line 31) and has an attribute old (line 29) so that the server can recognize a previously preempted ordinary customer in the queue. Ordinary customer objects exist in the queue as terminated process objects.

The server repeatedly selects the first ordinary customer in the queue as long as one exists (lines 43–44) and delays for its service time. When a service delay (line 53) is completed, a test for preemption is made by checking to see if the identity of the customer on which it began service *matches* that of the customer at the front of the queue (*if any*). If they *do not* match, no preemption occurred during the service (see line 55) because the ordinary customer on which it had begun service remains out of queue.

In summary then, we have included this example to

1. Indicate that even simple systems are sometimes best analyzed by simulation
2. Indicate again that analytic results can be extremely important and beneficial to simulation
3. Illustrate another handling of preemption
4. Illustrate a case where terminated process objects are used.

Model Program

```
U       SIMULATION #BEGIN#       #COMMENT# SINGLE-SERVER WITH PREEMPTIONS;
1            #REF#(HEAD) ORDINARY Q;
2            #REF#(ORDINARY ARRIVAL) JOB IN SERVICE;  #REAL# START TIME;
4            #REF#(SERVER UNIT) SERVER;    #REAL# UTILIZATION;
6            #INTEGER# I,U1,U2,U3,U4,U5,U6;
7            #INTEGER# NORDINARY;  #REAL# EFFECTIVE SERVICE;
9            #ARRAY# LAMBDA, MEAN SERVICE TIME [1:2];
10           #REAL# P,LAMBDA21,LAMBDA22;
11
11
11      PROCESS #CLASS# PRIORITY SOURCE;
12           #BEGIN#
12               #REAL# PRIORITY SERVICE TIME;
13           LOOP:
13           #INSPECT# JOB IN SERVICE   #DO#
14               #BEGIN#
14               REMAINING SERVICE:= SERVER.EVTIME - TIME;
15               FOLLOW (ORDINARY Q);     #COMMENT# PUT JOB AT HEAD OF Q;
```

```
17          ‡END‡;
20    PRIORITY SERVICE TIME := ERLANG (1/MEAN SERVICE TIME[1],2,U1);
21    ‡REACTIVATE‡ SERVER ‡DELAY‡  PRIORITY SERVICE TIME;
22    UTILIZATION := UTILIZATION + PRIORITY SERVICE TIME;
23    ‡REACTIVATE‡ ‡THIS‡ PRIORITY SOURCE  ‡DELAY‡
23          PRIORITY SERVICE TIME + NEGEXP(LAMBDAL1],U2);
24    ‡GO TO‡ LOOP;
25    ‡END‡ PRIORITY SOURCE
26    *************************************************************** ;
28
28    PROCESS ‡CLASS‡ ORDINARY ARRIVAL;
29    ‡BEGIN‡
29          ‡BOOLEAN‡ OLD;
30          ‡REAL‡ SERVICE TIME, REMAINING SERVICE;
31    ‡ACTIVATE‡ ‡NEW‡ ORDINARY ARRIVAL ‡DELAY‡ (‡IF‡ DRAW(P,U3)
31              ‡THEN‡ NEGEXP(LAMBDA21,U4)
32              ‡ELSE‡ NEGEXP(LAMBDA22,U5)  );
34    SERVICE TIME := REMAINING SERVICE
34              := ABS(NORMAL(0,1,U6));
35    INTO (ORDINARYQ);
36    ‡IF‡ SERVER.IDLE ‡THEN‡ ‡ACTIVATE‡ SERVER ‡AT‡ TIME;
38    ‡END‡ ORDINARY ARRIVAL;
41          ‡COMMENT‡ REMAIN IN Q AS A -TERMINATED- PROCESS OBJECT.
41    *************************************************************** ;
42
42    PROCESS ‡CLASS‡ SERVER UNIT;
43    ‡BEGIN‡ LOOP:
43    JOB IN SERVICE :- ORDINARYQ.FIRST;
44    ‡INSPECT‡ JOB IN SERVICE    ‡WHEN‡ ORDINARY ARRIVAL  ‡DO‡
45          ‡BEGIN‡
45          OUT;        ‡COMMENT‡ REMOVE JOB FROM Q;
47          ‡IF‡ ‡NOT‡ OLD ‡THEN‡
48              ‡BEGIN‡  OLD:=‡TRUE‡;  START TIME:=TIME;  ‡END‡;
53          HOLD (REMAINING SERVICE);
54          ‡IF‡ JOB IN SERVICE =/= ORDINARYQ.FIRST  ‡THEN‡
55              ‡BEGIN‡       ‡COMMENT‡ COMPLETED SERVICE;
56              NORDINARY:=NORDINARY+1;
57              EFFECTIVE SERVICE:=EFFECTIVE SERVICE+(TIME-START TIME);
58              UTILIZATION:=UTILIZATION+SERVICE TIME;
59              ‡END‡;
62          ‡END‡
63    ‡OTHERWISE‡ PASSIVATE;
66    ‡GOTO‡ LOOP;
67    ‡END‡ SERVER UNIT
68    *************************************************************** ;
70
70    ‡COMMENT‡               MAIN PROGRAM:  ;
71
71          ‡COMMENT‡ RANDOM STREAM SEEDS: ;
72    U1:=13; U2:=69; U3:=747; U4:=125; U5:=55; U6:=609;
78
78          ‡COMMENT‡ PRIORITY CUSTOMER PARAMETERS:  ;
79    LAMBDA[1]:=1;
80    MEAN SERVICE TIME[1]:=0.5;
81
81          ‡COMMENT‡ ORDINARY-CUSTOMER PARAMETERS:  ;
82    P:=0.9;  LAMBDA21:=0.2;  LAMBDA22:=0.15;
85    LAMBDA[2] := 1/ (P/LAMBDA21+(1-P)/LAMBDA22);
86          ‡COMMENT‡ ARRIVAL RATE FOR 2-PHASE HYPER-EXPONENTIAL DIST;
87    MEAN SERVICE TIME[2] :=  SQRT(2/3.1415926535);
88          ‡COMMENT‡ MEAN OF ABS(NORMAL(0,SIGMA)) = SIGMA*SQRT(2/PI);
89
89    ORDINARYQ :- ‡NEW‡ HEAD;
90    SERVER :- ‡NEW‡ SERVER UNIT;
91    ‡ACTIVATE‡ ‡NEW‡ ORDINARY ARRIVAL;
92    ‡ACTIVATE‡ ‡NEW‡ PRIORITY SOURCE;
93    HOLD(5000);
```

```
94              #COMMENT# TOTAL SIMULATION TIME;
95
95
95      SPACING(2);
96      OUTTEXT(#INPUT PARAMETERS:#);   OUTIMAGE;
98      #FOR# I:=1,2 #DO#
99          #BEGIN#
99          OUTINT(I,4);
100         OUTTEXT(#IF# I=1 #THEN# #   PRIORITY ARRIVAL:#
101                       #ELSE# #   ORDINARY ARRIVAL:# );
103         OUTTEXT(#   LAMBDA =#);   OUTFIX(LAMBDA[I],3,7);
105         OUTTEXT(#   MEAN SERVICE TIME =#);
106         OUTFIX(MEAN SERVICE TIME[I],3,7);   OUTIMAGE;
108         #END#;
111     EJECT(LINE+5);
112     OUTTEXT(#MEAN SERVICE-COMPLETION-TIME FOR ORDINARY ARRIVALS:#);
113     OUTIMAGE;
114     OUTTEXT(#   THEORETICAL:#);
115     OUTFIX(MEAN SERVICE TIME[2]*(1+LAMBDA[1]*MEAN SERVICE TIME[1]),
115               5,10);   OUTIMAGE;
117     OUTTEXT(#   SIMULATION: #);
118     OUTFIX(EFFECTIVE SERVICE/NORDINARY,5,10);   OUTIMAGE;
120     EJECT(LINE+2);
121     OUTTEXT(#SERVER UTILIZATION = #);
122     OUTFIX(UTILIZATION/TIME,5,8);   OUTIMAGE;
124     #END# SIMULATION;
124             #EOP#
124             FINIS
```

```
INPUT PARAMETERS:

    1    PRIORITY ARRIVAL:    LAMBDA =  1.000   MEAN SERVICE TIME =  0.500

    2    ORDINARY ARRIVAL:    LAMBDA =  0.194   MEAN SERVICE TIME =  0.798


MEAN SERVICE-COMPLETION-TIME FOR ORDINARY ARRIVALS:

    THEORETICAL:    1.19683

    SIMULATION:     1.17536


SERVER UTILIZATION =  0.49055
```

A FINITE SOURCE QUEUEING MODEL EXAMPLE[20]

System Description

The system depicted in Figure 6.7 is occupied by a finite number of units (customers). Each unit has a unique residence at which it

---

[20] An anlysis of this example may be found in Cooper [1972].

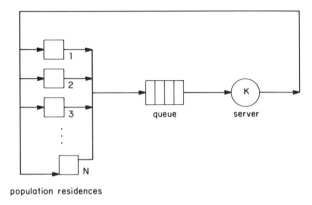

population residences

Figure 6.7   Finite source system

resides for a time (holding period), after which it joins the queue for service. Following a service completion, a unit returns to its residence to repeat the cycle. All holding times are drawn from an exponential distribution with parameter λ; all service times are drawn from an exponential distribution with parameter μ. The service station contains k ($k < N$) homogeneous servers which may operate in parallel, taking units from the queue on a first-come-first-served basis. Finally, we assume the steady-state distribution of the number of units in the system (in queue or in service) to be the measure of interest.

Model Realization

The model is designed to operate with an arbitrary number k of servers (as set by line 20). For this reason, it is convenient to collect idle servers in a set named idleserver. By doing so, the scenarios for sources (units) and servers are easily written in a form which is independent of their actual number. With this observation, the scenario for servers takes the following general form.

```
            process class server;
            ⟨declarations⟩;
Loop:   if the queue is empty then ⟨join the set of idle servers and
                                     become passive⟩
                        else
              begin
              ⟨take a unit from the queue⟩;
```

> delay (servicetime of unit);
> ⟨reactivate the unit for which
> service was just performed⟩;
> **end**;
> > **goto** loop;
> > **end** server scenario;

To interface with the above, the source scenario assumes the form given below.

> > process **class** source;
> Loop: delay(holding time);
> > **inspect** set of idle servers **when** not empty **do**
> > > **begin**
> > > ⟨remove a server from the set and schedule
> > > it for activation at current time⟩;
> > > **end**;
> > ⟨join the queue and become passive⟩;
> > **comment**: Will be reactivated by a server when service has been
> > completed; ⟨update statistics as explained below⟩;
> > **goto** Loop;
> > **end** source scenario;

The simulation program is designed to calculate and output estimates $\hat{P}_i$ of P_i, the steady-state probabilities of finding i $i = 0$, ..., n units in queue or in service. Data collection is guided by the regenerative methodology discussed earlier, so that a confidence interval can be reported for *each* point estimate $\hat{P}_i$, $i = 0, 1, \ldots, n$. Specifically, data for the estimations, estimations given by Equations (6.22, 6.31), are *updated* by lines 48–57 and the point estimates and confidence intervals calculated by lines 100–114. For the runs reported, the state with queue empty and servers idle was used as the regeneration point (see line 46), and the results are reported for ·20 units (line 8) and 500 iid blocks (line 11).

In summary then, we have presented this example.

1. To demonstrate a model program design strategy (the queue of idle servers) which makes the model program applicable to an arbitrary number of servers
2. To demonstrate the regenerative method.

Model Program

```
0    ‡bEGIN‡                ‡COMMENT‡  FINITE-SOURCE MODEL‡
1          ‡INTEGER‡ K,     ‡COMMENT‡ NUMBER OF SERVERS‡
```

```
3          #INTEGER# N;        #COMMENT# NUMBER OF SOURCES;
5          #REAL# LAMBDA,MU;
6          #INTEGER# BLOCK LIM;      #COMMENT# THE NUMBER OF IID BLOCKS;
8     N:=20;
9     LAMBDA:=1 ;
10    MU:=20;
11    BLOCK LIM := 500;
12    OUTTEXT(#N =#);   OUTINT(N,2);
14    OUTTEXT(#   LAMBDA =#);  OUTFIX(LAMBDA,2,6);
16    OUTTEXT(#   MU =#);   OUTFIX(MU,2,6);  OUTIMAGE;
19    OUTIMAGE;
20
20    #FOR# K := 1,2,8 #DO#
21    SIMULATION #BEGIN#
21         #ARRAY# P, AP, VAR P, COV TP, LOWER P, UPPER P  [0:N],
22         #REAL# START BLOCK, T, VAR T, KA, D;
23         #REAL# ONE, LASTIME;
24         #INTEGER# IN SYSTEM, TOTAL JOBS, I, NBLOCK, U1, U2;
25         #REF#(HEAD) JOB QUEUE, IDLE SERVER;
26         #COMMENT#
26    *****************************************************************
27
27    PROCESS #CLASS# SOURCE;
28    #BEGIN# #REAL# ARRIVETIME;
29    L: #REACTIVATE# #THIS# SOURCE #AT# TIME+NEGEXP(LAMBDA,U2);
30         #COMMENT# DELAY BEFORE GOING BACK FOR MORE SERVICE;
31    ARRIVETIME:=TIME;
32    ACCUM (P[INSYSTEM],LASTIME,ONE,0);
33    INSYSTEM:=INSYSTEM+1;
34    #INSPECT# IDLESERVER.FIRST #WHEN# SERVER #DO#   #BEGIN#
35         #ACTIVATE# #THIS# SERVER #AFTER# CURRENT;
36         OUT;  #COMMENT# REMOVE SERVER FROM Q;     #END#;
41    WAIT(JOBQUEUE); #COMMENT# REACTIVATE  AFTER SERVICE COMPLETION;
43    ACCUM (P[INSYSTEM],LASTIME,ONE,0);
44    INSYSTEM:=INSYSTEM-1;   #COMMENT# THE JOB IS DEPARTING THE SYSTEM;
46    #IF# INSYSTEM=0 #THEN#
47         #BEGIN#       #COMMENT# END OF A BUSY CYCLE (IID BLOCK).
47                       UPDATE STAT FOR P[T] CONFIDENCE INTERVAL;
48         NBLOCK:=NBLOCK+1;
49         T:=TIME-START BLOCK;    #COMMENT# LENGTH OF BUSY CYCLE;
51         VART:=VART+T∆2;
52         #FOR# I:=0 #STEP# 1 #UNTIL# N #DO#
53              #BEGIN#
53              AP[I]:=AP[I]+P[I];
54              VARP[I]:=VARP[I]+P[I]∆2;
55              COVTP[I]:=COVTP[I]+T*P[I];
56              P[I]:=0;
57              #END#;
60         #IF# NBLOCK = BLOCK LIM  #THEN#  #ACTIVATE# MAIN;
62         START BLOCK:=TIME;
63         #END#;
66    #GOTO# L;
67    #END# SOURCE
68    **************************************************************** ;
70
70    PROCESS #CLASS# SERVER ;
71    #BEGIN# #REF#(SOURCE)JOB .
72    L: #IF# JOBQUEUE.EMPTY #THEN# WAIT(IDLESERVER)
73         #ELSE# #BEGIN#
74              JOB :- JOBQUEUE.FIRST;
75              JOB.OUT;
76              TOTALJOBS:=TOTALJOBS+1;
77              HOLD(NEGEXP(MU,U1));  #COMMENT# SERVICE TIME;
79              #ACTIVATE# JOB #AFTER# CURRENT;
80         #END# ;
83    #GOTO# L;
84    #END# SERVER
```

```
85     ************************************************************** ;
87
87           ‡COMMENT‡   MAIN PROGRAM; ;
88
88     U1 := 501 ;
89     U2 := 1 ;
90     ONE := 1.0 ;
91     JOBQUEUE :- ‡NEW‡ HEAD;
92     IDLESERVER :- ‡NEW‡ HEAD ;
93     ‡FOR‡ I:= 1 ‡STEP‡ 1 ‡UNTIL‡ K ‡DO‡ ‡ACTIVATE‡ ‡NEW‡ SERVER;
95     ‡FOR‡ I:=1 ‡STEP‡ 1 ‡UNTIL‡ N ‡DO‡ ‡ACTIVATE‡ ‡NEW‡ SOURCE ;
97     PASSIVATE;             ‡COMMENT‡ RUN THE SIMULATION FOR A FIXED NUMBER
98                           OF IID BLOCKS (BUSY CYCLES);
99
99
99           ‡COMMENT‡ ESTIMATE EACH P[I] AND THE CONFIDENCE INTERVAL;
100
100
100    T:=TIME/NBLOCK;   ‡COMMENT‡ MEAN BUSY CYCLE;
102    VART := (VART-NBLOCK*T∆2)/(NBLOCK-1);
103    KA := 1.96 ∆2 / NBLOCK;
104           ‡COMMENT‡ 1.96 IS THE 95 PERCENT POINT ON THE NORMAL CURVE;
105    ‡FOR‡ I := 0 ‡STEP‡ 1 ‡UNTIL‡ N ‡DO‡
106           ‡BEGIN‡
106           AP[I]:=AP[I]/NBLOCK;
107           P[I]:=AP[I]/T;    ‡COMMENT‡ ESTIMATED POPULATION PROB;
109           VARP[I] := (VARP[I]-NBLOCK*AP[I]∆2)/(NBLOCK-1);
110           COVTP[I] := (COVTP[I]-NBLOCK*T*AP[I])/(NBLOCK-1);
111           D := (AP[I]*T-KA*COVTP[I]) ∆2
111                -(T∆2-KA*VART)*(AP[I]∆2-KA*VARP[I]);
112           LOWERP[I]:=(AP[I]*T-KA*COVTP[I]-SQRT(D)) / (T∆2-KA*VART);
113           UPPERP[I]:=(AP[I]*T-KA*COVTP[I]+SQRT(D)) / (T∆2-KA*VART);
114           ‡END‡;
117
117
117    ‡COMMENT‡ OUTPUT THE STATISTICS;
118
118    OUTTEXT(#**** K =#); OUTINT(K,2);
120    OUTTEXT(#   TOTAL JOBS =#); OUTINT(TOTALJOBS,5);
122    OUTTEXT(#   NUMBER OF IID BLOCKS =#); OUTINT(BLOCKLIM,5);
124    OUTIMAGE; OUTIMAGE;
126    OUTTEXT (# I    P[I]       CONFIDENCE INTERVAL #);
127    OUTTEXT(#(AT 95 PERCENT LEVEL)#);
128    OUTIMAGE;
129    OUTIMAGE;
130
130    ‡FOR‡ I := 0 ‡STEP‡ 1 ‡UNTIL‡ N ‡DO‡
131           ‡BEGIN‡
131           OUTINT(I,2);
132           OUTFIX(P[I],5,10);
133           SETPOS(21);
134           OUTCHAR($[$);
135           OUTFIX(LOWERP[I],5,8);
136           OUTCHAR($,$);
137           OUTFIX(UPPERP[I],5,8);
138           OUTTEXT(# ] = #);
139           OUTFIX(UPPERP[I]-LOWERP[I],5,8);
140           OUTIMAGE;
141           ‡END‡;
144    EJECT (‡IF‡ LINE ‡GREATER‡ 40 ‡THEN‡ 1 ‡ELSE‡ LINE+3);
147    ‡END‡ SIMULATION;
150    ‡END‡ OF PROGRAM;
150           ‡EOP‡
150           FINIS


N =20    LAMBDA = 1.00    MU = 20.00
```

```
**** K = 1     TOTAL JOBS = 2495     NUMBER OF ITD BLOCKS = 500

  I      P[I]       CONFIDENCE INTERVAL (AT 95 PERCENT LEVEL)

  0    0.16180      [  0.13579,  0.19711 ]  =  0.06133
  1    0.16603      [  0.14370,  0.19611 ]  =  0.05241
  2    0.14912      [  0.13244,  0.16891 ]  =  0.03647
  3    0.12953      [  0.11537,  0.14305 ]  =  0.02768
  4    0.10910      [  0.09124,  0.12421 ]  =  0.03297
  5    0.04491      [  0.07556,  0.10998 ]  =  0.03442
  6    0.06968      [  0.05166,  0.08402 ]  =  0.03237
  7    0.04155      [  0.02799,  0.05240 ]  =  0.02442
  8    0.03003      [  0.01645,  0.04120 ]  =  0.02476
  9    0.02215      [  0.01225,  0.03056 ]  =  0.01832
 10    0.01092      [  0.00314,  0.01759 ]  =  0.01445
 11    0.00731      [  0.00201,  0.01199 ]  =  0.00998
 12    0.00253      [ -0.00041,  0.00525 ]  =  0.00565
 13    0.00239      [ -0.00118,  0.00584 ]  =  0.00701
 14    0.00193      [ -0.00190,  0.00570 ]  =  0.00760
 15    0.00101      [ -0.00100,  0.00299 ]  =  0.00399
 16    0.00000      [  0.00000,  0.00000 ]  =  0.00000
 17    0.00000      [  0.00000,  0.00000 ]  =  0.00000
 18    0.00000      [  0.00000,  0.00000 ]  =  0.00000
 19    0.00000      [  0.00000,  0.00000 ]  =  0.00000
 20    0.00000      [  0.00000,  0.00000 ]  =  0.00000


**** K = 2     TOTAL JOBS = 1398     NUMBER OF ITD BLOCKS = 500

  I      P[I]       CONFIDENCE INTERVAL (AT 95 PERCENT LEVEL)

  0    0.35750      [  0.32500,  0.39278 ]  =  0.06777
  1    0.35201      [  0.33114,  0.37377 ]  =  0.04263
  2    0.16169      [  0.14351,  0.17868 ]  =  0.03517
  3    0.07838      [  0.06414,  0.09153 ]  =  0.02739
  4    0.03316      [  0.02205,  0.04354 ]  =  0.02150
  5    0.01216      [  0.00679,  0.01720 ]  =  0.01041
  6    0.00445      [ -0.00159,  0.01019 ]  =  0.01178
  7    0.00064      [ -0.00026,  0.00151 ]  =  0.00177
  8    0.00001      [ -0.00001,  0.00004 ]  =  0.00005
  9    0.00000      [  0.00000,  0.00000 ]  =  0.00000
 10    0.00000      [  0.00000,  0.00000 ]  =  0.00000
 11    0.00000      [  0.00000,  0.00000 ]  =  0.00000
 12    0.00000      [  0.00000,  0.00000 ]  =  0.00000
 13    0.00000      [  0.00000,  0.00000 ]  =  0.00000
 14    0.00000      [  0.00000,  0.00000 ]  =  0.00000
 15    0.00000      [  0.00000,  0.00000 ]  =  0.00000
 16    0.00000      [  0.00000,  0.00000 ]  =  0.00000
 17    0.00000      [  0.00000,  0.00000 ]  =  0.00000
 18    0.00000      [  0.00000,  0.00000 ]  =  0.00000
 19    0.00000      [  0.00000,  0.00000 ]  =  0.00000
 20    0.00000      [  0.00000,  0.00000 ]  =  0.00000


**** K = 8     TOTAL JOBS = 1278     NUMBER OF ITD BLOCKS = 500

  I      P[I]       CONFIDENCE INTERVAL (AT 95 PERCENT LEVEL)

  0    0.38479      [  0.35539,  0.41766 ]  =  0.06427
  1    0.37678      [  0.35476,  0.39901 ]  =  0.04425
  2    0.16998      [  0.15061,  0.18841 ]  =  0.03780
```

```
 3    0.05398     [ 0.04375,  0.06370 ]  =   0.01995
 4    0.01215     [ 0.00016,  0.01798 ]  =   0.01182
 5    0.00229     [ 0.00013,  0.00439 ]  =   0.00425
 6    0.00002     [-0.00002,  0.00007 ]  =   0.00009
 7    0.00000     [ 0.00000,  0.00000 ]  =   0.00000
 8    0.00000     [ 0.00000,  0.00000 ]  =   0.00000
 9    0.00000     [ 0.00000,  0.00000 ]  =   0.00000
10    0.00000     [ 0.00000,  0.00000 ]  =   0.00000
11    0.00000     [ 0.00000,  0.00000 ]  =   0.00000
12    0.00000     [ 0.00000,  0.00000 ]  =   0.00000
13    0.00000     [ 0.00000,  0.00000 ]  =   0.00000
14    0.00000     [ 0.00000,  0.00000 ]  =   0.00000
15    0.00000     [ 0.00000,  0.00000 ]  =   0.00000
16    0.00000     [ 0.00000,  0.00000 ]  =   0.00000
17    0.00000     [ 0.00000,  0.00000 ]  =   0.00000
18    0.00000     [ 0.00000,  0.00000 ]  =   0.00000
19    0.00000     [ 0.00000,  0.00000 ]  =   0.00000
20    0.00000     [ 0.00000,  0.00000 ]  =   0.00000
```

A COMPUTER SYSTEM MEMORY CONFLICT STUDY EXAMPLE

This example is the result of part of a study conducted for the U.S. Navy during 1973. While some of the results are reported in Franta [1974], the majority are found in the more obscure document [Patton, 1973]. The machine involved is the AN/UYK-7 military computer as employed in the shipboard real time command and control environment.

Characterization of the Modeled System

The system to be studied consists of a set of processors organized into one or more processor groups. Processors within a group are homogeneous in nature, whereas processors in different groups are different in nature. A processor's nature is determined by the characteristics of its command set. All processors share and operate from a single memory composed of several partially or completely interleaved modules or banks. The degree of interleaving is controlled by line 349 and in this listing is set to reflect complete interleave. Each bank has eight access ports, and a processing element accesses words in a bank through its assigned port (a given processor being assigned the same port number on all banks). Since a port cannot be shared, the total number of processors in the system is limited to eight.

Assume that processor i can execute instructions at a rate of m_i million instructions per second (MIPS). Theoretically then, n

processors can execute at a rate of $T = \Sigma_{i=1}^{n} m_i$ MIPS. This theoretical level is, of course, not generally realized as a result of processor memory bank contention. The objective of the simulation study is to characterize the achievable total instruction execution rate T', ($T' < T$). For this example, two processor groups are included. The first group contains the normal system processors (CPU's); the second group includes the input-output (channel) controllers (IOC's).

The contention patterns (and hence T') are determined by the manner in which programs executing in the processing elements reference memory modules. These reference patterns are, in turn, determined by the manner in which programs use the associated processor command set. Frequency counts on instruction usage were established (statistically) by examination of a large set of command and control programs. From the frequency counts, instruction profiles were constructed for use in the model program. These profiles are given by the data entries discussed in the next section.

Characterization of the Model Program

The organization of the model program is shown in Figure 6.8. It is driven by data sets contained on an input file named DATA. The information provided on the file DATA is organized as a series of problem descriptions, (data sets) with each problem set requiring a simulation run. The model program is organized so that it reads data sets and performs simulations as long as data sets exist on the file DATA.

The format of a dataset is consistent with the SIMULA free format conventions. To avoid errors within a data set, individual entries are identified by unique keywords. Each keyword begins in Column 1 of a data card, is of arbitrary length, and is recognized by an activation of procedure keyword as declared in lines 35–54. In the description that follows, the notation ⟨Cstring⟩ will denote the keyword given by the character string Cstring.

A problem is identified (and program execution begun) by a data set entry with keyword ⟨problem⟩, followed by system parameters in the form:

⟨problem⟩ numbanks numpgs mcycle runtime runbias runcount

begin
⟨establish the input file named DATA⟩   (lines 10-12)
next simulation: **Inspect** DATA **do**
    begin
        ⟨declaration of procedures for reading input data⟩   (lines 14-55)
        ⟨read system configuration parameters for the next
                                  'PROBLEM'⟩   (lines 57-63)
      simulation **begin**
        class processor group ( );   (lines 68-173)
            ⟨declaration of procedures and group attributes⟩   (lines 71-126)
            ⟨determine characteristics of the processors
                        in this group⟩   (lines 128-149)
            ⟨create and initialize the processing elements⟩   (lines 152-170)
        end processor group;

        process **class** processing element ( );   (lines 179-295)
            ⟨declaration of procedures and attributes⟩   (lines 182-258)
            ⟨scenario for each processing element⟩   (lines 260-295)
        end processing element;

        class memory request;   (lines 298-301)
            ⟨declaration of attributes for a request record⟩
        end memory request record;

        process **class** memory bank;   (lines 304-330)
            procedure enter;. . .;   (lines 306-313)
            ⟨scenario for memory banks⟩   (lines 318-328)
            end memory bank;
        ⟨create processor groups and memory banks⟩   (lines 336-347)
        ⟨run simulation and report results⟩
        end of simulation block;   (line 427)
    ⟨loop to find new data set for next 'PROBLEM'   (line 430)
    end of inspect DATA block;   (line 432)
end of model program;

Figure 6.8   Structure of model program

where

    numbanks = the number of memory banks in the configuration
      numpgs = the number of distinct processor groups
       mcycle = the memory cycle time (μ-seconds)

runtime = the runtime in μ-seconds of the simulation (after removal of the initial bias) between consecutive displays of statistics

runbias = the duration of the initial portion of the simulation after which statistic counters are *reset to zero* to eliminate initial bias (this value was determined experimentally)

runcount = the number of periods of length runtime included in the simulation.

Thus, the ⟨problem⟩ data set entry provides the general framework for a simulation and is established by lines 57–63. Specific information on program behavior and processing element characteristics are given next. Accordingly, the model program next expects to find the following entries in the data set:

⟨group⟩ maxpe,   instructions

where

maxpe = the number of processing elements in the group

instructions = the number of statistically unique instruction types each such element has in its instruction set.

In response to these entries, lines 336–342 of the model program create the processing groups. As an indirect result of these lines, for *each* group created, lines 128–149 are executed, thus establishing the characteristics of each processor in the group. These latter activities require entries with format

⟨Gamma⟩	Gamma
⟨IPW⟩	inst per word
⟨Umaster⟩	U master
⟨RNITM⟩	mode
⟨JUMPTM⟩	mode
⟨operand 1Tm⟩	mode
⟨operand 2TM⟩	mode
⟨instprob⟩	inst prob [i], i:=1, instructions
⟨instcost⟩	inst cost [i], i:=1, instructions
⟨insttype⟩	is type [i], i:=1, instructions
⟨instlength⟩	instlength [i], i:=1, instructions

where

> Gamma = a constant, reflecting the probability of obtaining and operand via the reference mode given by operand mode 1
>
> ipw = is the number of instructions per instruction word. The interaction between this parameter and the instruction lengths (given below) determine the frequency with which instruction words are fetched from memory.
>
> Umaster = a random number seed for generating all drawings within (for) elements of the group

and

> mode = determines the method of selecting the bank to be referenced on *consecutive references,* that is, for the read-next-instruction sequence (RNITM), for the jump sequence (JUMPTM) and when operands are read (operand 1 TM and operand 2 TM)), and has as its allowable values, the integers 1–4 with
>
> > 1 = implying that a transition matrix is to be used to determine bank references (a numbanks x numbanks matrix must follow directly)
> >
> > 2 = indicating that the next reference is selected from bank j with j an integer chosen uniformly on (1, numbanks)
> >
> > 3 = indicating that all references are from a single bank
> >
> > 4 = implying that banks are referenced sequentially.

The entries given by

> inst prob [i] = the unnormalized frequencies of occurrence of instruction i with
>
> instcost[i] = the time (μ-sec) required per execution of instruction i, and

istype[i] = specifying the type of instruction i, with
- 1 =   designating a jump
- 2 =   designating a no operand instruction
- 3 =   designating an instruction which requires an operand.

Finally,

inst length[i] = gives the fraction of an instruction word occupied by instruction i.

Next, lines 152–166 generate and initialize the processing elements of the group. This initialization requires a number, maxpe, of data entries of the form

⟨pe⟩ preg, qreg, bus[1], bus[2]

where

preg = determines the memory bank from which the first instruction is drawn
qreg = determines the bank from which the first operand is fetched
bus[1]
bus[2] = specify the memory access port which the processing element is to use for instruction and operand fetches respectively.

Thus, model organization is quite flexible. The data sets for the sample runs included are displayed in Figures 6.10 and 6.11. As can be seen from the figures, our sample runs employ two processor groups, designated CPU's and IOC's (input-output controllers), respectively. For elements of these groups, port assignments are as given by the entries for IOC_1 and CPU_1 in Table 6.6 (the table gives assignments for up to 3-CPU's and 2-IOC's).

Once the objects have been created and the simulation begun, model program behavior is governed by the scenario descriptions for processing elements and memory banks, each of which functions in the expected manner.

Specifically, memory banks cycle through the access ports, numbered one through eight (the lowest number reflecting highest priority), looking for and servicing posted processing element

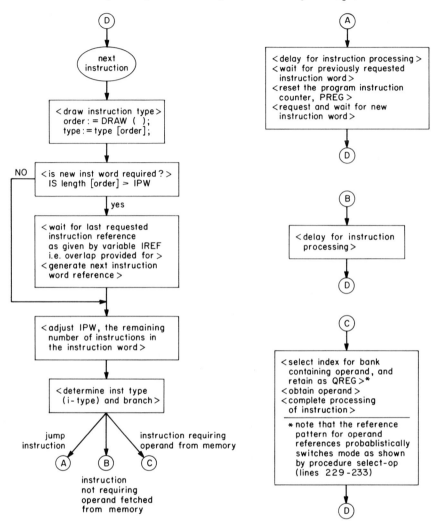

Figure 6.9   Processing element scenario

Table 6.6
Memory Port Assignments

Element	Instruction references	Operand references
IOC_1	1	1
IOC_2	2	2
CPU_1	4	3
CPU_2	6	5
CPU_3	8	7

```
PROBLEM  2 2 1.5 50.0 50.0  20
     ≠COMMENT≠ BANKS,GROUPS,CYCLE,RUNTIME,RUNBIAS,RUNCOUNT;
GROUP 1 22
     ≠COMMENT≠ MAXPE,INSTRUCTIONS;
GAMMA 0.8
IPW 2
UMASTER 16
RNITM 4
JUMPTM 2
OPERAND1TM 4
OPERAND2TM 2
INSTPROB
5257.0 2345.0  940.0 2188.0 1345.0 683.0 48.0 223.0 38.0
 148.0 1172.0  4.0   1839.0
 485.0 185.0 1672.0 12.0 142.0 88.0 29.0 88.0 22.0
INSTCOST
0   0.4 0.7 1.03 1.3 1.7 4.28 6.0 14.5 0.43 0.55 0.88 1.88
0.975 1.16 1.70 2.15 2.20 3.0 3.5 7.6 14.6
INSTTYPE
 3 3 3 3 3 3 3 3 3 1 1 1 1 2 2 2 2 2 2 2 2 2
INSTLENGTH
 2 2 2 2 2 2 2 2 2 2 2 2 2 2 1 1 1 1 1 1 1 1
PE 1 1 4 3
     ≠COMMENT≠ P,Q,BUS[1],BUS[2] ;


GROUP 1 9
GAMMA 0.9
IPW 10000
UMASTER 47
RNITM 2
JUMPTM 2
OPERAND1TM 4
OPERAND2TM 2
INSTPROB 10.0 20.0 30.0 20.0 9.0 5.0 3.0 2.0 1.0
INSTCOST 12.0 9.6 7.2 4.8 2.4 1.2 0.8 0.6 0.48
INSTTYPE 1 1 1 1 1 1 1 1 1 1
INSTLENGTH 0 0 0 0 0 0 0 0 0 0
PE 1 1 1 1
```

Figure 6.10   Data set for first simulation

requests. Processing elements post requests via the *procedure* obtain (lines 236–244), which remotely executes the procedure enter (lines 306–313) for the memory bank referenced. Posted requests are given by the auxilliary record objects created from the class memory requests declaration (lines 298–301). A processing element may wait for the reference to be satisfied, via procedure wait for (lines 247–255), or proceed in parallel with the request.

Because model behavior is not governed by the actual information requested but only by the delays incurred by those requests, simulation of the processor-momory (memory-processor) data exchange requires synchronization but no data transfer.

Processing elements endlessly fetch and execute instructions as shown by the life cycle scenario of Figure 6.9. As shown in this

```
PROBLEM  4 2 1.5 50.0 50.0   20
GROUP  1 22
GAMMA  0.8
IPW  2
UMASTER  16
RNITM  4
JUMPTM  2
OPERAND1TM  4
OPERAND2TM  2
INSTPROB
5257.0 2345.0 940.0 2188.0 1345.0 683.0 48.0 223.0 38.0
 148.0 1172.0 4.0  1839.0
 485.0 185.0 1672.0 12.0 142.0 88.0 29.0 88.0 22.0
INSTCOST
0   0.4 0.7 1.03 1.3 1.7 4.28 6.0 14.5 0.43 0.55 0.88 1.8ε
0.975 1.16 1.70 2.15 2.20 3.0 3.5 7.6 14.6
INSTTYPE
 3 3 3 3 3 3 3 3 3 1 1 1 1 2 2 2 2 2 2 2 2 2
INSTLENGTH
 2 2 2 2 2 2 2 2 2 2 2 2 2 1 1 1 1 1 1 1 1 1
PE  1 1 4 3


GROUP  1 9
GAMMA  0.9
IPW  10000
UMASTER  47
RNITM  2
JUMPTM  2
OPERAND1TM  4
OPERAND2TM  2
INSTPROB 10.0 20.0 30.0 20.0 9.0 5.0 3.0 2.0 1.0
INSTCOST 12.0 9.6 7.2 4.8 2.4 1.2 0.8 0.6 0.48
INSTTYPE 1 1 1 1 1 1 1 1 1 1
INSTLENGTH 0 0 0 0 0 0 0 0 0 0
PE  1 1 1 1
```

Figure 6.11   Data set for second simulation

figure, the model is organized so that the fetch of the next instruction word is overlapped with the execution of the instructions in the current instruction word. Furthermore, individual instructions can be one of three types as shown by the tags A, B, and C in Figure 6.9.

The model program (and so the model) was verified by setting its inputs to coincide with those associated with the assumptions of an available analytic model of a multiprocessor interleaved memory system (see Sastry [1975]). The output (MIPS) from the simulations so conducted compared favorably with those predicted by the analytic model, and so the model was considered verified; see Miharm [1972c] for a discussion of this verification technique. Model validation was made extremely difficult by the unavailability of data from an actual system. On the basis of certain preliminary data, we were able to ascertain only that the model was qualitatively correct.

Nevertheless, the model was used to investigate a battery of

Table 6.7
Simulation Results for 2-CPU, 2-IOC Configuration [a]

Degree of Inter- leave[b]	CPU1 (MIPS)	CPU2 (MIPS)	CPU3 (MIPS)	CPU Total CPU (MIPS)	Memory Refer- ences (MRPS)	IOC1 (MIPS)	IOC2 (MIPS)	Total IOC (MIPS)	IOC Memory Refer- ences (MRPS)	Total System (MIPS)
1	0.181	0.087	0.001	0.269	0.486	0.093	0.089	0.182	0.182	0.451
2	0.271	0.206	0.092	0.569	1.030	0.098	0.094	0.192	0.192	0.761
4	0.322	0.307	0.256	0.805	1.595	0.101	0.097	0.198	0.199	1.083
6	0.359	0.347	0.315	1.021	1.843	0.101	0.097	0.198	0.199	1.219
8	0.378	0.365	0.351	1.094	1.976	0.102	0.099	0.201	0.201	1.295
10	0.383	0.366	0.369	1.117	2.019	0.102	0.099	0.201	0.201	1.319
12	0.391	0.375	0.376	1.142	2.067	0.103	0.100	0.203	0.203	1.345
14	0.398	0.390	0.379	1.167	2.109	0.103	0.100	0.203	0.203	1.369
16	0.399	0.387	0.391	1.176	2.125	0.103	0.100	0.203	0.203	1.379

[a] Simulated time 1500 microseconds, $\lambda = 0.80$.
[b] Equal to number of memory modules in the model.

memory bank (numbanks, mcycle, groupsize, etc.) and processor configurations (maxpe, etc.). All simulation results reported here employed two processor groups: (i.e., numpgs=2) one group reflecting system processors (CPU's) and the other the input/output controllers (IOC's). The output included here was produced by the model program in response to the data sets of Figures 6.10 and 6.11. (In those outputs, G stands for group, T for time in microseconds, and the items reported are instructions and memory references per unit time.) Note in Figures 6.10 and 6.11 that the length of IOC instructions are set to zero so that fetches are not performed. The length of the transient period (runbias) as well as the required length of the simulation runs ($T = 1000$ and occasionally $T = 1500$), were determined experimentally from outputs such as those shown. Each run required about 20 seconds of Cyber-74 processor time at a total cost of about $3.00. From these runs, a series of tables (Tables 6.7–6.10) and graphs (such as Figures 6.12 and 6.13) were prepared to reflect the performance of various systems.

To conclude, we readily admit this example is lengthy, but we believe a report on one actual system study is necessary to clearly demonstrate the applicability of the scenario approach to model realization on a grand scale.

Table 6.8
Simulation Results for 3-CPU, 2-IOC Configuration [a]

Degree of Inter- leave[b]	CPU1 (MIPS)	CPU2 (MIPS)	CPU3 (MIPS)	Total CPU (MIPS)	CPU Memory Refer- ences (MRPS)	IOC1 (MIPS)	IOC2 (MIPS)	Total IOC (MIPS)	IOC Memory Refer- ences (MRPS)	Total System (MIPS)
1	0.163	0.106	0.001	0.270	0.485	0.093	0.089	0.182	0.182	0.452
2	0.248	0.201	0.108	0.557	1.005	0.098	0.094	0.192	0.192	0.749
4	0.313	0.301	0.279	0.893	1.611	0.100	0.097	0.197	0.197	1.090
6	0.342	0.332	0.324	0.998	1.800	0.101	0.098	0.199	0.200	1.197
8	0.369	0.351	0.349	1.008	1.928	0.102	0.099	0.201	0.201	1.269
10	0.383	0.365	0.371	1.119	2.025	0.103	0.099	0.202	0.202	1.321
12	0.393	0.375	0.375	1.143	2.068	0.103	0.099	0.202	0.202	1.345
14	0.389	0.375	0.387	1.151	2.083	0.103	0.100	0.203	0.203	1.354
16	0.393	0.383	0.397	1.173	2.121	0.103	0.100	0.203	0.203	1.377

[a] Simulated time 1500 microseconds, $\lambda = 0.80$.
[b] Equal to number of memory modules in the model.

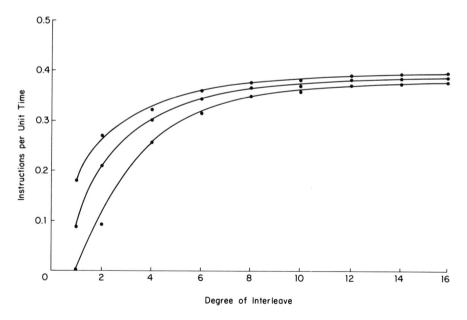

Figure 6.12   Individual Processor Performance for CPU's in a 3-CPU, 2-IOC Configuration

Table 6.9
Multiprocessor Performance Ratios for CPU's in a 2-CPU, 2-IOC Configuration[a]

Degree of Interleave	Physical Memory Modules								
	1	2	4	6	8	10	12	14	16
1	1.222	1.406	1.616	1.705	1.744	1.814	1.833	1.872	1.879
2		1.470	1.671	1.782	1.822	1.827	1.871	1.903	1.896
4			1.728		1.847		1.884		1.913
6				1.830			1.884		
8					1.856				1.924
10						1.882			
12							1.884		
14								1.918	
16									1.911

[a] Total processor performance to performance of a 1×1 AN/UYK-7 processor.

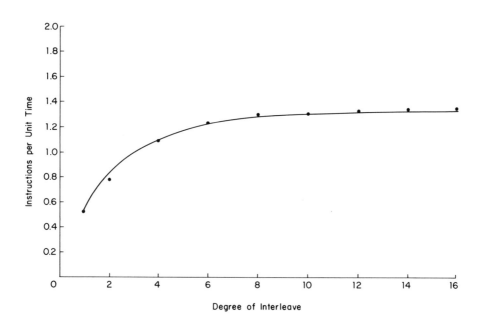

Figure 6.13   Total Processor Performance for CPU's in a 3-CPU, 2-IOC Configuration

Table 6.10

Multiprocessor Performance Ratios for CPU's in a 3-CPU, 2-IOC Configuration[a]

Degree of Interleave	Physical Memory Modules								
	1	2	4	6	8	10	12	14	16
1	1.222	1.466	1.880	2.136	2.290	2.354	2.431	2.506	2.523
2		1.565	1.935	2.186	2.291	2.400	2.418	2.537	2.548
4			2.122		2.387		2.516		2.557
6				2.352			2.516		
8					2.475				2.599
10						2.507			
12							2.542		
14								2.602	
16									2.611

[a] Total processor performance to performance of a 1×1 AN/UYK-7 processor.

Model Program

```
0     ≠BEGIN≠              ≠COMMENT≠  MULTI-PE MEMORY CONFLICT MODEL;
1     ≠INTEGER≠ NUMBANKS,NUMPGS;
2     ≠REAL≠ MCYCLE;
3     ≠INTEGER≠ GROUP SIZE;  ≠COMMENT≠ NO. OF BANKS INTERLEAVED,
5     ≠REAL≠ RUN TIME;
6     ≠INTEGER≠ RUN COUNT,RUNS;
7     ≠REAL≠ RUNBIAS;
8     ≠REF≠(INFILE) DATA;  ≠TEXT≠ BUFFER;
10
10    BUFFER:-BLANKS(80);  DATA:-≠NEW≠INFILE(#DATA#);
12     DATA.OPEN(BUFFER,≠NOTEXT≠);
13
13    NEXT SIMULATION:  ≠INSPECT≠ DATA ≠DO≠
14    ≠BEGIN≠
14
14    ≠COMMENT≠
14    ***********************************;
15    ≠PROCEDURE≠ IN REAL ARRAY (A,N);
16    ≠NAME≠ A;  ≠ARRAY≠ A;  ≠INTEGER≠ N;
19    ≠BEGIN≠
19    ≠INTEGER≠ I;
20    ≠FOR≠ I:=1 ≠STEP≠ 1 ≠UNTIL≠ N ≠DO≠
21      A[I]:=INREAL;
22    ≠END≠ IN REAL ARRAY
23    ***********************************;
25
25    ≠PROCEDURE≠ IN INT ARRAY (A,N);
26    ≠NAME≠ A;  ≠INTEGER≠≠ARRAY≠ A;  ≠INTEGER≠ N;
29    ≠BEGIN≠
29    ≠INTEGER≠ I;
30    ≠FOR≠ I:=1 ≠STEP≠ 1 ≠UNTIL≠ N ≠DO≠
31      A[I]:=ININT;
32    ≠END≠ IN INT ARRAY
33    ***********************************;
35
35    ≠PROCEDURE≠ KEYWORD(T);  ≠TEXT≠T;
```

```
37    ‡BEGIN‡   ‡TEXT‡ J;
38    LOOP:INIMAGE;   ‡IF‡ ENDFILE ‡THEN‡
40    ‡BEGIN‡
40    EJECT(‡IF‡ LINE ‡GREATER‡ 55 ‡THEN‡ 1 ‡ELSE‡ LINE+5);
43    OUTTEXT(#EOF ENCOUNTERED WHILE SCANNING FOR  #);
44    OUTTEXT(T);   OUTTEXT(#‡.#);   OUTIMAGE;   ‡GOTO‡ TERMINATE;
48    ‡END‡;
51    J:-TEXT(INTEXT(T.LENGTH));   ‡IF‡ J%=T ‡THEN‡ ‡GOTO‡ LOOP;
54    ‡END‡ OF KEYWORD
55    ******************************************;
57
57    KEYWORD(#PROBLEM#);
58    NUMBANKS:=ININT;
59    NUMPGS:=ININT;
60    MCYCLE:=INREAL;
61    RUNTIME:=INREAL;
62    RUNBIAS:=INREAL;
63    RUN COUNT:=ININT;
64
64    SIMULATION ‡BEGIN‡
64
64
64    ‡REF‡(MEMORY BANK) ‡ARRAY‡ MBANK[1:NUMBANKS] ;
65    ‡REF‡(PROCESSOR GROUP) ‡ARRAY‡ PEG[1:NUMPGS] ;
66    ‡INTEGER‡   I,G;
67
67    ‡COMMENT‡
67    ***************************************************************** ;
68
68
68    ‡CLASS‡ PROCESSOR GROUP(MAXPE,INSTRUCTIONS) ;
69    ‡INTEGER‡ MAXPE,INSTRUCTIONS ;
70    ‡BEGIN‡ ‡COMMENT‡
70        THIS OBJECT REPRESENTS THE OPERATING CHARACTERISTICS
70        OF A GROUP OF PROCESSING ELEMENTS.  THERE EXIST
70        -MAXPE- PROCESSING ELEMENTS, EACH WITH
70        -INSTRUCTIONS- DISTINCT COMMANDS.  THE REFERENCE ARRAYS
70        -RNIBANK-, -OPBANK-, AND -JMPBANK- DENOTE DISTRIBUTIONS
70        USED AS ROWS WITHIN
70        TRANSITION MATRICES DETERMINING THE BANKS FOR INSTRUCTION
70        AND OPERAND REFERENCES.  THE ARRAY -INSTCOST-
70        PROVIDES THE EXECUTION TIMES OF THE INSTRUCTIONS.
70        A COMMAND IS A JUMP WITH PROBABILITY -ALPHA-
70        AND REQUIRES AN OPERAND WITH PROBABILITY -BETA-.
70        THE NEXT INSTRUCTION WORD IS UTILIZED AFTER
70        THE CURRENT COMMAND WITH PROBABILITY -GAMMA-.
70        FINALLY, THE GENERATION OF THIS OBJECT RESULTS IN
70        THE DATA NECESSARY TO DEFINE THESE STRUCTURES
70        BEING READ FROM THE FILE -DATA-
70    ********************************;
71
71    ‡CLASS‡ VECTOR ;
72    ‡BEGIN‡
72    ‡ARRAY‡ X[1:NUMBANKS] ;
73    IN REAL ARRAY(X,NUMBANKS);
74    CONVERT(X,NUMBANKS);
75    ‡END‡ OF VECTOR
76    ****************************************;
78
78    ‡PROCEDURE‡ READ(P);   ‡NAME‡ P;   ‡REF‡(VECTOR) ‡ARRAY‡ P;
81    ‡BEGIN‡ ‡INTEGER‡ I;
82    ‡FOR‡ I:=1 ‡STEP‡ 1 ‡UNTIL‡ NUMBANKS ‡DO‡
83     P[I]:-‡NEW‡ VECTOR;
84    ‡END‡ OF READ
85    ****************************************;
87
87    ‡PROCEDURE‡ CONVERT(A,N);   ‡NAME‡ A;   ‡ARRAY‡ A;   ‡INTEGER‡ N;
```

```
91     #BEGIN#
91     #INTEGER# I;   #REAL# SUM,ACC;
93     SUM:=ACC:=0;
94     #FOR# I:=1 #STEP# 1 #UNTIL# N #DO#
95      SUM:=SUM+A[I];
96     #FOR# I:=1 #STEP# 1 #UNTIL# N #DO#
97     #BEGIN#
97      A[I]:=A[I]/SUM;   A[I]:=ACC:=ACC+A[I];
99     #END#;
102    A[N]:=1.0;
103    #END# OF CONVERT
104    ***********************************;
106
106    #PROCEDURE# SETUP(MODE,Z);   #NAME# MODE,Z;
108    #INTEGER# MODE;   #REF#(VECTOR) #ARRAY# Z;
110    #BEGIN# MODE:=ININT;   #IF# MODE=1 #THEN# READ(Z);
113    #END# OF SET UP
114    ***********************************;
116
116
116    #REF#(VECTOR)#ARRAY# RNIBANK,JMPBANK,OPBANK1,OPBANK2[1:NUMBANKS];
117    #INTEGER# #ARRAY# CLENGTH[1:INSTRUCTIONS];
118    #INTEGER# #ARRAY# ISTYPE[1:INSTRUCTIONS];
119
119    #INTEGER# TOTREFS;
120    #INTEGER# RMODE,JMODE,OMODE1,OMODE2;
121    #INTEGER# INST PER WORD;
122    #ARRAY# INSTPROB,INSTCOST[1:INSTRUCTIONS] ;
123    #REF#(PROCESSING ELEMENT) #ARRAY# PE[1:MAXPE] ;
124    #REAL# GAMMA;
125    #INTEGER# I,J;
126    #INTEGER# UMASTER;
127
127    #COMMENT# READ GROUP DESCRIPTIONS;
128
128    KEYWORD(#GAMMA#);   GAMMA := INREAL;
130    KEYWORD(#IPW#);   INST PER WORD := ININT;
132    KEYWORD(#UMASTER#);   UMASTER:=ININT;
134    KEYWORD(#RNITM#);   SETUP(RMODE,RNIBANK);
136    KEYWORD(#JUMPTM#);   SETUP(JMODE,JMPBANK);
138    KEYWORD(#OPERAND1TM#);   SETUP(OMODE1,OPBANK1);
140    KEYWORD(#OPERAND2TM#);   SETUP(OMODE2,OPBANK2);
142    KEYWORD(#INSTPROB#);   IN REAL ARRAY(INSTPROB,INSTRUCTIONS),
144    CONVERT(INSTPROB,INSTRUCTIONS);
145    KEYWORD(#INSTCOST#);   IN REAL ARRAY(INSTCOST,INSTRUCTIONS),
147    KEYWORD(#INSTTYPE#);   IN INT ARRAY(ISTYPE,INSTRUCTIONS);
149    KEYWORD(#INSTLENGTH#);   IN INT ARRAY(CLENGTH,INSTRUCTIONS),
151
151    #COMMENT#   SET UP THE PE#S FROM THIS GROUP.
151               THEY ARE ACTIVATED AT MCYCLE TO PREVENT THEIR
151               ACTION FROM STARTING UNTIL ALL IS READY ;
152
152    #FOR# I:= 1 #STEP# 1 #UNTIL# MAXPE #DO#
153    #BEGIN#
153    KEYWORD(#PE#);
154    PE[I] :- #NEW# PROCESSING ELEMENT(#THIS# PROCESSOR GROUP) ;
155    #INSPECT# PE[I] #DO#
156    #BEGIN#
156    #INTEGER# II;
157    II := RANDINT(1,100000000,UMASTER) ;
158    UGAMMA :=        II+3000 ;
159    URNI :=          II+4000 ;
160    UJMP :=          II+5000 ;
161    UOP :=           II+6000 ;
162    UCOMMAND:=       II+7000 ;
163    PREG:=ININT;   QREG:=ININT;
165    IN INT ARRAY(BUS,2);
```

```
166     #END# OF INSPECT PE BLOCK ;
169     #ACTIVATE# PE[I] #DELAY# MCYCLE ;
170     #END# OF LOOP ON PE;
173     #END# OF PROCESSOR GROUP
174     ***************************************************************** ;
176
176
176     #REAL# #PROCEDURE# CLOCK ;
177       CLOCK := .05*MCYCLE ;
178
178     #COMMENT#
178     ***************************************************************** ;
179
179
179     PROCESS #CLASS# PROCESSING ELEMENT(GROUP) ;
180     #REF#(PROCESSOR GROUP) GROUP ;
181     #BEGIN# #COMMENT#
181         THIS OBJECT REPRESENTS A PROCESSING ELEMENT (CPU)
181         IN THE MULTIPROCESSOR ENVIRONMENT.  ITS BEHAVIOR
181         IS DETERMINED BY DATA CONTAINED IN THE
181         PROCESSOR GROUP DENOTED BY -GROUP-  ;
182
182     #INTEGER# PREG ;
183     #INTEGER# QREG;
184     #INTEGER# REQCOUNT,TOTAL ;
185     #INTEGER# ITYPE;
186     #INTEGER# URNI,UJMP,UOP,UCOMMAND,UGAMMA;
187     #INTEGER##ARRAY# BUS[1:2];
188     #INTEGER# ORDER;
189     #INTEGER# IPW;
190     #REF#(MEMORY REQUEST) IREF,OREF;
191
191
191     #COMMENT#   THE BODY OF THIS PROCESS OPERATES
191               WHILE CONNECTED TO THE PROCESSOR GROUP;
192
192     #INSPECT# GROUP #DO#
193     #BEGIN#
193
193     #COMMENT#
193         THE SELECT MEMORY BANK PROCEDURES OPERATE RELATIVE TO A
193         MODE SWITCH.   THE FOLLOWING MODES ARE CURRENTLY DEFINED:
193               1 = TRANSITION MATRIX
193               2 = UNIFORMLY RANDOM
193               3 = NO CHANGE FROM PREG
193               4 = PHASED REFERENCES (CIRCULAR).
193
193     ******************************************;
194
194     #INTEGER# #PROCEDURE# SELECT(M,BANK,REG,U);
195     #NAME# U ;
196     #INTEGER# M,U ;
197     #INTEGER# REG;
198     #REF#(VECTOR) #ARRAY# BANK ;
199     #BEGIN#
199     #SWITCH# MODE:= TM, UN, NC, PB;
200     #GOTO# MODE[M] ;
201
201     TM:
201     SELECT:=DISCRETE(BANK[REG].X,U)+1;
202     #GOTO# EXIT ;
203
203     UN:
203     SELECT := RANDINT(1,NUMBANKS,U) ;
204     #GOTO# EXIT ;
205
205     NC:
```

```
205    SELECT := PREG ;    ≢GOTO≢ EXIT ;
207
207    PB:
207    SELECT := ≢IF≢ PREG=NUMBANKS ≢THEN≢ 1
208                        ≢ELSE≢ PREG+1 ;
210
210    EXIT:
210
210    ≢END≢ OF SELECT
211    ************************************;
213
213    ≢INTEGER≢ ≢PROCEDURE≢ SELECT RNI ;
214    ≢BEGIN≢
214     ≢COMMENT≢           ;
215     SELECTRNI:=≢IF≢(ENTIER(PREG/GROUPSIZE)*GROUPSIZE)%=PREG +THEN≢
216     PREG+1 ≢ELSE≢ PREG-GROUPSIZE+1
217    ≢END≢ OF SELECT RNI
218    ************************************;
220
220    ≢INTEGER≢ ≢PROCEDURE≢ SELECT JMP ;
221    ≢BEGIN≢
221     ≢COMMENT≢           ;
222      ≢INTEGER≢ X;
223     X:=RANDINT(1,NUMBANKS+GROUPSIZE,UJMP);
224     SELECTJMP:=≢IF≢X#NUMBANKS ≢THEN≢ X ≢ELSE≢ X-NUMBANKS
226    ≢END≢ OF SELECT JMP
227    ************************************;
229
229    ≢INTEGER≢ ≢PROCEDURE≢ SELECT OP ;
230    ≢BEGIN≢
230    SELECT OP:=≢IF≢DRAW(GAMMA,UGAMMA) ≢THEN≢
231            SELECT(OMODE1,OPBANK1,QREG,UOP)  ≢ELSE≢
232            SELECT(OMODE2,OPBANK2,QREG,UOP);
233    ≢END≢ OF SELECT OP
234    ************************************;
236
236    ≢PROCEDURE≢ OBTAIN(P,BANK,BUS);
237    ≢NAME≢ P;
238    ≢INTEGER≢ BUS;
239    ≢INTEGER≢ BANK;
240    ≢REF≢(MEMORY REQUEST) P;
241    ≢BEGIN≢
241    P:=≢NEW≢ MEMORY REQUEST(≢THIS≢ PROCESSING ELEMENT);
242    MBANK[BANK].ENTER(P,BUS);
243    TOTREFS:=TOTREFS+1;
244    ≢END≢ OF OBTAIN
245    ************************************;
247
247    ≢PROCEDURE≢ WAIT FOR (P);
248    ≢REF≢(MEMORY REQUEST) P;
249    ≢BEGIN≢
249    LOOP: ≢IF≢ %P.COMPLETED ≢THEN≢
250    ≢BEGIN≢
250    PASSIVATE;
251    ≢GOTO≢ LOOP;
252    ≢END≢;
255    ≢END≢ OF WAIT FOR
256    ************************************;
258
258    ≢SWITCH≢ DO:= JUMP,NOOPERAND,OPERAND;
259
259    ≢COMMENT≢  *** THE BODY OF -PROCESSING ELEMENT- CLASS: *** ;
260
260    IPW:=INST PER WORD;
261    OBTAIN(IREF,PREG,BUS[1]);
262    ≢COMMENT≢    BEGIN THE ACTION OF THE PE ;
263
```

```
263     NEXT INSTRUCTION :
263       TOTAL := TOTAL+1 ;
264     ORDER:=DISCRETE(INSTPROB,UCOMMAND)+1;
265     ITYPE:=ISTYPE[ORDER];
266     ≠IF≠ CLENGTH[ORDER] > IPW ≠THEN≠
267     ≠BEGIN≠
267     WAIT FOR (IREF);
268     IPW:=INST PER WORD;
269     PREG:=SELECT RNI;
270     OBTAIN(IREF,PREG,BUS[1]);
271     ≠END≠;
274     IPW:=IPW-CLENGTH[ORDER];
275
275     ≠GOTO≠ DO[ITYPE];
276
276     JUMP:
276     ≠IF≠ INSTCOST[ORDER]>0 ≠THEN≠ HOLD(INSTCOST[ORDER]);
278     WAIT FOR(IREF);
279     PREG:=SELECT JMP;
280     OBTAIN(IREF,PREG,BUS[1]);
281     WAIT FOR(IREF);
282     IPW:=0;
283     ≠GOTO≠ NEXT INSTRUCTION;
284
284     NO OPERAND:
284     HOLD(INSTCOST[ORDER]);
285     ≠GOTO≠ NEXT INSTRUCTION;
286
286     OPERAND:
286     QREG:=SELECT OP;
287     OBTAIN(OREF,QREG,BUS[2]);
288     WAIT FOR(OREF);
289     ≠IF≠ INSTCOST[ORDER]>0 ≠THEN≠  HOLD(INSTCOST[ORDER]);
291     ≠GOTO≠ NEXT INSTRUCTION;
292
292
292     ≠END≠ OF INSPECTION BLOCK ;
295
295     ≠END≠ OF PROCESSING ELEMENT
296     ****************************************************************** ;
298
298
298     ≠CLASS≠ MEMORY REQUEST(OWNER);
299     ≠REF≠(PROCESSING ELEMENT) OWNER ;
300     ≠BEGIN≠
300     ≠BOOLEAN≠ COMPLETED;
301     ≠END≠ OF MEMORY REQUEST
302     ****************************************************************** ;
304
304
304     PROCESS ≠CLASS≠ MEMORY BANK;
305     ≠BEGIN≠ ≠COMMENT≠
305        THIS OBJECT REPRESENTS A MEMORY MODULE.  THE ARRAY -PORT-
305        REPRESENTS THE POSSIBLE PATHS INTO THIS MODULE.  THE
305        PROCEDURE -ENTER- IS USED TO MAKE MEMEORY REQUESTS INTO THE
305        RESPECTIVE PORTS;
306
306     ≠PROCEDURE≠ ENTER(P,N);
307     ≠REF≠(MEMORY REQUEST) P;
308     ≠INTEGER≠ N;
309     ≠BEGIN≠
309     PORT[N]:-P;
310     SIZE:=SIZE+1;
311     ≠IF≠ IDLE ≠THEN≠ ≠ACTIVATE≠ ≠THIS≠ MEMORY BANK ≠DELAY≠ CLOCK;
313     ≠END≠ OF ENTER
314     ***********************************;
316
```

```
316        ≠REF≠(MEMORY REQUEST) ≠ARRAY≠ PORT[1:8];
317        ≠INTEGER≠ SIZE,I;
318
318        LOOP:
318        ≠IF≠ SIZE#0 ≠THEN≠ PASSIVATE;
320        ≠FOR≠ I:=1 ≠STEP≠ 1 ≠UNTIL≠ 8 ≠DO≠
321        ≠IF≠ PORT[I]=/=≠NONE≠ ≠THEN≠
322        ≠BEGIN≠
322        SIZE:=SIZE-1;
323        HOLD(MCYCLE);
324        PORT[I].COMPLETED:= ≠TRUE≠;
325        ≠IF≠ PORT[I].OWNER.IDLE ≠THEN≠
326        ≠ACTIVATE≠ PORT[I].OWNER ≠DELAY≠ CLOCK;
327        PORT[I]:- ≠NONE≠;
328        ≠GOTO≠ LOOP;
329        ≠END≠
330        ≠END≠ OF MEMORY BANK
332        *****************************************************≠**≠*** ;
334
334
334        ≠COMMENT≠  EXECUTION OF SIMULATION BLOCK STARTS HERE:  ;
335
335
335        ≠COMMENT≠ SET UP THE GROUPS OF PROCESSING ELEMENTS;
336
336        ≠FOR≠ I:=1 ≠STEP≠ 1 ≠UNTIL≠ NUMPGS ≠DO≠
337        ≠BEGIN≠ ≠INTEGER≠ J,K;
338        KEYWORD(#GROUP#);
339        J:=ININT; K:=ININT;
341        PEG[I]:-≠NEW≠ PROCESSOR GROUP(J,K);
342        ≠END≠;
345
345        ≠COMMENT≠  SET UP THE MEMORY BANKS ;
346
346        ≠FOR≠  I:= 1 ≠STEP≠ 1 ≠UNTIL≠ NUMBANKS ≠DO≠
347        MBANK[I]  :- ≠NEW≠ MEMORY BANK ;
348
348        ≠COMMENT≠
348           -GROUP SIZE- IS THE NUMBER OF BANKS INTERLEAVED TOGETnER.
348           -NUMBANKS- MUST BE A MULTIPLE OF -GROUP SIZE-.
348           THE ENTIRE SIMULATION MAY BE RUN FOR DIFFERENT GROUP ⊃IZES
348           VIA THE FOLLOWING LOOP:   ;
349
349        ≠FOR≠ GROUP SIZE := 1  ≠DO≠
350
350         ≠BEGIN≠
350         ≠REAL≠ GTIME;
350         ≠IF≠NUMBANKS<GROUPSIZE ≠THEN≠ ≠GOTO≠ ENDGROUP;
353         ≠IF≠%(ENTIER(NUMBANKS/GROUPSIZE)*GROUPSIZE=NUMBANKS)≠THEN≠
354         ≠GOTO≠ ENDGROUP;
355
355        ≠COMMENT≠ RUN FOR INITIAL BIAS ;
356
356        HOLD(RUNBIAS);
357         GTIME:=TIME;
358
358        ≠COMMENT≠ CLEAR THE COUNTERS FOR STATISTICS;
359
359        ≠FOR≠ I:=1 ≠STEP≠ 1 ≠UNTIL≠ NUMPGS ≠DO≠ ≠INSPECT≠ PEG[I] +DO≠
361        ≠BEGIN≠
361        TOTREFS:=0;
362        ≠FOR≠ J:=1 ≠STEP≠ 1 ≠UNTIL≠ MAXPE  ≠DO≠  PE[J].TOTAL := 0 ;
364        ≠END≠;
367
367
367        EJECT(1);
```

```
368      OUTTEXT (# G   GAMMA,  RMODE,  JMODE,  OMODE1,  OMODE2 #);   OUTIMAGE;
370      #FOR# G:=1 #STEP# 1 #UNTIL# NUMPGS #DO#   #INSPECT# PEG[G] #DO#
372        #BEGIN#
372        OUTINT(G,2);   OUTFIX(GAMMA,2,7);    OUTINT(RMODE,7);
375        OUTINT(JMODE,7);  OUTINT(OMODE1,8);  OUTINT(OMODE2,8);  OUTIMAGE;
379        #END#;
382      OUTIMAGE;
383      SYSOUT.SETPOS(11);
384      OUTTEXT (#G, TOTAL GROUP INST,  TOTREFS,  TOTAL INST#);
385      OUTIMAGE;  OUTIMAGE;
387
387
387      #FOR# RUNS:=1 #STEP# 1 #UNTIL# RUN COUNT #DO#
388      #BEGIN#
388        #REAL# TIMX;   #INTEGER# TOTAL INST;
390
390      #COMMENT#   RUN THE SIMULATION ;
391
391      HOLD(RUN TIME);
392
392
392      #COMMENT#   PRINT SUMMARY OF RESULTS;
393
393
393       TIMX:=TIME-GTIME;
394      OUTTEXT(#T=#);  OUTFIX(TIMX,0,6);
396      #FOR# G:=1 #STEP# 1 #UNTIL# NUMPGS #DO#   #INSPECT# PEG[G] #DO#
398      #BEGIN#     #INTEGER# SUM,J;
399      SYSOUT.SETPOS(11);   OUTINT(G,1);   OUTTEXT(#  (#);
402      #FOR# J:=1 #STEP# 1 #UNTIL# MAXPE #DO#
403      #INSPECT# PE[J] #DO#
404      #BEGIN#
404      SUM:=SUM+TOTAL;
405      OUTFIX(TOTAL/TIMX,3,6);
406      #END# OF INSPECT PE BLOCK;
409      OUTTEXT(# )=#);  OUTFIX(SUM/TIMX,3,7);
411      OUTFIX(TOTREFS/TIMX,3,7);
412      TOTALINST:=TOTALINST+SUM;
413      #IF# G #LESS# NUMPGS   #THEN# OUTIMAGE
414                             #ELSE# SYSOUT.SETPOS(SYSOUT.POS+5);
416      #END# OF LOOP ON PE GROUPS;
419      OUTFIX(TOTAL INST/TIMX,3,7);
420      OUTIMAGE;
421
424      #END# OF LOOP ON DIFFERENT GROUP SIZES ;
427
427      #END# OF SIMULATION BLOCK;
430
430      #GOTO# NEXT SIMULATION;
431
431          #COMMENT#  LOOP UNTIL EOF IS REACHED ON FILE -DATA-
432
432      #END# OF INSPECT DATA BLOCK;
435
435      TERMINATE: OUTTEXT(# PROGRAM TERMINATION#) ;   OUTIMAGE;
437      DATA.CLOSE(##);
438      #END# ;
438                #EOP#
438                FINIS
```

Simulation Output

```
G  GAMMA, RMODE, JMODE, OMODE1, OMODE2
1   0.80      4      2      4       2
2   0.90      2      2      4       2

        G, TOTAL GROUP INST,  TOTREFS,  TOTAL INST
```

```
T=    50.   1  ( 0.400 )=   0.400   0.700
           2  ( 0.080 )=   0.080   0.080            0.480
T=   100.   1  ( 0.340 )=   0.340   0.610
           2  ( 0.100 )=   0.100   0.100            0.440
T=   150.   1  ( 0.340 )=   0.340   0.640
           2  ( 0.100 )=   0.100   0.100            0.440
T=   200.   1  ( 0.355 )=   0.355   0.660
           2  ( 0.100 )=   0.100   0.105            0.455
T=   250.   1  ( 0.360 )=   0.360   0.672
           2  ( 0.104 )=   0.104   0.104            0.464
T=   300.   1  ( 0.373 )=   0.373   0.697
           2  ( 0.110 )=   0.110   0.110            0.483
T=   350.   1  ( 0.371 )=   0.371   0.691
           2  ( 0.111 )=   0.111   0.111            0.483
T=   400.   1  ( 0.367 )=   0.367   0.685
           2  ( 0.117 )=   0.117   0.117            0.483
T=   450.   1  ( 0.369 )=   0.369   0.689
           2  ( 0.118 )=   0.118   0.118            0.487
T=   500.   1  ( 0.370 )=   0.370   0.688
           2  ( 0.116 )=   0.116   0.116            0.486
T=   550.   1  ( 0.358 )=   0.358   0.673
           2  ( 0.116 )=   0.116   0.118            0.475
T=   600.   1  ( 0.358 )=   0.358   0.670
           2  ( 0.117 )=   0.117   0.117            0.475
T=   650.   1  ( 0.363 )=   0.363   0.675
           2  ( 0.115 )=   0.115   0.117            0.478
T=   700.   1  ( 0.360 )=   0.360   0.670
           2  ( 0.116 )=   0.116   0.117            0.476
T=   750.   1  ( 0.364 )=   0.364   0.671
           2  ( 0.116 )=   0.116   0.117            0.480
T=   800.   1  ( 0.361 )=   0.361   0.666
           2  ( 0.116 )=   0.116   0.117            0.477
T=   850.   1  ( 0.360 )=   0.360   0.666
           2  ( 0.118 )=   0.118   0.118            0.478
T=   900.   1  ( 0.361 )=   0.361   0.668
           2  ( 0.118 )=   0.118   0.118            0.479
T=   950.   1  ( 0.359 )=   0.359   0.664
           2  ( 0.119 )=   0.119   0.119            0.478
T=  1000.   1  ( 0.359 )=   0.359   0.665
           2  ( 0.121 )=   0.121   0.121            0.480


G   GAMMA,  RMODE,  JMODE,  OMODE1,  OMODE2
1   0.80      4       2        4        2
2   0.90      2       2        4        2


            G,  TOTAL GROUP INST,  TOTREFS,  TOTAL INST

T=    50.   1  ( 0.400 )=   0.400   0.760
           2  ( 0.100 )=   0.100   0.100            0.500
T=   100.   1  ( 0.350 )=   0.350   0.660
           2  ( 0.100 )=   0.100   0.100            0.450
T=   150.   1  ( 0.360 )=   0.360   0.673
           2  ( 0.107 )=   0.107   0.107            0.467
T=   200.   1  ( 0.370 )=   0.370   0.695
           2  ( 0.105 )=   0.105   0.105            0.475
T=   250.   1  ( 0.384 )=   0.384   0.724
           2  ( 0.108 )=   0.108   0.112            0.492
T=   300.   1  ( 0.390 )=   0.390   0.730
           2  ( 0.113 )=   0.113   0.113            0.503
T=   350.   1  ( 0.383 )=   0.383   0.714
           2  ( 0.114 )=   0.114   0.117            0.497
T=   400.   1  ( 0.382 )=   0.382   0.715
           2  ( 0.117 )=   0.117   0.120            0.500
T=   450.   1  ( 0.387 )=   0.387   0.724
           2  ( 0.120 )=   0.120   0.120            0.507
T=   500.   1  ( 0.384 )=   0.384   0.722
           2  ( 0.120 )=   0.120   0.120            0.504
```

```
T=   550.   1   ( 0.376 )=   0.376   0.704
            2   ( 0.118 )=   0.118   0.120          0.495
T=   600.   1   ( 0.377 )=   0.377   0.702
            2   ( 0.118 )=   0.118   0.118          0.495
T=   650.   1   ( 0.374 )=   0.374   0.695
            2   ( 0.118 )=   0.118   0.120          0.492
T=   700.   1   ( 0.377 )=   0.377   0.700
            2   ( 0.119 )=   0.119   0.120          0.496
T=   750.   1   ( 0.377 )=   0.377   0.697
            2   ( 0.119 )=   0.119   0.119          0.496
T=   800.   1   ( 0.376 )=   0.376   0.696
            2   ( 0.120 )=   0.120   0.120          0.496
T=   850.   1   ( 0.376 )=   0.376   0.698
            2   ( 0.119 )=   0.119   0.120          0.495
T=   900.   1   ( 0.376 )=   0.376   0.696
            2   ( 0.120 )=   0.120   0.121          0.496
T=   950.   1   ( 0.378 )=   0.378   0.701
            2   ( 0.122 )=   0.122   0.123          0.500
T=  1000.   1   ( 0.379 )=   0.379   0.703
            2   ( 0.123 )=   0.123   0.123          0.502
```

```
EOF ENCOUNTERED WHILE SCANNING FOR  ≠PROBLEM≠.
PROGRAM TERMINATION
```

CHAPTER 7
Constructs Using SIMULA

We have now come a good distance in our development of the process (scenario) view of simulation. Via several examples we have hopefully demonstrated the natural applicability and flexibility of the scenario view and the SIMULA language. In this chapter we develop certain additonal structures which demonstrate a somewhat different aspect of SIMULA's flexibility, namely, its *extendability* and *adaptability*. In particular we investigate SIMULA's potential for supporting the modeling views associated with SIMSCRIPT, GPSS, and ASPOL. Familiarity with these languages is not necessary in reading the chapter, since a summary of the essential features of each language is included.

SIMULA AND THE SIMSCRIPT EVENT VIEW

The event approach to simulation is characterized by the concepts supported by the SIMSCRIPT language, and by SIMSCRIPT 11.5 [Kiviat, 1968] in particular. Because the application of SIMULA is a relatively straightforward approach, we briefly consider its use to support the SIMSCRIPT notions of entitites (resources with attributes), event routines and event notices, and set definitions.

Entities

In SIMSCRIPT entities are a collection of attributes grouped into a named object. We may realize both *permanent* and *transient* entities via class declarations. For example, the declaration

    class ship (size,weight,cargo);
    real size, weight, cargo;
    begin ⟨operational statements⟩ end;

would correspond to a SIMSCRIPT entity called ship with attributes size, weight, and cargo. The operational portion of the object is not critical to the entity definition, but can be used to establish values when the object is created. Functionally, after creation, the operating statements play no further role, and the object exists strictly as a *data object.* One such definition is, of course, necessary for each intended entity.

Event Routines and Event Notices

Event routines cause changes in system state and schedule times for other future events. SIMSCRIPT thus dictates that we model a system from the viewpoint of potential events. In SIMULA, specification and scheduling of event routines is quite simple. Event routine declarations take the form

> process **class** event name (parameters);
> ⟨specifications⟩;
> **begin** ⟨body of event routine⟩ **end**;

An event can be scheduled with a statement such as

> **activate new** event name (parameters) **at** time;

with generation of the event notice handled automatically by SIMULA. If reference to the event is necessary, perhaps for possible cancellation, the above must be emended to

> **ref**(event name)X;
>
> .
>
> .
>
> .
>
> x :-**new** event name (parameters);
> **activate** x **at** time;

and the possible cancellations effected by the

> cancel (x);

In the above outline we have indicated parameters, because they represent one way of providing communication between the body of the event routine and other structures in the model program.

Set Definitions

In SIMSCRIPT sets are owned by entities and contain other entities as members. Further, entity membership may be simultaneously to more than one set. In SIMULA, as we have stated, an object can have membership in only a *single* set at a time. This limitation is circumvented by having a SIMULA object *represented indirectly* in each of several sets. To do so we define, for example,

> link **class** membership (main object);
>> **ref** (process) main object;
>> **begin**. . .**end**;

So that objects generated from the declaration

> process **class** job;
> **begin**. . .**end**;

can be simultaneous members of several sets. If x refers to such an object, then the statement pair

> **new** membership(x).into(queue1);
> **new** membership(x).into(queue2);

for example, provides representation for the object referenced by x in both the set queue1 *and* the set queue2, by using auxiliary records as introduced in Chapter 5.

SIMULA AND GPSS

GPSS provides a series of predefined resource, active, and operational objects. Transaction objects (the active objects) flow through a program composed of statistical and operational objects. When a transaction flows into an operational entity (also known as blocks), its predefined operational sequence is executed on *behalf* of the entering transaction. Once a given transaction begins its flow through the operational blocks, it continues until its progress is *blocked* by the unavailability of a known resource, or *delayed* to simulate an activity. When a transaction becomes blocked or delayed, a next transaction is selected and its progress (flow) is continued until it also becomes blocked or delayed. The pattern is repeated. The flexibility of GPSS is determined by the resource types it allows and the richness of the operational blocks. A complete account is given in Gordon [1975].

To sketch the adaptability of SIMULA to the GPSS view, we will consider only the transaction, storage and facility resources, and the delay construct.

Facility

A facility is a resource that can be engaged by only one transaction at a time. A facility is thus busy (if engaged) or not busy. A transaction engages a facility by flowing into a SEIZE block. Transactions attempting to engage a busy facility become blocked, after becoming a member of a FCFS queue associated with the facility resource. An engaged facility is released by the holding transaction flowing through a RELEASE block. When a release is executed, the facility is immediately assigned to the first blocked transaction in the queue, if any. The transaction to which the assignment is made becomes unblocked and is eligible to continue its sojourn through operational entities (blocks).

Storages

A storage is a resource with a capacity greater than one. Portions of the capacity can be allocated to (i.e., be engaged by) different transactions, provided that the totality of allocations is less than or equal to the capacity. A transaction engages a portion of the capacity by flowing through the ENTER block, and releases an engaged portion by flowing through the LEAVE block. Transactions attempting to engage a larger than currently available portion of the capacity are entered into an associated queue and their advance through operational blocks is halted. An engaged portion is vacated by the LEAVE block, and when vacated, *all* transactions blocked and in the facility queue are given a chance to engage their requested fractional capacities.

Delays

Delays are provided for by the ADVANCE block. It functions as a direct analog of the SIMULA hold ( ) procedure and delays a transaction a specified number of time units.

Transactions

Transactions are generated by the GENERATE block. When generated, a transaction begins its sojourn through operational blocks, usually beginning with the block which follows the generate block in the program deck. Their existence is transient, and terminated by their entrance into a TERMINATE block.

EXAMPLE 7.1   We consider the simple single server queueing system. A fragment of the GPSS program which simulated the system is given below, with ancillary comments to clarify the structure.

	GENERATE 5,0	{generate one transaction every 5 time units} transaction flows through operational blocks beginning with next unit
	SEIZE SERVER	{engage facility named server}
	ADVANCE 4,1	{delay t time units, with t uniformly distributed between 3 and 5}
Operational Blocks	RELEASE SERVER . . .	{release server for reassignment}
	TERMINATE 1	{terminate existence of transaction and increment count of number of terminations}
	END	

For this (and all GPSS model programs) we have generated transactions flowing through the operational blocks of the model program.

Thus, as stated earlier, GPSS supports the process view of simulation, but in a more restrictive way than does SIMULA. We should, therefore, be able to write a "GPSS like" system in SIMULA. For the GPSS constructs considered, we could organize the realization as follows.

```
simulation begin
real ⟨static variables⟩;
    begin
        real array ⟨block count statistics⟩;
        class facility;  begin. . .end facility;
        class storage; begin. . .end storage;
```

```
process class transaction;
    begin
integer ⟨standard attributes and standard parameters⟩;
procedure seize(f); ref(facility)f; begin. . .end;
procedure release(f); ref(facility)f; begin. . .end;
procedure enter(s,n); ref(storage)s; integer n; begin. . .end;
procedure leave(s,n); ref(storage)s; integer n; begin. . .end;
        {other block action procedures};
end transaction;

transaction class customer; begin
{GPSS like model program in terms of operational blocks};
end customer description;
⟨main program for startup, display of results⟩;
    end program;
end simulation;
```

We define facility resources via

```
class facility; begin ref(head)fq;

comment a facility is an equipment of unit capacity which may
        be used (held) sequentially by transactions;

ref(transaction) holder;
Boolean procedure busy;
busy:-holder =/= none;
fq:- new head;
end facility;
```

which specifies a queue on which unhonored requests can be placed, and a busy nonbusy flag. Our philosophy will be to delay generation of a facility object until it is *first* referenced. Thus the procedure SEIZE must bear the generation responsibility and can be defined as follows.

```
procedure seize(f);
ref(facility)f;
begin
    If f = = none then f:- new facility;
    If f.busy then
            begin
            into(f.fq);
            passivate;
```

saction;

The var... ...s used as *actual* parameters in the GPSS-like program must, of course, be declared as type **ref**(facility).Queued (blocked) requests are advanced by the RELEASE procedure, the definition of which follows.

```
procedure release(f);
ref(facility)f;
inspect f do
    begin
    if holder =/= this transaction then ERROR;
    if fq.empty then holder:- none else
        activate fq.first delay 0;
    end release;
```

Storages can be realized in several ways. We select one which allows the capacity of a storage to accompany its generation via **new** storage(capacity); by defining **class** storage as follows.

```
class storage(capacity);
integer capacity;
begin
ref(head)q; integer available space;
    procedure check q;
    comment used by LEAVE block construct;
    begin ref( linkage)x;
    x:- q;
    for x:- x.suc
        while x =/= none and available space > 0 do
            activate x qua transaction;
    end check q;
q:- new head;
available space:=capacity;
end storage;
```

This definition is then mated with the procedure declarations which emulate the operational blocks ENTER and LEAVE. We emulate ENTER with

```
procedure enter(sto,number units requested);
ref(storage)sto; integer number units requested;
```

```
        inspect sto when storage do
        begin
            if number units requested > capacity then errors;
            into(q);
            for q:- q
            while number units requested > available space
                do passivate;
            out;
            available space:=available space-number units requested;

        end enter;
```

and LEAVE with

```
        procedure leave(sto,number units returned);
        ref(storage)sto; integer number units returned;
        inspect sto when storage do
        begin
            available space:=available space + number units returned;
            if available space > capacity then error;

            comment allow transactions in storage queue to retry
                    their ENTER operation;

            check q;
        end leave;
```

EXAMPLE 7.2   We repeat Example 7.1 using the SIMULA "GPSS-like" constructs.

```
        transaction class customer;
        begin
        activate new customer delay 5;
        seize(server);
        hold(uniform(3,5,u));
        release(server);
            .
            .
            .
        end customer description;
```

The variable SERVER must be declared at the outset by ref(facility) SERVER. To begin and control the simulation we might give as the main program

    u: = 5291;
    activate new customer **delay** 0;
    hold ( );
    ⟨statements to display performance statistics⟩;
    end program;

Much of the material presented here is from Vaucher [1971, 1973]. The ideas here can be pursued to the point where a GPSS program is massaged by a preprocessor and then executed using constructs such as those developed here. The interested reader is referred to Houle [1974] for additional material on this point.

SIMULA AND ASPOL

In some situations the scheduling constructs of SIMULA are too rich, and confinement to a simpler framework is desirable. A viable but simple scheme might dictate, for example, that *process synchronizations* be governed by *event variables.* Imagine that such variables are declared by the statement

    event $e_1, e_2, \ldots, e_n$;

and that associated with each such variable is a *Boolean value,* a *set,* and a *queue* (an ordered set). Processes become members of and leave the event variable set or queue as a result of the execution of the procedures wait(e), set(e), and queue(e). Assuming the Boolean value associated with the event variable identifier, the effect of each procedure is as follows.

Wait(e)   If the value of e is **false**, the executing process is passivated after joining the set associated with the event variable. If e has value **true**, then the value of e is toggled and the executing process is allowed to continue.

Set(e)   This causes the value of e to be set to **true**, if the associated set and queue are empty. Otherwise, all processes booked on the event variable's set as well

as the highest priority process in its FCFS queue are
scheduled for reactivation at the current time.

Queue(e)   If the value of *e* is **true**, the executing process is
allowed to continue and the value of *e* is toggled.
Otherwise, the executing process is made a member
of the FIFO queue associated with *e* and then made
passive (passivated).

We may view the execution of wait(e) or queue(e) as event selection. For a given variable the totality of event selections may be a
mixture of queue and wait selections. The execution of set( ) can
then be viewed as event occurrence and the passive processes, which
become scheduled for activation at the then current time, may be
thought of as having recognized the event occurrence. The mechanisms
described are in fact the only process communication primitives
employed in the language ASPOL [MacDougall, 1973]. Although the
primitives are sufficient to account for process interactions in a
variety of scenario descriptions, the ASPOL language was designed specifically as a general purpose vehicle for simulating computer systems.
The language also supports the storage and facility concepts of GPSS.
Note, in this context, that a facility may now be thought of as an
event variable, so that SEIZE becomes queue(e) and RELEASE
becomes set(e).

Having just considered a SIMULA realization of storages and
facilities, we concentrate here on a realization of event variables. A
discussion of certain details (such as scope of definition of an event
variable and the concept of an array of event variables) is omitted.
A full accounting can be had by consulting MacDougall [1973].

For our purposes we will declare event variables via

ref(event)$e_1, e_2, \ldots, e_n$;

rather than

event e_1, e_2, e_n;

and invoke the associated procedures with

e.set,

e.queue

e.wait

rather than

> set(e)
>
> queue(e)
>
> wait(e)

Having so stated, it remains to specify the operational routines set, queue, and wait which become local to the declaration of the **class** event as shown below.

```
class event;
begin ref(head)waits,queues;
        Boolean occurred;
        procedure set;
        comment event occurrence procedure;

        if waits.empty and queues.empty then
        occurred := true else
        begin ref(process)P;

            comment schedule activations for all processes
                    in event variable set;

            for p:-waits.first      while p=/=none do
            begin p.out;activate p after current;end;
            comment schedule activation for process at
                    head of FCFS event variable queue;

            If ⌐queues.empty then

                begin
                p:-queues.first;p.out;
                activate p after current;
                end;

        end of set;

        procedure wait;
        comment set event selection procedure;
            begin
            if ⌐occurred then
                begin
```

```
                 current.into(waits);
                 passivate;
                 end
                           else
                 occurred:=false
                 end of wait;

          procedure queue;
          comment procedure for event selection via a FCFS queue;
             begin
             if ⌐ occurred then
                 begin
                 current.into(queues);
                 passivate;
                 end
                             else
                 occurred:=false
          end of queue;


             comment generate event variable set and queue heads;

                 waits:-new head;
                 queues:-new head
          end of event;
```

In ASPOL each process object has as one of its attributes a priority value, and in reality the queue associated with an event variable is ordered by the *static priority* values of its member processes. This ordering can be accommodated in SIMULA by associating a priority attribute with *class* process and redefining the procedure named queue as shown below.

```
          procedure queue;

          comment: assume process objects with an attribute
          'priority', with larger values of 'priority' reflecting
          lower priority;

          if occurred then occurred:=false else
             begin ref(linkage)y; ref(process)z;
             y:- queues;
```

```
if ⌐queues.empty then
   begin
   if queues.last qua process.priority ≤ current.priority
   then y:- queues.last
   else for z:- y.suc while z.priority ≤ current.priority
        do y:- z;
   end;
current.follow(y);
passivate;
end of queue;
```

EXAMPLE 7.3   The event indicator synchronization construct is particularly useful in situations where process objects must initiate and then wait for completion of activities of unknown or variable duration. This situation is frequently encountered when constructing operating system models, and an elaborate example has been given by MacDougall [1973]. We consider a much simpler example. Imagine that class C objects generate, activate, and wait for completion of the activities of a class A and a B object. If the A and B activity times are unknown a priori, then event indicators (variables) serve to coordinate the activity of the C object with those of the A and B objects. For C objects we have

```
process class c;
   .
   .
   .
ref(event)eventa,event b;
   .
   .
   .
eventa:-new event;
eventb:-new event;
activate new a(eventa) after current;
activate new b(eventb) after current;

comment wait for both A and B object completions;
eventa.wait; eventb.wait;
```

with the declarations of a and b taking the following forms.

```
process class a(e);          process class b(e);
ref(event)e;                 ref(event)e;
```

```
        begin                           begin
          .                               .
          .                             .   .
          .                               .
exit:   e.set                  exit:    e.set
        end a;                          end b;
```

A GENERAL "WAIT UNTIL" CONSTRUCT

Many of the constructs we have discussed contain *implicit* "wait until" algorithms. The event and facility constructs contained, for example, "wait until taken from queue" algorithms which governed the reactivation times for processes waiting for a given event or the right to control a facility, respectively. The construct

   hold(t);

is an explicit "wait until" construct and insures that the executing process will not be advanced until the system clock has advanced to a time equal to the current time plus the increment t. For hold( ) we have, in essence, written

   wait until(system time=current system time + t);

It is a generalization of this idea which we now explore. Specifically, we shall realize a generalized construct of the form

   wait until(condition);

where "condition" is a Boolean expression of arbitrary complexity.[1] When executed by a process, the *intended* semantics dictates that the executing process become passive *until* the Boolean expression first becomes *true*. Thus, wait-until generalizes not only the hold construct, but also the wait procedure associated with event variables, and the wait-until procedure given in Chapter 5.

EXAMPLE 7.4   Consider a situation in which model program logic requires that a process passivate until the number of entries in a set, referenced by the variable s, is less than 5, or until a period of time

---

[1] The language SOL [Knuth, 1964] was probably the first process-oriented language to contain a wait until construct. Although GPSS is a predecessor to SOL, it does not qualify because its use of "wait until" is more implicit than discussed here, or as found in SOL.

given by INTERVAL has elapsed. Using wait-until, we account for this situation by writing

tout:=time+interval;

wait until (s.cardinal < 5 **or** time = tout);

As discussed in Vaucher, [1973], realization of the wait-until construct requires four elements. They include:

1. A *procedure* named wait-until to be used by processes
2. A list, waitq, where processes passivated by wait-until are collected (established as a result of **ref**(head)waitq; wait q:-**new** head;)
3. A *monitor* (established as a result of **ref**(wait monitor)monitor; monitor:-**new** wait monitor); which examines passivated processes booked on waitq and schedules reactivations at opportune times
4. A global Boolean variable, action, used for communication between blocked processes and the monitor.

The procedure wait-until is actually quite simple and is given next.

```
                procedure wait until(b);
                name b;Boolean b;
                begin
                    if b then goto exit;
                    into(waitq);
                    if monitor.idle then activate
                    monitor after nextev;
loop:           passivate;
loop 1:         if not b then goto loop;
                    out;
                    action:=true;
                exit;
                end waituntil;
```

The procedure is written so that if the Boolean condition *b* is initially true, the invoking process is allowed to proceed. Otherwise, it is entered into waitq and made passive. Notice that the procedure is responsible for the continual testing of *b*, leading *eventually* to the continuation of any process blocked by its falsity. It is the responsibility of the monitor (declared below) to activate the passivated processes so that they may execute the line labeled Loop1 to test b. Such activations should be done, of course, only at epochs when it is possible that b may be true. Further, notice that when b becomes true, the process continues after setting action to true and removing itself from the set waitq. Finally, the statement to activate the monitor is necessary since it will be passive if there are *no* processes blocked as a result of having executed the wait-until procedure.

Next we specify the monitor whose structure is governed by the observation that a process passivated by "wait until" must remain passivated *at least* until the system state has been altered (an exception to this remark concerns the variable or function time, and will be discussed below). This is true because only a system state ch nge can alter attributes referenced in b. Processes booked on waitq must, therefore, be activated to recheck b following events. These activations are performed by the monitor, whose definition is given next.

```
process class wait monitor;
begin ref (process) pt;
start:   if waitq.empty then passivate;
         action:=false;
         pt:-waitq.first;
loop:    if pt= =none then goto wait;
         activate pt;
         if action then goto start;
         pt:-pt.suc;
         goto loop;
wait:    reactivate this wait monitor after nextev;
         goto start;
end      wait monitor;
```

Since the variable nextev (see Chapter 5) refers to the next event notice in *SQS*, the monitor is activated after each normal system event. The monitor considers the exit of a process from waitq as an event, so that it *restarts* its scan through waitq when a process signals continuance by setting action to **true**.

The realization is quite general in the sense that arbitrary Boolean expressions b are allowed. The exceptional cases alluded to earlier are those for which b contains the variable time, and Example 7.4

is in this category. For these cases a basic difficulty stems from the fact that time is advanced in discrete jumps.

To clarify the situation, consider the following two statements:

(a) WAIT UNTIL (TIME=15);

(b) WAIT UNTIL (TIME>15);

and imagine them executed at TIME=10. Further assume that the next notice in SQS has an event time of 20. When the monitor is activated as the *last* event at TIME=10 (which it will be), neither condition is satisfied. The next activation will be at a time of 20. The net effect is that the process which executed (a) will *never* be reactivated, and the process which executed (b) will not be reactivated until time=20 (rather than time=15 + Δt which is more meaningful).

Several candidate solutions exist, including activating the monitor every Δt time units. For most situations the most satisfactory solution is to appropriately lace the set SQS with *dummy* event notices to force the activation of the monitor at known critical times. Such dummy notices are easily constructed by generating *and* scheduling activation times for objects from the *empty* class declaration.

    process **class** alarm; ;

The situation described in Example 7.4 is then *correctly* realized if the coding presented there is changed to

    TOUT:=TIME+INTERVAL;
    activate new alarm **at** TOUT;
    WAIT UNTIL (S.CARDINAL<5 or TIME=TOUT);

Statements such as (a) and (b) above should, of course, be replaced by

    (a) hold(15-time)

and

    (b) hold(15-time+ Δt),

respectively.

The capability provided by WAIT UNTIL is generally known as *interrogative* scheduling, whereas that scheduling capability provided by hold( ) and *activate* is referred to as *imperative*. While the interrogative form provided by wait-until is general, it is costly because after each imperative event, *each* process passivated by the interrogative form must be tested. Efficiency is better served if several monitors are used, one for each possible delay form. Further, if the processes can be ordered in the individual monitor sets so that only the first or last need be tested, the overhead is further reduced. A moment's thought will, in fact, convince the reader it is for these very reasons that

> **activate** this process **at** TOUT;

is preferable to

> wait until(TIME=TOUT);

EXAMPLE 7.5   Given the existence of a monitor and its associated wait-until procedure, we may realize the solution to the mutual exclusion example of Chapter 5 by the following code.

```
process class P;
begin
A1:
    wait until(AR1>0 and AR3>0);
    AR1:=AR1-1;AR3:=AR3-1;
    hold(activity1 time);
    AR1:=AR1+1;
A2:
    waituntil (AR2>0);
    AR2:=AR2-1;
    hold(activity2 time);
    AR2:=AR2+1;
A3:
    waituntil(AR1>0);
    AR1:=AR1-1;
    hold(activity3 time);
    AR1:=AR1+1; AR3:=AR3+1;
end p scenario;
```

As comparison of the two solutions shows, the form used here places the burden of activation attempts on the monitor rather than on the *P* objects. Although structurally more appealing than the original version, the coding given here is less efficient (in terms of computer time).

Next, we consider a slightly more time-efficient realization of the procedure "wait-until" and the class "wait monitor." In the above realization, after each event, the monitor activates all processes blocked in waitq so that each process can recheck its Boolean expression. An improvement (time-wise) is obtained if the monitor itself takes up the responsibility of rechecking the Boolean condition for each process represented in waitq, and activates a process only in the event that its Boolean expression is found to be **true**.

To enable the monitor to do the rechecking, we introduce an auxiliary class,

```
link class record(condition);
    name condition; Boolean condition;
begin
    ref(process) owner;
owner:- current;
end record;
```

and let each process be represented in waitq by an auxiliary record object from this class. Then, the procedure "wait-until" will take the following form.

```
procedure wait until(b)
    name b; Boolean b;
if ⌐b then
    begin
    new record(b).into(waitq);
    if monitor.idle then
        activate monitor after nextev;
    passivate;
    end of wait until;
```

And, the monitor has the following structure.

```
process class wait monitor;
begin ref(record) P;
start:  if waitq.empty then
        begin passivate, goto start; end;
    for p:-waitq.first, P.suc while P =/= none do
        if P.condition then
                begin
                P.out;
                activate P.owner;
                goto start;
```

```
        end;
reactivate this wait monitor after nextev;
goto start;
end wait monitor;
```

Note that the variable, action, has been eliminated.

Finally, we note that the simulation system can be completely redefined by creating *new* classes designed to replace SIMSET and/or SIMULATION. Such redefinition can be completely effected within the confines of SIMULA itself, at the expense, perhaps, of safeguarded variables.

CHAPTER 8

The Cost of Simulation

The cost of simulation is determined by the amount of work—human and computer—necessary to the steps shown in Figure 1.4. We have addressed the factors contributing to human work, and here we concentrate on those factors that influence the amount of work done by the computer (i.e., for steps 3–5 of figure 1.4). These factors include:

(a) The complexity of the model
(b) The simulated time necessary to collect sufficient data to yield valid statistics
(c) The overhead incurred in supporting events (processes)

with the work precipitated measured in *expended* computer time.

In fact, the most severe liability of simulation may be the excessive amount of computer time it often requires. From the modeling side, we abstract and simplify to keep the complexity of the model low. It is difficult to discuss this aspect, since determining the correct degree of correspondence (detail) between the system and simulation model is an art, and little useful information has been written on the subject.

From the statistical side, we develop variance reduction sampling techniques to minimize the number of observations of a response variable required for a given statistical precision. A great deal is written on this subject and the reader is referred to Fishman [1975] and Kleijnen [1974]. In this chapter we discuss two additional factors affecting the cost of simulation, namely, those associated with the selection of the time advance mechanism and the physical data structure employed for the sequencing set.

THE TIME ADVANCE MECHANISM

The time advance mechanism can influence (b) and (c). In Chapter 1 we identified two time advancement mechanisms—the unit-time

advance and event-advance mechanisms.[1] In situations where both
are applicable, response estimates with the smaller variance are generally given by models that use the event-advance mechanism. To illustrate, consider the model of Figure 8.1, consisting of a single service
station with two servers to which a finite population of six customers
repeatedly come for service. Service times are exponentially distributed with parameter $\mu = 0.2$. Following service, a customer returns to
a uniquely assigned holding station, where he remains for an exponentially distributed (parameter $\lambda = 0.067$) amount of time, following which he again enters the system for an additional service. The
cycle is repeated endlessly by each of the six customers. Imagine we
are interested in P_n, $n = 0, 1, ..., 6$, the steady-state probabilities of
the system containing n customers. The system described is a variant
of a queueing model known as the "repairman model" and has been
analyzed mathematically (see Cooper, [1972]). We thus have exact
values for the P_i. We can develop both unit-time and event-advance
simulation models, run each to simulate H hours of operation, and
compare the estimates to each other and the theoretical values.

An experiment of this kind was conducted by Emshoff and Sisson
[Emshoff, 1970], for which the service and holding times are in
minutes and H is 200 hours. They recorded

$E(n) = \Sigma_{i=0}^{6} nP_n$, and their results are summarized in Figure 8.2.[2]
As shown in Table 8.1, the event-advance model produced not only a
sharper estimate, but it did so in a third the computer time.

The event-advance model required the least computer time
because no overhead is incurred at those time points where no state
change occurs.

On the basis of experimental evidence together with some theoretical evidence (see Emshoff [1970]), we prefer the event to unit
advance when *both* are applicable. This advance reduces overhead
but requires the maintenance of a sequencing set. Our attention,

---

[1] Unit-time advance models can be used to represent any system, but event-advance
models cannot. In particular, event-advance models are inappropriate when state variables
change in a continuous rather than discrete manner.

[2] We must, of course, select a time increment for the unit-advance model. Since state
changes (which in reality should occur between increments) can in the model occur only at
increment points, our intuition suggests the unit should be small. Exactly how small is
necessary was, for this model, determined to be 0.25 min (see Emshoff [1970] for a
discussion).

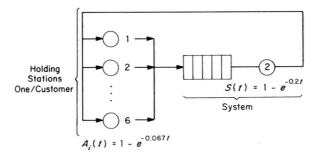

Figure 8.1 Finite customer queueing model

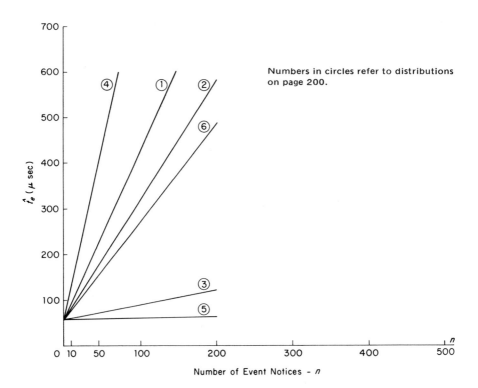

Figure 8.2 $D_s = L$: Test results. (Numbers in circles refer to numbers associated with the distributions listed above)

Table 8.1
Comparison of unit and Event Advance Models

Estimation Method	$E(n)$	360/65 Computer Time Required to Simulate 200 Hours
Theoretical value	1.811	–
Unit-advance (1/4 min interval)	1.868	0.36 min
Event advance	1.835	0.12 min

therefore, naturally turns to the structure of the sequencing set and to the *access routine* alogirthms which manipulate it.

SEQUENCING SET PHYSICAL DATA STRUCTURE

As stated earlier, the record of scheduled events is generally kept in objects known as event notices which are collected and organized by event time in a data structure called the sequencing set S. To schedule an event, we first *generate* an event notice. Next, to maintain time order in the set S, the notices it contains are *scanned* to determine the proper insertion point where the new notice is inserted to complete the scheduling. The details of these operations are given in Chapter 5 (procedures *activate,* hold, rank, passivate, etc.) for the SIMULA system which employs the linear list as the *physical data* structure for S. In this section we first examine the environment in which the sequencing set is manipulated, and then for that environment, examine structures which have characteristics more desirable than those associated with the linear list structure.

In essence the physical data structure used for S must mitigate the task of isolating the notice(s) with minimal valued event time(s) in a dynamically changing collection of notices. In order to mitigate the isolation task, it is *desirable* to keep the notices in S *ordered* by increasing event time values. Thus *insertion* of a new notice requires a *scan* of the notices in S in order to locate the correct insertion point. Further, the computer time required to insert a notice (in S) is proportional to the number of notices scanned. Therefore, it is convenient and conventional to take the scanning of one notice as the *basic unit* for a *complexity analysis* of the physical data structure.

EXAMPLE 8.1 The worst case complexity (scans required to locate insertion point for a new notice) of the linear list structure is $0(n)$ for a set S containing n notices, and obviously occurs when the scan begins at the the right (left) end of the list, and the notice being inserted has an event time smaller (larger) than all n notices in the set.

We are more interested in the expected (average) complexity than the worst case complexity. Unfortunately, analytic determination of the average complexity is very difficult when, as is usually the case, event times are determined by stochastic drawings. We can, however, proceed experimentally and obtain estimates for the average number of scans required to insert a notice under various conditions. Such estimates would be adequate for the linear list structure. As we shall find, however, alternate physical data struc- tures will require occasional *restructuring*, the frequency of which is unknown (again due to the stochastic nature of the event times).

In this chapter we therefore use t_e, the computer time expended to insert a new notice into S as the basic unit of complexity, because it accounts for the number of scans required, and when necessary, the time for restructuring operations.

The computer time t_e required to schedule an event is functionally dependent on many parameters. Considering the more important parameters, we have

$$t_e = f(n,\ t,\ F_s(x),\ C,\ D_s,\ 0), \tag{8.1}$$

with

n = number of notices in the sequencing set S
t = event time for the event being scheduled
$F_s(x)$ = distribution of the event times given by the n notices in S, this distribution is generally unknown
C = computer on which the simulation is run
D_s = physical data structure used to realize (support) S
0 = scheduling operation used.

Unfortunately Equation (8.1) is not directly useful because f is unknown and parameters such as $F_s(x)$ cannot often be determined.

We can, however, proceed experimentally and by fixing n, C, D_s, and 0 obtain estimates $\hat{t}_e$ of $E(t_e)$, the expected time required to schedule an event.[3] Then, by repeated experiments, we can compare the effects of various D_s and n on $\hat{t}_e$.

To obtain $\hat{t}_e$, we select for 0 the primitive hold(th) and conduct experiments with $F_{th}(x)$ given by each of the six distributions listed below. The hold(th) primitive was chosen because it is typically used and requires delete (rather than generate), scan of S, and insertion operations.

Unimodal Continuous
1. Negative exponential (average of 1).
2. Uniform distribution over the interval [0 to 2].
3. Uniform distribution over the interval [0.9 to 1.1].

Bimodal Continuous
4. 90 percent probability—uniform over the interval [0 to S]. 10 percent probability—uniform over the interval [100 S to 101 S] where S is such as to give the distribution an average of unity.

Discrete
5. "th" is constant with value of unity.
6. "th" is assigned the values 0, 1, or 2 with equal probabilities.

These six distributions were chosen after extensive preliminary experimentation.[4] They are all representative of various kinds of simulation problems, yet they differ widely in their characteristics, and reflect attempts to emphasize the good and bad points of the various structures D_s. The distributions fall in three categories.

In the 1st two categories, it is highly unlikely that two event notices will be scheduled for the same time. The first distribution is typical of queueing situations; it represents randomness in events and sets no upper bound on "th." The second and third distributions are representative of the simple form of the GPSS "ADVANCE" statement. The second distribution has the highest ratio of variance

---

[3] For all results reported here, C=Cyber 74, and tests were made using the standard PASCAL compiler.

[4] The tests were repeated for each candidate structure D_s. For each F, and n, j hold operations were performed, with $j = 10000$ for $n = 1$ to $j = 4000$ when $n \geqslant 200$.

to average that can be obtained with the uniform distribution, whereas the third distribution provides a relatively constant value for "th." The bimodal distribution (4) gives the highest ratio of variance to average of the six distributions, and its narrow peaks should give trouble to the time mapping algorithms.

The Discrete Category is typical of clocked digital circuit simulations where time is represented by an integer variable.

$D_s = L$—The Linear Circular List

As stated, SIMULA currently employs the linear list as the physical structure for S. Even for this simple structure, knowledge of $F_{th}(x)$ is *not* sufficient to determining $F_s(x)$, necessary to finding $E(t_e)$. The results of our tests are depicted in Figure 8.2. As expected, the values $\hat{t}_e$ vary linearly with n. Further, the slopes of the lines are ordered much as we might expect.

For actual simulations, $F_s(x)$ is influenced simultaneously by several distributions $F_{th}(x)$, rather than by a single one as for the experiments reported. This observation generally makes $F_s(x)$ bi- or multimodal, so that the curve for distribution "4" would be typical of many simulations and suggests a potentially high cost per hold operation. Obviously, the major portion of the time t_e is devoted to scanning S, and we naturally seek alternative data structures D_s, which might *reduce* the number of scans required to execute hold(th). Many alternatives have been investigated, and two, the indexed list and two level structures, when tested, consistently produce much lower estimates for $\hat{t}_e$. We consider next their physical structures and then, for each companions to Figure 8.2.

$D_s = \text{IL}$—The Indexed List with Dummy Notices

The indexed list algorithm (reported originally in Vaucher et al. [1975]) attempts to produce lower values of $\hat{t}_e$ by the following means. The range of event times represented in the set S is estimated and divided into a number du (heuristically determined) of equal-sized intervals of width DT. The intervals are bounded by "dummy notices" which are pointed to by the elements of an index list. Insertions are made by identifying the correct interval, and then linearly scanning the notices associated with that interval for the proper insertion point. A single overflow interval is included for event times which fall outside the estimated range.

The variable ICURRENT indicates the index pointer to the current interval, and LOWERBOUND gives the simulated time for the beginning of that interval. The last pointer of the array delimits the overflow portion of the list, and as dummy notices migrate to the extreme left, they are moved to their proper place in the overflow segment.

EXAMPLE 8.2   To illustrate we set $du = 4$, $DT = 1$ and imagine that initially D_s has the following structure where an "x" denotes a dummy notice. Suppose that initially we have four event notices, TIME = 0.5 and LOWERBOUND = 0.

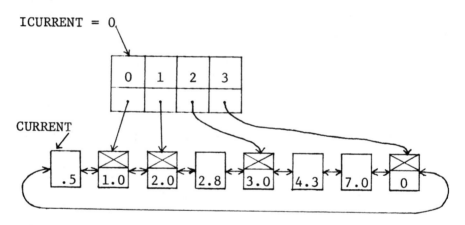

Then following HOLD (8.2), we have TIME = 2.8; LOWER-BOUND = 2, and D_s appears as:

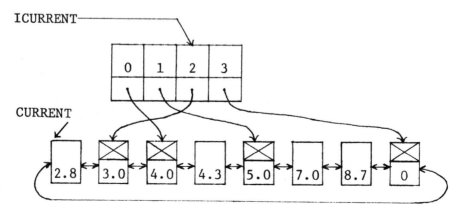

After HOLD (3.9), TIME = 4.3; LOWERBOUND = 4, and D_s has the form:

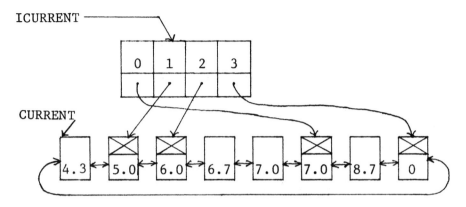

The physical data structure and the procedure hold are specified by the code segment given next. Incorporation of these notions into the SIMULA simulation system would require respecification of class simulation.

Access Algorithm for D_s = IL.

```
Simset begin
link class event notice;
begin real evtime;
    Boolean dummy;
end of event notice;

    ref(event notice) array pointer[0:100] ;
    integer icurrent, du;
    real lowerbound, dt;
    ref(event notice) current;

procedure hold(t); real t;
begin
    ref(event notice)y; integer i;
current:-pointer[du] .suc;
inspect current do
    begin
    if t>0 then evtime:=evtime+t;
    if evtime < suc qua eventnotice.evtime then goto exit;
    out;
```

```
        i:=entier((evtime-lowerbound)/dt);
        if i ≥ du then i:=du else i:=mod(icurrent+i,du);
        y:-pointer[i].pred;
        for y:-y while y.evtime > evtime do y:-y.pred;
        follow(y)
        end;
    for current:-pointer[du].suc   while current.dummy
    inspect current do
        begin comment:move dummy to overflow segment;
        lowerbound:=lowerbound+dt;
        icurrent:=icurrent+1;
        out;
        evtime:=lowerbound+du*dt;
        y:-pointer[du].pred;
        for y:-y while y.evtime>evtime do y:-y.pred;
        follow(y);
        end;
    exit:;
    end of hold;
```

⟨initialization: requires creation of dummy event notices placed in a circular doubly-linked list⟩

.

.

.

end of program;

The worst case complexity for insertion remains $0(n)$ and occurs when all scheduled times fall outside the estimated range. As for the D_s = L structure, the average complexity could not be analytically determined (owing to the difficulty of determining the distribution of event times in the set) and was, therefore, experimentally estimated.

The structure D_s = IL was tested in the same manner as was D_s = L, given earlier. For the tests, the settings du = 30 and

$$
DT := \begin{cases} 200 \times E(th) & n = 1 \\ \dfrac{8}{(n-1)} + 0.07 & \times E(th) \qquad n > 1 \end{cases} \tag{8.2}
$$

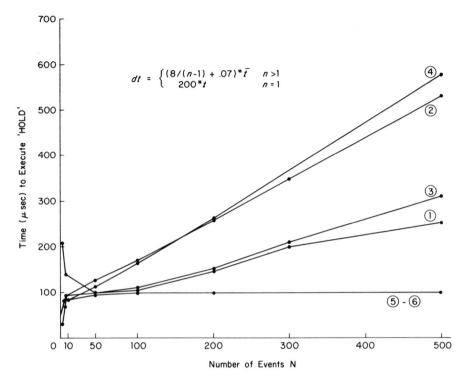

$$dt = \begin{cases} (8/(n-1) + .07)*\bar{t} & n > 1 \\ 200*t & n = 1 \end{cases}$$

Figure 8.3 D_s = IL test results

were used.[5] Figure 8.3 contains performance results, which indicate its superiority over the simple linear list algorithm.

As Figure 8.3 shows, the IL structure is sensitive to distribution "4," a type likely encountered. An attempt to overcome this dependence on n, as well as the sensitivity to $F_{th}(x)$, is given by D_s = TL, the two-level structure.

D_s = TL—The Two-Level Structure

The TL algorithm and its associated physical data structure are motivated in part by the indexed list (IL) algorithm and in part by

---

[5] Equation 8.2 was empirically obtained, and based on the observation that DT should be inversely proportional to n, and directly proportional to E(th). It was derived by Vaucher et al. [1975].

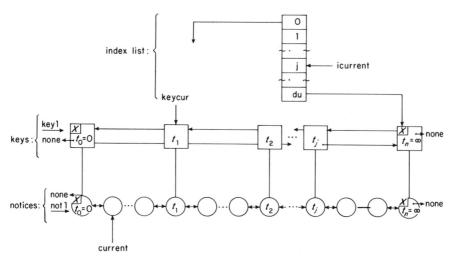

X denotes a dummy key or event notice

Figure 8.4   Data structure for the two-level algorithm

the notion of balanced trees, or more specifically, 3-2 trees. The basic idea of the TL algorithm is to limit the number of notices that must be scanned for an insertion. This requirement is met by dynamically creating for each interval a list of secondary keys and associating them with the right boundary dummy key. Each secondary key points to the beginning of a sublist of notices within an interval (see Figures 8.4 and 8.5). Whenever one of these sublists becomes unbalanced, that is, too large, the structure is adjusted either by moving the notice to the adjacent list or by creating a new sublist with its associated secondary key. The TL access algorithm given on the following pages uses the following variables:

$$
\begin{aligned}
&du = \text{number of intervals} \\
&dt = \text{width of interval} \\
&current = \text{points to first event notice} \\
&keycur = \text{points to ``key'' whose sublist contains} \\
&\qquad\qquad\quad current \\
&icurrent = \text{points to the element of the index list whose} \\
&\qquad\qquad\qquad\;\; \text{interval contains current} \\
&lowerbound = \text{lower bound of interval containing current} \\
&pointer[0:du] = \text{sequential representation of the index list} \\
&n\,\text{lim} = \text{maximum number of notices per sublist}
\end{aligned}
$$

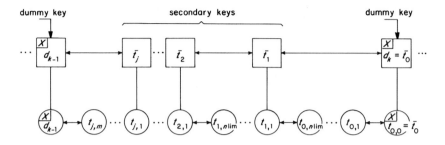

$d_k = d_{k-1} + dt; \quad \bar{t}_j \leq \cdots \leq \bar{t}_2 \leq \bar{t}_1 \leq \bar{t}_0 = d_k; \quad t_{,i} = \bar{t}_i \text{ for } 0 \leq i \leq j;$

$m \leq n\lim; \quad t_{j,m} \leq \cdots \leq t_{j1} \leq \cdots \leq t_{2,1} \leq t_{1,n\lim} \leq \cdots \leq t_{1,1} \leq t_{0,n\lim} \leq \cdots \leq t_{0,1} \leq t_{0,0} = \bar{t}_0;$

Figure 8.5   Details of the two-level algorithm data structure

The field identifiers for notice nodes are "suc," "pred," and "evtime" with their obvious interpretation, and those for dummy and secondary key nodes are "pred," "suc," "segment" (a pointer to its notice node), "number" (indicating the current size of a sub-list), "dummy" (differentiating secondary and dummy keys), and "evtime." As for $D_s = L$ and $D_s = IL$, experiments were conducted to estimate $\bar{t}_e$, using Equation (8.2) for dt, and $du = 30$. The value for the parameter n lim was determined by the following method.

It should be obvious that the two-level structure is designed to reduce the dependence of the search time on n. The value of n lim used was determined by analyzing the worst case behavior of the TL algorithm, denoted by $c_w(n)$ using key comparisons as basic units, which occurs when all n notices are associated with the same dummy key, and the notice being inserted has an event time smaller than all other notices in the structure. That is,

$$c_w(n) = \frac{n}{n \lim} + n \lim \tag{8.3}$$

Under these conditions $c_w(n)$ is minimized by setting n lim to $\sqrt{n}$, thus $c_w(n)$ is $0(\sqrt{n})$. Obviously, this selection does not account for the overhead incurred in maintaining a balanced structure.

Experimentally, we confirmed that for the distributions tested, the setting n lim $= \sqrt{n}$ does indeed result in best algorithm performance, except when n is very small. We therefore suggest the setting

$$n \lim = \max (8, \sqrt{n}) \qquad (8.4)$$

We further note here that the algorithm (given next) is written in such a way that n lim can be changed dynamically. For instance, if n is not known, the scheduling procedure can keep track of the number of events in the system and increase n lim at appropriate times.

Access Algorithm for $D_s = TL$[6]

```
Simset begin
link class event notice;
begin real evtime; end;

link class key;
begin real evtime;
    ref(eventnotice) segment;
    integer number;
    Boolean dummy;
end of key;

    real dt,lowerbound;
    integer icurrent,nlim,du;
    ref(key) keyl,keycur;
    ref(eventnotice) notl,current;
    ref(key)array pointer [0:100] ;

procedure adjust (x); ref(key)x;
comment: invoked after a notice has been inserted in x's segment in order to
    limit the maximum number of notices to nlim. The procedure takes out the
    left-most notice of x's segment and puts it in the segment of either an
    already existing key to the left of x or a new key to be created to the
    left of x;
begin ref(key)xp; ref(event notice)y;
xp:-x.pred; y:-xp.segment.suc;
if xp.dummy or xp.number=nlim then
    begin xp:-new key; xp.precede(x); end;
inspect xp do
    begin
```

---

[6] See Franta [1976] for a PASCAL implementation. Note also that an additional pointer must be added to realize the cancel operation.

```
      number:=number+1;
      segment:-y; evtime:=y.evtime;
      end;
   end of adjust;

procedure schedule(y); ref(event notice)y;
comment:inserts the notice y into the list;
begin
      ref(key)x; ref(event notice)P; integer i; real t;
   t:=y.evtime;
   i:=entier((t-lowerbound)/dt);
   if i ⩾ du then i:=du else i:=mod(icurrent+i,du);
   x:-pointer[i] .pred;
   for x:-x while x.evtime > t do x:-x.pred;
   x:-x.suc; P:-x.segment;
   for P:-P while P.evtime > t do P:-P.pred;
   y.follow(P);
   if x.number < nlim then x.number:=x.number+1 else adjust(x);
   end of schedule;

procedure move dummy;
comment: removes the left-most dummy key together with its associated
      dummy notice, and re-inserts them in the overflow area;
begin
      ref(key) x,x1; ref(event notice)y1;
   for x:-keyl.suc while x. number = o do inspect x do
      begin comment move the dummy key x and its associate event notice;
      lowerbound:=lowerbound+dt;
      evtime:=segment.evtime:=lowerbound+du*dt;
      out; segment.out;
      x1:-pointer[du] .pred;
      for x1:-x1 while x1.evtime > evtime do x1:-x1.pred;
      y1:-x1.segment;
      for y1:-y1.suc while y1.evtime < evtime do number:=number+1;
      follow(x1);segment.precede(y1);
      inspect suc qua key do number:=number-x. number;
      if not x1.dummy and x1.number+number ⩽ nlim then
          begin comment remove x1 key and merge its segment with x's segment;
          x1.out;number:=number+x1.number;
          end;
      icurrent:-icurrent+1;
      end of inspect x;
   end of move dummy;
```

```
procedure hold(t); real t;
begin
current:-not1.suc; keycur:-key1.suc;
if t > 0 then current.evtime:=current.evtime+t;
if current evtime ⩾ current.suc qua event notice.evtime then
    begin
    current.out;
    keycur.number:=keycur.number-1;
    schedule(current);
    if keycur.number=0 then
        begin
        if keycur.dummy then move dummy
                        else keycur.out;
        end;
    end;
end of hold;


⟨initialization of the list structure⟩
    .

    .
    .

end of program;
```

With the settings given by Equations (8.2) and (8.4) and $du = 30$, the TL structure was also tested under the environment described earlier. The results are shown in Figure 8.6.

It should be clear from Figures 8.3 and 8.6 that the performance of the TL algorithm is superior to the IL algorithm except for small values of n, and so by implication is definitely superior to the linear list approach graphically depicted in Figure 8.2. Further note that the estimates of t_e produced are not only *nearly* independent of n, but of $F_{th}(x)$ as well.

One factor contributing to the superior performance of the TL algorithm is its uiform handling of the overflow list (i.e., the right-most sublist). Specifically, the overflow portion is structured in the same way as the remainder of the subintervals, so that as it migrates to the left it does not become an excessively long linear list, and therefore does not require restructuring. Further, we observed the same insensitivity of du and dt as reported for $D_s = IL$ as long as its value had the proper order of magnitude.

An interesting question is whether it is fruitful to continue the structuring of the event set toward the direction of balanced trees. Intuitively, one would surmise that further levels of indexing will

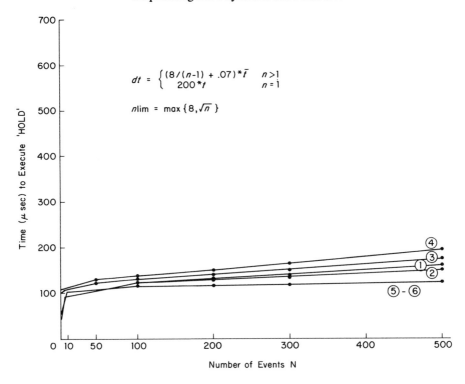

$$dt = \begin{cases} (8/(n-1) + .07)*\bar{t} & n>1 \\ 200*t & n=1 \end{cases}$$

$$n\text{lim} = \max\{8, \sqrt{n}\}$$

Figure 8.6 Two-level algorithm: test results

reduce the efficiency since the set is changing rapidly and rebalancing becomes the major operation. Preliminary experiments indicate that further structuring results in a deterioration in performance, although the results of Gonnet [1976] are not in agreement with these findings.

DISCUSSION

The reported performance (i.e., estimates $\hat{t}_e$) for the IL and TL structures must be considered indicative rather than conclusive, because to be useful structures, we must know du, dt, and n. For instance, for distribution 5, the choice,

$$du = 2, \ dt = E(th) \qquad \forall n$$

is clearly optimal.

Fortunately, as we have said, the access algorithms are *robust* in these parameters. We must, however, be able to produce reasonable *estimates* for *du, dt,* and $E(n)$ for actual simulations (as opposed to the controlled environment of the tests).

Generally, we wish to base the values of *du* and *dt* on $E(n)$, as well as the mean μ_s and variance σ_s^2 of the distribution of event times contained in S.[7] We can use the TL structure to obtain estimates of these parameters from *pilot runs*. The determination of the functional relationship between μ_s, σ_s^2, $E(n)$, and the pair *du, dt* is for most distributions an open question and remains an area for further research.

If such relationships can be found, Figure 8.6 suggests that the cost of simulation (particularly large simulations) can be significantly reduced through reduced overhead.

Of course, structures such as $D_s = L$ or $D_s = \text{HEAP}$ (as reported in Gonnet [1976]) do not require such parameterization.

---

[7] Such parameters are applicable only if the distribution on S becomes (is) stationary, a state often realized.

APPENDIX A[1]

An ALGOL Summary

SIMULA may be considered an extension of ALGOL-60, and to understand and appreciate SIMULA the reader must be familiar with the basic features of ALGOL-60. We give here a very short summary. Complete accounts can be found in Bauman [1964] and Ekman [1965].

ALGOL 60, at a functional level is similar to FORTRAN in that it is intended for solution of numeric and scientific problems. The importance of the ALGOL language, however, lies not so much in its functional capabilities as in the underlying structure that hosts those capabilities. As we shall see, ALGOL programs operate under a discipline which contrasts sharply with the simplicity of FORTRAN. This discipline establishes a protocol that provides useful guidelines for program creation.

ARITHMETIC

Algol's arithmetic capabilities, in terms of both data types and operators, are similar to those of FORTRAN. The same basic operators and a similar set of built-in functions are provided. Variables (data) may be of real, integer, switch, or Boolean type. All variables in an ALGOL program must have a type declaration.

EXAMPLE A.1

    real alpha, b, mag;
    integer gamma;
    Boolean c;

These statements declare alpha, *b,* and mag to be real variables, gamma to be an integer variable, and *c* a Boolean or logical variable.

Statements are delineated by the semicolon. Boldface items are to

[1] This section relies quite heavily on Chapter 2 of *Concepts of Programming Languages* by Mark Elson. Copyright 1973 by Science Research Associates, Inc. Reprinted by permission.

be considered *single* symbols and are usually referred to as *keywords.* Expressions may be arbitrarily complex, with a combination of precedence rules and parentheses dictating the evaluation order. ALGOL is very liberal and allows an arbitrary expression wherever a numeric value is required.

ARRAYS

ALGOL's features for defining arrays are very broad.

1. ALGOL allows specification of both upper and lower bounds. Given the declaration

real array $a[3:5,-4:-3]$;

we may visualize a as follows:

$$a_{3,-4} \qquad a_{3,-3}$$
$$a_{4,-4} \qquad a_{4,-3}$$
$$a_{5,-4} \qquad a_{5,-3}$$

2. ALGOL allows use of arbitrary expressions for dimension specifications:

integer array $b[n + 1:3 \times n+4]$;[2]

At the time of definition of b, which is *not* prior to program execution, n is evaluated and the bounds of b are set accordingly. See Example A.6 for details.

LOOPS, BRANCHES, AND CONDITIONALS

ALGOL has powerful features for conditional execution including the *if then else* construct.

EXAMPLE A.2

if $a+b<100$ **then go to** repeat **else** $a:=a+10$;

If the sum of a and b is less than 100, control is transferred to the

---

[2] In ALGOL (and SIMULA), multiplication is denoted by x rather than *. See Appendix D.

statement labeled repeat (note that labels are given as names). Otherwise *a* is incremented by 10 (the symbol := is the ALGOL assignment operator), and execution continues with the next statement. It is also possible in ALGOL for the statement following *then* and the one following *else,* or both, to be a collection of statements (a compound statement) delineated by a *begin end* pair.

We note at this point, after observing evaluation of truth-value expressions, that Boolean variables can take on true or false values. The operators used with such data are ¬(not), ∧(and), ∨(or), ⊃(implies), and ≡(equivalent to).

Iteration in ALGOL takes the form:

sum:=0;

for i:=j **step** k **until** n+2 **do**

sum:=sum+a[i] ;

This sequence of statements adds selected elements of array *a,* depending on the values of *j, k,* and *n*; *i* is initialized to the value of *j* and incremented by the value of *k.* The iteration stops when *i* exceeds *n* + 2 (or if *k* is negative, when *n* + 2 exceeds *i*). Again the summation statement could be a compound statement.

Another form of ALGOL loop allows iteration while a given condition is true. Thus, the iteration below continues as long as *a* = *b,* with *i* having the value 1.

for i:=1 **while** a=b **do**

statement;

Finally, a for-statement may employ a combination of the above forms. For example,

for i:=1,50,5 **step** 1 **until** 10, i+2 **while** i ≤ 20 **do**

will select for index i the values

1,50,5,6, . . ., 10,12,14, . . ., 18, 20

CONDITIONAL EXPRESSIONS

Having looked at the conditional statement, we now observe more general ways in which conditional specifications may be used.

EXAMPLE A.3

    a:=b+**if** i>j **then** c **else** d+5;

a is to be assigned the sum of b and either of two values, one of which is selected by evaluation of the conditional expression $i > j$. If i is greater than j, a is assigned the value of $b + c$, otherwise a is assigned the value of $b + d + 5$.

    go to if d+f>j **then** k3 **else** k4;

If $d + f$ is greater than j, then transfer is made to $k3$; otherwise transfer is made to $k4$.

THE BLOCK CONCEPT AND PROGRAM STRUCTURE

A complete ALGOL program, which we shall also designate a block, consists of the keyword **begin**, a sequence of declarations, a sequence of statements, and finally the keyword **end**.

EXAMPLE A.4 The following statements are an example of an ALGOL program. (In ALGOL, ↑ is the exponentiation operator; outreal an output statement.)[3]

```
begin
    real a, b;
    integer i;
    b:=a↑i;
    outreal(b);
end;
```

The above program is also an example of a block, which is itself a valid ALGOL statement. Further, as we just stated, a program, or block, consists of, among other things, a sequence of statements. This phenomenon leads us to the notion of a nest of blocks, because any block may contain another block as one of its statements. Such nests are the basis of the ALGOL program structure.

EXAMPLE A.5 The test below denotes a series of ALGOL state-

---

[3] The procedure outreal is not be found in SIMULA, as Figure 4.1 indicates.

ments, highlighting block initiations (labeled) and terminations. The drawing below illustrates the logical block nestings implied.

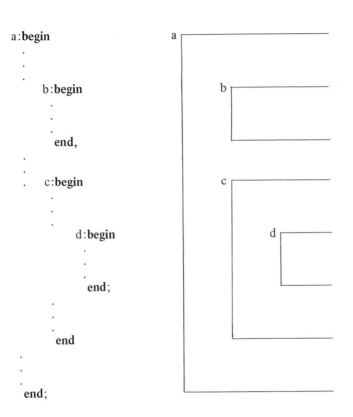

```
a:begin
   .
   .
   .
      b:begin
         .
         .
      end,
   .
   .
   .  c:begin
         .
         .
         .
            d:begin
               .
               .
            end;
         .
         .
      end
   .
   .
   .
end;
```

SCOPE OF NAMES

We have seen that a block may include declarations of names to be used in the block. Let us now investigate the relation of these declarations to names referred to within a block.

As one might expect, if a reference to a name declared in a block occurs within that block, the reference is to the data item described by the declaration. For the situation depicted below, the reference to x denotes the x given in the declaration, regardless of the context in which block a occurs in a program.

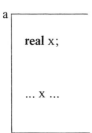

Now consider a somewhat more complex situation:

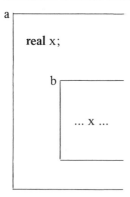

Block b contains reference to x but no declaration for it. However, bs *containing block a* contains a declaration for x, so the reference to x in b is resolved to this declaration.

Now consider the following program:

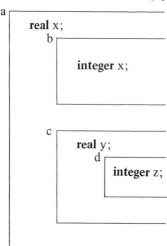

The names x, y, and z are known within blocks and resolved to declarations as indicated below.

Block	Resolution
a	x declared in a
b	x declared in b
c	x declared in a
	y declared in c
d	x declared in a
	y declared in c
	z declared in d

The general rule for resolving a name to a declaration is as follows:

> If the name is declared in the block containing the reference, then that is the appropriate declaration, and the data item is said to be *local* to the block. Otherwise the containing block is searched for a declaration, then its containing block, and so on, until a declaration of the name is found. The reference is resolved to the first declaration found. In these cases, the data item is said to be *nonlocal* to the block in which the reference occurs.

We can now speak of the *scope* of a declaration of a name as being the block in which the declaration appears, plus all contained blocks not providing a new declaration of the same name. This stratification of the naming process provides a flexible means for selective sharing or privacy of names within blocks.

ALLOCATION OF STORAGE FOR DATA

The block structuring of ALGOL hosts another language flexibility that we shall consider, first in terms of storage management.

In ALGOL, storage for a variable is allocated only upon entry to the block in which the variable is declared and that storage is freed upon exit from the block. This requires *dynamic allocation*, and storage for data is required only while that data is needed in a program.

Now let us look at the language implications of this storage scheme. Its most significant value is that one can calculate the dimensions of an array before entering the block in which that array is declared. Upon entry to the block, the array comes into being with the desired bounds.

EXAMPLE A.6   Consider the program:

```
begin
    integer n;
    inint (n);
    begin
        real a [1:n,1:n+1] ;
        .
        .
        .
    end;
    .
    .
    .
end;
```

In the outer block we calculate *n* (in this case by reading it), and then the block using array *a* is entered. At the time of entry, *n* and *n* + 1 are evaluated to provide the bounds for *a*.

A second important language aspect of storage management can also be seen in the above example. Since storage for *a* is freed when the inner block has finished execution and terminated, any values assigned to elements of *a* are lost. If the block is reentered later in execution, a new *a* comes into being; the old *a* and the values of its elements are not restored.

This loss of data values does cause problems in some cases. Suppose that a certain block, nested deeply within an ALGOL program, must record information abouts its executions during a program run. (It may of course be executed any number of times.) No other block needs this information, so use of private data variables declared in the block seems in order. Yet each time the block's execution is terminated, the values of these data elements will be lost. One solution is to require an outer block to make the declarations (and to ensure that no other containing blocks modify the data elements or redeclare the names).

An alternate solution is provided by the concept of *own* variables as supported by ALGOL. Storage for variables declared as own is *static* and permanent. Thus the values for variables so declared are *retained* upon exit from the block in which the *own* declaration appears, and they may be referenced upon subsequent entrance to that block. The own feature has not proven itself and is not available in SIMULA.

PROCEDURES AND PARAMETERS

Proper procedures and *function procedures* are ALGOL analogs of FORTRAN *subroutines* and *functions,* respectively. A procedure is closely related to a block from the standpoint of a program structure as we have described it. In fact, the body of a procedure is a block. Procedures differ from blocks in their mode of initiation and termination, and in their ability to accept parameters from a calling block.

EXAMPLE A.7   Declarations for a function procedure named *p*, having two formal parameters *x* and *y*.

```
real procedure p(x,y);
     value x;
     real x;
     real array y;
     begin
     .
     .
     .
     end;
```

When *p* is *referenced* (called), the *actual* parameter associated with formal parameter *x* will be passed to the procedure by *value,* whereas the actual parameter associated with *y* will be passed by *name.* This difference is discussed in detail in Appendix C and outlined here as follows:[4] If a formal parameter is to be received by value, every reference to that parameter in the called procedure yields the value of the actual parameter at the time of the call. If a formal parameter is received by name, every such reference yields the value of the actual parameter at the time of the reference.

x is declared to represent a real quantity, *y* a real array. Note that no bounds are given for *y*. Instead, the bounds are passed as a logical part of the array actual parameter, so that subscripted references to *y* can be interpreted correctly.

---

[4] See also Appendix B.

The body of the procedure follows as a normal ALGOL block, and the returned value of the procedure is the last value assigned to the name p.

An ALGOL procedure is invoked only as a result of an explicit reference to it, either within an expression (for a function procedure) or in an invoking statement consisting solely of the procedure name and actual parameter list (for a proper procedure). A procedure definition is skipped if encountered during normal sequential statement execution.

The point of return from a function procedure or proper procedure is analogous to that in FORTRAN. Labels can be passed to proper procedures and used as return points by means of "go to's" for procedures containing label formal parameters.

A procedure name is considered to be declared in the block containing the procedure definition; its scope is as for any other name. It can, of course, be invoked only from a point in the program at which its name is known.

RECURSION

An ALGOL procedure can call itself during its execution just as it can call other procedures. This type of call is known as a *recursive call*.

EXAMPLE A.8   Consider a procedure, factorial, designed to evaluate the factorial of its positive-integer formal parameter n. Its declaration is given as:

```
integer procedure factorial (n);
    integer n;
    factorial:=if n<3 then n else n x factorial (n-1);
```

If $n < 3$, then factorial $(n) = n$. Otherwise factorial $(n) = n$ x factorial $(n - 1)$. Thus, for clarification,

```
factorial (4) = 4 x factorial (3)
            = 4 x (3 x factorial (2))
            = 4 x (3 x 2)
            = 24
```

When a procedure calls itself recursively, it is as though it were calling an *identical copy of itself* located at the same point in the block structure. Thus new copies of local data are created for each level of a recursive call.

APPENDIX B

ALGOL and SIMULA Differences

1. The default parameter mode is not call by name as in ALGOL-60, but rather call by value or call by reference.
   The situation is summarized by Table B.1.
2. All variables are initialized in SIMULA upon entry into the block where they are declared.

Type	Initial Value
real,integer	0
ref	none
Boolean	false
text	notext

3. The concept of OWN variables present in ALGOL-60 is absent

Table B.1
Transmission Modes for Class Parameters and Procedure Parameters

Parameter Type	Transmission Mode		
	by VALUE[a]	by REFERENCE	by NAME
real, integer, Bool., char.	D	////	0[b]
ref	////	D	0[b]
text	0	D	0[b]
real array, Boolean array, integer array, char. array	0	D	0[b]
ref array, text array	////	D	0[b]
procedure identifier	////	D[b]	0[b]
label	////	D[b]	0[b]
switch	////	D[b]	0[b]

[a] Consult Appendix C for a summary discussion of transmission modes.
[b] Forbidden for class parameters transmission.
Note: 0 = optional mode; D = default; //// = forbidden for class & procedure parameters transmission.

in SIMULA. Our summary of ALGOL, therefore, only
broached the subject.

4. The ALGOL type string has been replaced by the concept of a
   text.

5. SIMULA contains as extensions to ALGOL-60

   Call by reference
   The class and reference variable concepts
   Coroutines (resume, detach)
   Input-output facilities

APPENDIX C

Argument Transfer Modes: A Refresher[1]

We summarize here the effects of the three procedure parameter transmission models, referred to as calls by (1) value, (2) name, and (3) reference.

(1) A formal parameter called by value has much the same properties as a local quantity declared at the outermost level of the procedure block. The only difference is the fact that while the latter is initialized according to standard SIMULA conventions, a formal parameter called by value is initialized by the value obtained by evaluating the corresponding actual parameter at the instant of call.

EXAMPLE C.1   The program segment

```
procedure p1(i); integer i;
begin integer j;  . . .
        for j := 1 step 1 until i do . . .
end of p1;
. . .
p1(5)
```

will act as though replaced by

```
procedure p1;
begin integer i,j; i :=5;
        . . . . . . .
        for j := 1step 1 until i do . . .
end of p1;
. . .
p1;
```

(2) Conversely, a parameter called by name is never evaluated at the time the procedure is invoked. Instead each time control encounters a name parameter in the procedure body, the corresponding actual parameter (which may be an expression) is re-evaluated, and the

---

[1] This summary is abstracted from Activate SIMULA, by Karel Babcicky, *SIMULA Newsletter,* vol. 3, no. 3, August 1975, pp. 15–18.

result of this computation is subsequently used instead of the formal parameter. The next effect of this handling allows us to consider that when invoked, every occurrence in the procedure body of a formal parameter called by name is *textually* replaced by the corresponding actual parameter. (Possible name conflicts arising from such program modifications are systematically resolved by the compiler.)

EXAMPLE C.2   Consider the segment:

```
array a[1:5] ; integer i;
procedure p2(r); name r; real r;
begin real x;
        r := . . .;
        x := r . . .;
end of p2;
. . .
p2(a[i]);
```

An equivalent program segment which does not use the name parameter is given by:

```
array a [1:5] ; integer i;
procedure p2;
begin real x;
        a [i]  := . . .;
        x := a [i] . . .;
end of p2;
. . .
p2;
. . .
```

(3) Call by reference in a way represents a compromise between call by value and by name. It is available only for certain types of parameters, namely those that reference either data structures or program components. The underlying idea is that the corresponding actual parameter is evaluated at the call execution, and the result of this evaluation, which must be a reference (to a data structure or program component), is then used in place of the formal parameter wherever this is encountered.

EXAMPLE C.3   Consider:

```
text s;
procedure p3(t); text t; comment implied call be reference;
```

```
begin . . .
      outtext (t);
end of p3;
. . .
p3(s);
```

This sequence behaves as though written as follows:

```
text s;
procedure p3;
begin text t; t :- s; . . .
      outtext (t); . . .
end of p3;
. . .
p3;
```

Call by name becomes more and more inefficient as the number of encountered occurrences of a name parameter increases. Call by value becomes inefficient when copying initial values for individual elements of large arrays and so on, becomes necessary. Neither of these disadvantages can be found with a reference call, and for this reason the reference is, as can be seen from the table B.1, the SIMULA default transmission mode for array, procedure, and text (not discussed) parameters.

APPENDIX D

Representation of Symbols

The previous information is useless if we cannot *prepare our input, access the compiler, produce output,* and *interpret diagnostic messages.* Unfortunately these matters are implementation dependent, and it seems only fair to supply this information for each of them or, as we have chosen, for none of them. The one possible exception concerns input preparation. To aid input preparation and the reading of our program listings, a self-explanatory listing is included.

SIMULA Symbol	Normal Representation	Alternate Representation	Punch for Normal Representation
A – Z a –z	A – Z	A – Z	12-1 – 0-9
0 – 9	0 – 9	0 – 9	0 – 9
+	+	+	12
−	−	−	11
x	*	*	11-8-4
/	/	/	0-1
↑	↑	'POWER'	11-8-5
÷	:/	'DIV' or '/'	8-2,0-1
>	>	'GREATER'	11-8-7
⩾	⩾	'NOT LESS'	12-8-5
=	=	'EQUAL'	8-3
≠	¬=	'NOT EQUAL'	12-8-6,8-3
⩽	⩽	'NOT GREATER'	8-5
<	<	'LESS'	12-0
∧	∧	'AND'	0-8-7
∨	∨	'OR'	11-0
≡	≡	'EQUIV'	0-8-6
= =	= =	'IDENT'	8-3,8-3
¬	¬	'NOT'	12-8-6
=/=	=/=	'NOT IDENT'	8-3,0-1,8-3
⊃	→	'IMPL'	0-8-5
.	.	.	12-8-3
, (comma)	,	,	0-8-3
:	:	..	8-2
;	;	.,	12-8-7
'₀	' (apos.)	'	8-4

SIMULA Symbol	Normal Representation	Alternate Representation	Punch for Normal Representation
(	(	(	0-8-4
)	)	)	12-8-4
[	[	(/	8-7
]	]	/)	0-8-2
:=	:=	..=or .=	8-2,8-3
:-	:-	..-or.-	8-2,11
↓	↓	''	11-8-6
''	$	$	11-8-3
(blank)	space	space	
delimiter	'DELIMITER'	'DELIMITER'	

SIMULA Symbol	Usual Representation
activate	'ACTIVATE'
after	'AFTER'
array	'ARRAY'
at	'AT'
before	'BEFORE'
begin	'BEGIN'
Boolean	'BOOLEAN'
class	'CLASS'
.	
.	
.	

etc. for remainder of keyword symbols, where ' is the apostrophe which appears as the symbol $\neq$ in our program listings.

APPENDIX E

A Histogram Display Routine

A histogram display routine

```
0     #PROCEDURE# PLOT HISTO (A,B,M,LENGTH,WIDTH);
1         #REAL# #ARRAY# A,B;   #INTEGER# M,LENGTH,WIDTH;
3     #COMMENT#
3         A[1:M]              FREQUENY VECTOR (MAY BE INTEGER OR REAL)
3                             A[I]=OBSERVATIONS WITH VALUE IN THE RANGE
3                                  B(I-1) .LT. VALUE .LE. B(I)
3
3         B[1:M-1]            INTERVALS (NEED NOT BE EQUALLY SPACED)
3
3         M                   DIMENSION OF A-VECTOR
3
3         LENGTH              MAXIMUM LENGTH OF THE PLOT
3                             (IF LESS THAN 10, IT IS RESET TO 50)
3                             THE LENGTH IS NOT LIMITED TO A PAGE.
3
3         WIDTH               MAXIMUM WIDTH
3                             (IF LESS THAN 50, IT IS RESET TO 130)
3                             WIDTH-28 BECOMES THE WIDTH OF THE
3                             MIDDLE M-2 INTERVALS;
4     #BEGIN#
4         #INTEGER##ARRAY# IA(/1:M/),COL(/0:M/);
5         #BOOLEAN# #ARRAY# MARKED(/1:M/);
6         #CHARACTER# #ARRAY# CHAR(/1:140/);
7         #INTEGER# EDGE,I,J,K,VK,C,FRAC,PWIDTH;
8         #REAL# MAXFREQ,XMAX,VSCALE,RANGE,FACTOR,VFACTOR;
9         #BOOLEAN# REALFREQ;
10        #CHARACTER# BLANK,STAR,DASH;
11
11    #IF# M #LESS# 3 #THEN# #GOTO# EXIT;
13    #IF# LENGTH #LESS# 10 #THEN# LENGTH:=50;
15    #IF# LENGTH #GREATER# 100 #THEN# LENGTH:=100;
17    #IF# WIDTH #LESS# 50 #OR# WIDTH #GREATER# 130 #THEN# WIDTH:=130;
19    BLANK:=$ $; STAR:=$*$; DASH:=$-$;
22    #IF# LINE #NOT EQUAL# 1 #THEN# EJECT(1);
24
24    #COMMENT#  CHOOSE THE WIDTH OF M-2 INTERVALS SUCH THAT,IF EQUALLY
24    SPACED, EACH INTERVAL WOULD BE AN INTEGER NUMBER OF COLUMNS;
25
25    COL(/0/):=11;
26    EDGE:=5;  #COMMENT# WIDTH OF LEFT-MOST AND RIGHTMOST INTERVALS;
28    PWIDTH:=WIDTH-COL(/0/)-2*EDGE-7;
29              #COMMENT# MAXIMUM WIDTH OF M-2 INTERVALS;
30    #IF# M #GREATER# PWIDTH+2 #THEN# M:=PWIDTH+2
31      #ELSE# PWIDTH:= (PWIDTH:/(M-2)) *(M-2);
33
33    #COMMENT# ***** MAP B-VECTOR TO A VECTOR OF COLUMN NUMBERS;
34
34    COL[1]:=COL[0]+EDGE;       #COMMENT# FOR OBSERVATIONS .LE. B(1);
36    #FOR# J:=2 #STEP# 1 #UNTIL# M-1 #DO#
37            #BEGIN#
37            COL[J]:=COL[1]+PWIDTH*(B[J]-B[1])/(B[M-1]-B[1]);
38            #IF# COL(/J/) #LESS# COL(/J-1/) #THEN#
39                    #BEGIN#
39                    OUTTEXT(# ERROR IN B VECTOR OF HISTOGRAM#);
40                    OUTIMAGE;
```

```
41                          ‡GOTO‡ EXIT;
42                          ‡END‡;
45            ‡END‡;
48    COL[M]:=COL[M-1]+EDGE;        ‡COMMENT‡ FOR OBSERVATIONS .GT. B[M-1];
50
50    ‡COMMENT‡ ***** VERTICAL SCALING;
51
51    MAXFREQ:=0;
52    ‡FOR‡ J:=1 ‡STEP‡ 1 ‡UNTIL‡ M ‡DO‡
53            ‡BEGIN‡
53            ‡IF‡ A(/J/) ‡LESS‡ 0.0 ‡THEN‡ ‡BEGIN‡
54                    OUTTEXT(#NEGATIVE FREQ IN HISTOGRAM#); OUTIMAGE;
56                    ‡GOTO‡ EXIT;  ‡END‡;
60            ‡IF‡ A(/J/) ‡GREATER‡ MAXFREQ ‡THEN‡ MAXFREQ:=A(/J/);
62            ‡IF‡ A(/J/)%=ENTIER(A(/J/)) ‡AND‡ A(/J/)%=0.0
62                    ‡THEN‡ REALFREQ := ‡TRUE‡;
64                    ‡COMMENT‡  COMPILER GIVES -1 FOR ENTIER(0.0);
65            ‡END‡;
68    ‡IF‡ MAXFREQ=0.0 ‡THEN‡ ‡GOTO‡ EXIT;
70    ‡IF‡ REALFREQ
70            ‡THEN‡ VSCALE:=MAXFREQ/LENGTH
71            ‡ELSE‡ VSCALE:=ENTIER((MAXFREQ+LENGTH-1)/LENGTH);
73    LENGTH:=MAXFREQ/VSCALE;
74    ‡FOR‡ J:=1 ‡STEP‡ 1 ‡UNTIL‡ M ‡DO‡ IA(/J/):=A(/J/)/VSCALE;
76
76    ‡COMMENT‡ ***** SCALE Y VALUES TO BE PRINTED AS XXXX.XXX FORMAT;
77
77    RANGE:= ‡IF‡ REALFREQ ‡THEN‡ 10000 ‡ELSE‡ 10000000;
80    ‡FOR‡ VK:=VK+1 ‡WHILE‡ VSCALE ‡LESS‡ 0.1 ‡DO‡
81            VSCALE:=VSCALE*10.0;
82    ‡FOR‡ VK:=VK-1 ‡WHILE‡ VSCALE*LENGTH ‡NOT LESS‡ RANGE ‡DO‡
83            VSCALE:=VSCALE/10.0;
84    VFACTOR:= 10.0 ‡POWER‡ VK;
85    ‡IF‡ VK%=0 ‡THEN‡  ‡BEGIN‡
86            SETPOS(COL(/0/)-5);
87            OUTCHAR($E$); OUTINT(-VK,4); OUTIMAGE;   ‡END‡;
93    EJECT(3);
94    FRAC:= ‡IF‡ REALFREQ ‡THEN‡ 3 ‡ELSE‡ 0;
97    ‡FOR‡ J:=COL[0] ‡STEP‡ 1 ‡UNTIL‡ COL[M] ‡DO‡  CHAR[J]:=BLANK;
99
99    ‡COMMENT‡ ***** CONSTRUCT ONE LINE IMAGE AT A TIME AND OUTPUT;
100
100   ‡FOR‡ I:= LENGTH ‡STEP‡ -1 ‡UNTIL‡ 1 ‡DO‡
101           ‡BEGIN‡
101           CHAR[COL[0]]:=CHAR[COL[M]]:=BLANK;
102           ‡FOR‡ J:=1 ‡STEP‡ 1 ‡UNTIL‡ M ‡DO‡
103           ‡IF‡ IA(/J/)=I ‡THEN‡  ‡BEGIN‡
104                   ‡FOR‡ C:=COL[J-1] ‡STEP‡ 1 ‡UNTIL‡ COL[J]  ‡DO‡
105                           CHAR[C] := STAR; ‡END‡
107           ‡ELSE‡ ‡IF‡ IA(/J/)=I+1 ‡THEN‡
110                   ‡FOR‡ C:=COL[J-1]+1 ‡STEP‡1 ‡UNTIL‡ COL[J-1 ‡DO‡
111                           CHAR[C] := BLANK;
112           OUTFIX(I*VSCALE,FRAC,9);
113           SETPOS(COL(/0/));
114           ‡FOR‡ C:= COL(/0/) ‡STEP‡ 1 ‡UNTIL‡ COL(/M/) ‡DO‡
115                   OUTCHAR(CHAR(/C/));
116           OUTIMAGE;
117           ‡END‡;
120
120   ‡COMMENT‡ ***** OUTPUT BOTTOM LINE;
121
121   SETPOS(COL(/0/));
122   ‡FOR‡ C:= COL(/0/) ‡STEP‡ 1 ‡UNTIL‡ COL(/M/) ‡DO‡ OUTCHAR(DASH);
124   OUTIMAGE;
125
125   ‡COMMENT‡ ***** SCALE X VALUES TO BE PRINTED IN XXX.XXX FORMAT;
126
```

```
126    XMAX:=ABS(B(/M-1/));
127    #IF# -B(/1/)   #GREATER# XMAX #THEN# XMAX:= -B(/1/);
129    K:=0;
130    #FOR# K:=K+1 #WHILE# XMAX #LESS# .1 #DO# XMAX:=XMAX*10.0;
132    #FOR# K:=K-1 #WHILE# XMAX #NOT LESS# 1000 #DO# XMAX:=XMAX/10.0;
134    FACTOR:=10.0 #POWER# K;
135
135    #COMMENT# ***** MARK X-AXIS UNDER EACH COLUMN;
136
136    #FOR# I:=1 #STEP# 1 #UNTIL# M-1 #DO# MARKED(/I/):=#FALSE#;
138    #FOR# I:=1,2,3 #DO#
139            #BEGIN#
139            #FOR# J:=1 #STEP# 1 #UNTIL# M-1 #DO#
140                #IF# #NOT# MARKED[J] #AND# POS #LESS# COL[J]-4 #THEN#
141                    #BEGIN#
141                    MARKED(/J/):=#TRUE#;
142                    SETPOS(COL(/J/)-4);
143                    OUTFIX(B(/J/)*FACTOR,3,8);
144                    #END#;
147            #IF# I=1 #AND# K%=0 #THEN#   #BEGIN#
148                    SETPOS(COL(/M/)+3);
149                    OUTCHAR($E$); OUTINT(-K,4);   #END#;
154            #IF# POS #GREATER# 1 #THEN# OUTIMAGE
155                    #ELSE# #GO TO# MARKED ALL;
157            #END#;
160    MARKED ALL:;
161
161    #COMMENT# ***** OUTPUT THE FREQUENCY VECTOR;
162
162    OUTIMAGE; OUTIMAGE;
164    OUTTEXT(#  LIMITS:        HISTOGRAM:  #);
165    #IF# VK%=0 #THEN# #BEGIN#
166            OUTCHAR($E$); OUTINT(-VK,4);   #END#;
171    OUTIMAGE; OUTIMAGE;
173    SETPOS(13);
174    #FOR# J:=1 #STEP# 1 #UNTIL# M #DO#
175            #BEGIN#
175            #IF# POS #GREATER# WIDTH-9 #THEN# #BEGIN#
176                    OUTIMAGE; OUTREAL(B(/J-1/),4,12) #END#;
180            OUTFIX(A(/J/)*VFACTOR,FRAC,10);
181            #END#;
184    OUTIMAGE;
185    EXIT:;
186    #END# PLOT HISTO;
```

APPENDIX F

Procedures for the Normal Distribution

Books on simulation have almost traditionally contained an appendix which presented a battery of statistical tables (see, for example, Fishman [1973], Mihram [1972b]). Here we resist such temptation and instead present routines for the calculation of the cumulative normal distribution and its inverse.

CUMULATIVE NORMAL DISTRIBUTION

The cumulative normal distribution is given by

$$P(x) = \frac{1}{\sqrt{2\pi}} \int_{-\infty}^{x} e^{-t^2/2} \, dt \tag{F.1}$$

and is approximated[1] by

$$\text{Norm}(x) = 1 - \frac{1}{2}[1 + d_1 x + d_2 x^2 + d_3 x^3 + d_4 x^4$$
$$+ d_5 x^5 + d_6 x^6]^{-16} + \epsilon(x) \tag{F.2}$$

with

$$|\epsilon(x)| < 1.5 \cdot 10^{-7} \tag{F.3}$$

and d_1, d_2, ..., d_6 constants. The appropriate constants and algorithm are seen in the accompanying listing of **procedure** norm(x).

INVERSE OF THE CUMULATIVE NORMAL DISTRIBUTION

We define the inverse of the cumulative distribution to be given by that point x_p which, for a given value P, $0 < P < 0.5$, and $0 \leq x_p < \infty$, is so as to make

$$P = \frac{1}{\sqrt{2\pi}} \int_{x_p}^{\infty} e^{-t^2/2} \, dt \tag{F.4}$$

---

[1] All approximations are taken from *The Handbook of Mathematical Functions*, by M. Abramowitz, National Bureau of Standards, June 1964, pp. 931–933.

The approximation is given by

$$\text{norminv}(P) = x_P = \frac{t - c_0 + c_1 t + c_2 t^2}{1 + d_1 t + d_2 t^2 + d_3 t^3} + \epsilon(P), \quad t = \sqrt{\ln \frac{1}{P^2}} \quad \text{(F.5)}$$

with

$$| \epsilon(P) | < 4.5 \cdot 10^{-4} \quad \text{(F.6)}$$

Although the error (F.6) is tolerable for simulation applications, it can be improved to something near (F.3) by first using (F.5) and then performing a double Newton iteration on the function P-norm(Z_i) with $Z_0 = x_p$ from (F.5). This approach is employed in the procedure norminv(P) shown in the accompanying listing, and produces (on the Cyber 74) $| \epsilon(P) | < 10^{-6}$.

Note that the procedure NORMINV(Z) presented in this appendix actually returns the value NORMINV defined by

$$Z = \frac{1}{\sqrt{2\pi}} \int_{-\alpha}^{NORMINV} e^{-t^2/2} \, dt \quad \text{(F.6)}$$

where $0 < Z < 1$, $-\infty < \text{NORMINV} < +\infty$

```
U     #REAL# #PROCEDURE# NORM(X); #REAL# X;
2     #COMMENT# COMPUTES NORMAL CUMULATIVE DISTRIBUTION FUNCTION
2               WITH 7 DIGITS OF ACCURACY;
3     #BEGIN#
3           #REAL# D1,D2,D3,D4,D5,D6, Y,CDFN;
4
4           D1:=.0498674347U ; D2:=.02114 10061 ; D3:=.00327 76263 ;
7           D4:=.0000J 8003U ; D5:=.0000U 8890b ; D6:=.0000U 5383U ;
10
10    Y:=ABS(X);
11    CDFN:= #IF# Y #LESS# .0000U0001         #THEN# 0.5  #ELSE#
13          #IF# Y #GREATER# 10.0              #THEN# 0.0  #ELSE#
15          .5/(((((((D6*Y+D5)*Y+D4)*Y+D3)*Y+D2)*Y+D1)*Y+1.0)#POWER# 16;
16    NORM:= #IF# X #GREATER# 0.0 #THEN# 1.0-CDFN #ELSE# CDFN;
19    #END# OF NORM
20    ******************************************************************** ;
22
22
22
22    #REAL# #PROCEDURE# NORMINV(Z); #REAL# Z;
24    #COMMENT# COMPUTES INVERSE OF NORMAL CUMULATIVE DISTRIBUTION;
25    #BEGIN#
25          #REAL# C0,C1,C2, D1,D2,D3;
26          #REAL# P,Y,SQRT2PI,CDFN1;
27          #INTEGER# I;
28
28          C0:=2.515517; C1:=0.802853; C2:=0.010328;
31          D1:=1.432788; D2:=0.189269; D3:=0.001308;
34          SQRT2PI:=2.506628274631U0 ; #COMMENT# SQRT(2*PI);
36
36    #IF# Z #LESS# 0.0 #OR# Z #GREATER# 1.0 #THEN#
37          #BEGIN#
37          OUT.IMAGE;
38          OUTTEXT(# *** NORMINV ERROR.  Z NOT IN (0,1). #);
39          OUT.IMAGE;
```

```
40          #GOTO# EXIT;
41          #END#;
44   P:= #IF# Z #LESS# 0.5 #THEN# Z #ELSE# 1.0-Z;
47   #IF# P #LESS# .00000000604 #THEN# CDFNI:=7.0
48   #ELSE##BEGIN#
49          Y:=SQRT(-LN(P*P));
50          CDFNI:=Y-((C2*Y+C1)*Y+C0)/(((D3*Y+D2)*Y+D1)*Y+1.0);
51          #END#;
54   CDFNI:=CDFNI*SIGN(Z-0.5);
55
55          #COMMENT# NEWTON-RAPHSON ITERATION TO IMPROVE ACCURACY:  ;
56   #FOR# I:=1,2 #DO#
57   CDFNI:=CDFNI+SQRT2PI*(Z-NORM(CDFNI))*EXP(0.5*CDFNI*CDFNI);
58   EXIT:;
59   NORMINV:=CDFNI;
60   #END# OF NORM INV
61   **************************************************************** ;
```

References

Adiri, I. and Avi-Itzhak, B., A Time-Sharing Queue with a Finite Number of Customers, *JACM,* vol. 16, no. 2, April 1969.

Ahrens, J. H. and Dieter, U., Computer Methods for Sampling form the Exponential and Normal Distributions, *CACM,* vol. 15, no. 10, October 1972, pp. 873–882.

Bauman, Feliciano M., Bauer, F. L., and Samuelson, K., *Introduction to ALGOL,* Englewood Cliffs, N.J.: Prentice-Hall, 1964.

Bennett, R. P. et al., *SIMPAC User's Manual,* System Development Corporation, TM-602/000/00, April 1962.

Betz, Frederick and Mitroff, Ian I., Representational Systems Theory, *Management Science,* vol. 20, no. 9, May 1974, pp. 1242-1252.

Birtwhistle, Graham M., Dahl, Ole-Johan, Myhrhaug, Bjorn, and Nygaard, Kristen, *SIMULA Begin,* Studentlitteratur, Auerbach, 1973a.

Birtwhistle, Graham M., SIMULA: Its Features and Prospects, Technical Report No. S-44, Norwegian Computing Center, February 1973b.

Box, G. E. P. and Jenkens, G. M., *Time Series Analysis Forecasting and Control,* San Francisco: Holden-Day, 1970.

Buxton, J. N. (ed.), Simulation Programming Languages, *Proceedings of the IFIP Working Conference on Simulation Programming Languages,* Oslo, 1967, North-Holland, 1968.

Chaitin, Gregory J., Randomness and Mathematical Proof, *Scientific American,* January 1975, pp. 47-52.

Cheng, P. S., Trace Driven System Modeling, *IBM Systems Journal,* vol. 8, no. 4, 1969, pp. 280-289.

Clint, M., Program Proving: Coroutines, *Acta Informatica,* 2, 1973, pp. 50-63.

Control Data Corporation, *SIMULA Reference Manual,* 1971, Revision (July 1971).

Conway, R. W., Some Tactical Problems in Digital Simulation, *Management Science,* vol. 10, 1963, pp. 47-61.

Cooper, Robert B., *Introduction to Queueing Theory,* New York: Macmillan, 1972.

Cotton, Ira W., Remarks on Stably Updating Mean and Standard Deviation of Data, *CACM,* vol. 18, no. 2, August 1975, p. 458.

Crane, M. A. and Iglehart, D. L., Simulating Stable Stochastic Systems, I: General Multi-Server Queues, *JACM,* vol. 21, 1974, pp. 103–113.

Crane, M. A. and Iglehart, D. L., Simulating Stable Stochastic Systems, III: Regenerative Processes and Discrete Event Simulations, *Operations Research,* 23, 1975b, pp. 33–45.

Crane, M. A. and Iglehart, D. L., Simulating Stable Stochastic Systems, IV: Approximation Techniques, *Management Science,* vol. 21, 1975a, pp. 1215–1224.

Dahl, Ole-Johan, Myhrhaug, Bjorn, and Nygaard, Kristen, *Common Base Language,* Pub. no. 5-22, Norwegian Computing Center, October 1970.

Dahl, Ole-Johan, Discrete Event Simulation Languages, *Programming Languages,* NATO Advanced Study Institute, F. Gennys (ed.), New York: Academic Press, 1968, pp. 349–395.

Dahl, Ole-John and Hoare, C. A. R., Hierarchical Program Structure, in *Structured Programming,* by O.-J. Dahl, E. W. Dijkstra, and C. A. R. Hoare, New York: Academic Press, 1972.

Dahl, Ole-Johan and Nygaard, K., SIMULA—An Algol-Based Simulation Language, *CACM,* vol. 9, no. 9, 1966, pp. 671–687.

Donovan, J. J., Alsop, J. W., and Jones, M. M., A Graphical Facility for an Interactive Simulation System, *Proceedings of IFIPS Congress,* 1968.

Ekman, Torgil and Froberg, Carl-Erik, *Introduction to ALGOL Programming,* Studentlitteratur, Lund, Sweden, 1965.

Elson, Mark, *Concepts of Programming Languages,* Chicago: SRA, 1973.

Emshoff, James R. and Sisson, Roger L., *Design and Use of Computer Simulation Models,* New York: Macmillan, 1970.

Fishman, George, *Concepts and Methods in Discrete Event Digital Simulation,* New York: Wiley, 1973.

Franta, W. R. and Maly, Kurt, An Efficient Data Structure for the Simulation Event Set, *CACM,* in press.

Franta, W. R. and Houle, P. A., Comments on Models of Multi-Processor Multi-Memory Bank Computer Systems, *Proceedings Winter Simulation Conference,* 1974, pp. 87–97.

Gafarian, A. V., Ancker, C. J., Jr., and Morisaku, T., *The Problem of the Initial Transient with respect to Mean Value in Digital Computer Simulation and the Evaluation of Some Proposed Solutions,* ISE TR 77-1, Univ. of Southern California, February, 1977.

General Electric Company, *SIMCOM User's Guide,* Information System Operations, TR-65-1-149010, 1964.

Gonnet, Gaston H., Heaps Applied to Event Driven Mechanisms, *CACM,* vol. 19, no. 7. July 1976, pp. 417-418.

Gonzalez, T., Shani, Sartaj, and Franta, W. R., An Efficient Algorithm for the Kolmogorov Smirnov and Lilliefors Tests, *ACM Transactions on Mathematical Software,* vol. 3, no. 1, March, 1977, pp. 60-64.

Gordon, Geoffrey, *The Application of GPSS V to Discrete System Simulation,* Englewood Cliffs, N.J.: Prentice-Hall, 1975.

Greenberger, M. et. al., *On-Line Computation and Simulation: The OPS-3 System,* Cambridge, Mass.: M.I.T. Press, 1965.

Halachmi, Baruch and Franta, W. R., A Diffusion Approximate Solution to the G|G|K Queueing System, *The International Journal of Computers and Operations Research,* (in press).

Hansen, Per Brinch, *Operating System Principles,* Englewood Cliffs, N.J.: Prentice-Hall, 1973.

Hansen, Per Brinch, Structured Multi-Programming, *CACM,* vol. 15, no. 7, July 1972, pp. 574-578.

Hanson, Richard J., Stably Updating Mean and Standard Deviation of Data, *CACM,* vol. 18, no. 1, January 1975, pp. 57-58.

Hills, Robin, Simulation Model Structures, *Proceedings Simula Users Conference,* Oslo, Norway, Sept. 24-25, 1973.

Hoare, C. A. R., Monitors: An Operating Systems Structuring Concept, *CACM,* vol. 17, no. 10, October 1974, pp. 549-557.

Houle, P. A. and Franta, W. R., On the Structural Concepts of SIMULA and Simulation Modeling, *Proc. Summer Computer Simulation Conference,* 1974, pp. 55-60, Reprinted in *SIMULA Newsletter,* vol. 3, no. 2, May 1975, pp. 8-16, Oslo, Norway. Also printed in Australian Computer Journal, vol. 7, no. 1, March 1975, pp. 39-45.

IBM United Kingdom Limited Data Centre, *CSL User's Manual,* London, 1966.

IBM, *Simulation Evaluation and Analysis Language (SEAL) System Reference Manual,* January 17, 1968.

Iglehart, D. L., Simulating Stable Stochastic Systems, V: Comparison of Ratio Estimators, *Naval Research Logistic Quarterly,* vol. 22, no. 3, September 1975a.

Iglehart, Donald L., *Statistical Analysis of Simulations,* TR 86-18, Control Analysis Corporation, July 1975b.

Iglehart, D. L., *The Regenerative Method for Simulation Anaylsis,* TR 86-20, Control Analysis Corporation, October 1975c.

Jensen, Kathleen and Wirth, Miklaus, *Pascal User Manual and Report,* Springer-Verlag, #18 in Series Lecture Notes in Computer Science, 1974.

Jills, P. R., *SIMON–A Computer Simulation Language in ALGOL, Digital Simulation in Operations Research,* S. H. Hollingdale (ed), New York: Elsevier North-Holland, 1967.

Kiviat, Philip J., Villaneuva, R. and Markowitz, H. M., *The Simscript II Programming Language,* Englewood Cliffs, N.J.: Prentice-Hall, 1968.

Kiviat, Philip J., Simulation Languages, Appendix C, *Computer Simulation Experiments with Models of Economic Systems,* by Thomas H. Naylor, New York: Wiley, 1971.

Kleinrock, Leonard, *Queueing Systems Volume 1: Theory*, New York: Wiley, 1975, *Volume 2: Applications,* New York: Wiley, 1976.

Kleijnen, Jack P. C., *Statistical Techniques in Simulation: Part I,* New York: Marcel Dekker, 1974.

Knuth, Donald, *The Art of Computer Programming, Vol. 2,* Seminumerical Algorithms, Reading, Mass.: Addison-Wesley, 1971.

Knuth, Donald and McNeley, J. L., SOL–A Symbolic Language for General Purpose Systems Simulation, *IEEE Transactions on Electronic Computers,* August 1964, pp. 401–408.

Lavenberg, S. S. and Slutz, D. R., Regenerative Simulation of a Queueing Model of an Automated Tape Library, *IBM Journal of Research and Development,* vol. 19, no. 5, September 1975b, pp. 463–475.

Law, Averill M., Efficient Estimators for Simulated Queueing Systems, *Management Science,* 22, 1, September 1975, pp. 30–41.

MacDougall, Myron H. and MacAlpine, J. Stuart, Computer System Simulation with Aspol, *Proceedings Symposium on the Simulation of Computer Systems,* June 19–20, 1973, pp. 92–103.

Martin, Francis F., *Computer Modeling and Simulation,* New York: Wiley, 1968.

Mihram, Danielle and Mirham, G. Arthur, Human Knowledge, The Role of Models, Metaphore and Analogy, *International Journal General Systems,* vol. 1, 1974, pp. 41–60.

Mihram, G. Arthur, The Modeling Process, *IEEE Transactions on Systems, Man and Cybernetics,* vol. SMC-2, no. 5, November 1972a, pp. 621–629.

Mihram, G. Arthur, *Simulation: Statistical Foundations and Methodology,* New York: Academic Press, 1972b.

Mihram, G. Arthur, Some Practical Aspects of the Verification and Validation of Simulation Models, *Opns. Res. Qtrly.,* vol. 23, no. 1, 1972c, pp. 17–29.

Mills, Harlen, Top Down Programming in Large Systems, pp. 41–55, *Debugging Techniques in Large Systems,* Randall Rustin (ed.), Englewood Cliffs, N.J.: Prentice-Hall, 1970.

Naylor T. H. (ed.), The Design of Computer Simulation Experiments, Durham, N.C.: Duke University Press, 1969.

Parente, R. J., *A Language for Dynamic System Description,* IBM Advanced Systems Development Division Technical Report 17-180, 1966.

Paree, Howard (ed.), *Hierarchy Theory: The Challenge of Complex Systems,* The International Library of Systems Theory and Philosophy, New York: George Braziller, 1973.

Parslow, R. D., AS: An ALGOL Simulation Language, *IFIP Working Conference on Simulation Languages,* Oslo, Norway, 1967.

Patton, P. C., Franta, W. R., and Houle, P. A., A Study of System Performance in a 3PCU/2IOC AN/UYK-7 Multi-Processor, A Report to the Raytheon Service Company, October 1973.

Petrone, L., On a Simulation Language Completely Defined onto the Programming Language PL/I, *IFIP Working Conference on Simulation Languages,* Oslo, Norway, 1967.

Pritscher, A. A. and Kiviat, P. J., *Simulation with Gasp II,* Englewood Cliffs, N.J.: Prentice-Hall, 1969.

Rogeberg, Thomas, Simulation and Simulation Languages, pub. no. 5-48, Norwegian Computing Center, October 1973.

Sargent, Robert G., Statistical Analysis of Simulation Output Data, *Proceedings Symposium on the Simulation of Computer Systems,* August 10-12, 1976, pp. 39–50.

Sastry, Kuchibhotla and Kain, Richard, On the Performance of Certain Multi-Processor Computer Organizations, *IEEE Transactions on Computers,* vol. C-24, no. 11, November 1975, pp. 1066–1074.

Schmidt, J. W. and Taylor, R. E., *Simulation and Analysis of Industrial Systems,* Homewood, Ill.: Richard D. Irwin, 1970.

United States Steel Corporation, *Simulation Language and Library (SILLY),* Engineering and Scientific Computer Services, February 1968.

Vaucher, J. G. and Duval, Pierre, A Comparison of Simulation Event List Algorithms, *CACM,* vol. 10, no. 4, April 1975, pp. 223–230.

Vaucher, J. G., Simulation Data Structures Using SIMULA 67, *Proceedings Winter Simulation Conference,* 1971, pp. 255–260.

Vaucher, J. G., A "Wait-Until" Algorithm for General Purpose Simulation Languages, *Proceedings Winter Simulation Conference,* 1973, pp. 177–183.

Williams, J. W. J., The Elliott Simulator Package (ESP), *Computer Journal,* VI, January 1964, pp. 328–331.

Wyman, Paul F., Improved Event-Scanning Mechanisms for Discrete Event Simulation, *CACM,* vol. 18, no. 6, June 1975. pp. 350–353.

Zeigler, Bernard P., A Conceptual Basis for Modeling and Simulation, *International Journal General Systems,* vol. 1, 1974, pp. 213–228.

INDEX